The World War II Bookshelf

CITADEL BOOKS BY JAMES F. DUNNIGAN

The Next War Zone

The Perfect Soldier

THE
WORLD WAR II
BOOKSHELF

Fifty Must-Read Books

JAMES F. DUNNIGAN

CITADEL PRESS
Kensington Publishing Corp.
www.kensingtonbooks.com

CITADEL PRESS BOOKS are published by

Kensington Publishing Corp.
850 Third Avenue
New York, NY 10022

All Kensington titles, imprints, and distributed lines are available at special quantity discounts for bulk purchases for sales promotions, premiums, fund-raising, educational, or institutional use. Special book excerpts or customized printings can also be created to fit specific needs. For details, write or phone the office of the Kensington special sales manager: Kensington Publishing Corp., 850 Third Avenue, New York, NY 10022, attn: Special Sales Department, phone 1-800-221-2647.

CITADEL PRESS and the Citadel logo are Reg. U.S. Pat. & TM Off.

First printing: May 2004

10   9   8   7   6   5   4   3   2   1

Printed in the United States of America

Library of Congres Control Number: 2004100514

ISBN: 0-8065-2609-2

To John Dunnigan, Jr., a World War II veteran who was a great guy who never let you down

CONTENTS

Three
THE WAR IN RUSSIA   119

Four
THE WAR IN THE PACIFIC   145

INTRODUCTION

The World War II Bookshelf is full of information about books you may not have read, or even heard of. But if you want to really understand World War II, these are the books that can fill in the gaps in your knowledge of the largest and bloodiest war ever fought.

You're probably wondering why, if these books are so important, they aren't all best-sellers. Well, some of them are, but just as it isn't unusual for it to take years—sometimes decades—to gauge the historical importance of events, this can also be the case with books that describe these events. Important titles may go out of print, too, and not be readily available, but thanks to eBay and online booksellers (like Amazon.com), many can be obtained for about what they cost when first published.

Ranking the top fifty books is another matter. Tens of thousands of books have been written on World War II, and even a short list of the essential ones yields several hundred excellent works. Getting down to only fifty leaves us with the cream, and ranking them is a challenge, because among them are books which occupy first place in one of five catagories I've set forth. (Your criteria for what is more important may differ from mine, but that's okay.) The first five are those books that add the most knowledge to whatever you thought you knew about World War II.

1. *The American Soldier* by S. A. Stouffer et al., is about not only what American soldiers thought about World War II but how

those opinions were collected, organized, and presented in a convincing fashion. This two-volume set represents the results of the U.S. Army opinion survey (among the troops) during World War II—the first time anything like this was ever done. The results are a remarkable portrait of what American troops felt as they were prepared for combat, and after they went into action. Many of the soldiers' opinions found here ring true after half a century.

2. *The United States Strategic Bombing Survey.* They don't call World War II "The Big One" for nothing, and the "big" referred to the extent of the destruction, caused by millions of tons of bombs dropped in Europe and the Pacific. This work covers the destruction in great detail. There is no more definitive work on the war's efforts to smash things and kill people.

3. *Soviet Casualties and Combat Losses in the Twentieth Century* by G.F. Krivosheev. Until the Cold War ended, willful ignorance in the West kept secret the extent to which the Russians had been responsible for defeating Nazi Germany. The startling revelation reported first in this book was the staggering Russian death toll from the war: 30 million. Much additional detail is provided on where and when those people were killed.

4. *Reporting World War II* edited by Samuel Hynes, Anne Matthews, Nancy Caldwell Sorel, and Roger J. Spiller. The interpretation of history changes over time, as new generations take a different point of view or decide that the past looks different from where they stand. Well, here's a reality check. This two-volume anthology of some of the best journalism to come out of the war is unlike what is written today. A different style of writing was in vogue sixty years ago, and a different sensibility, but these pieces reflect what the observers saw and understood.

5. *United States Army in World War II* by various authors. A hidden gem. This is the official U.S. Army history of the war.

Many volumes were written by famous historians (and authors of numerous other books), covering numerous topics of importance that were never fully dealt with anywhere else. A treasure for the World War II buff.

The remaining forty-five books are ranked according to how much each is likely, in my estimation, to increase your knowledge and understanding of World War II.

You'll note that I've included in *The World War II Bookshelf* few biographies or accounts of the experiences of individual soldiers. Nor are there many volumes dedicated to individual battles or campaigns. These have been largely omitted because, given a list of only fifty books about a war this large, the greater issues need to be understood first. Remember, to truly understand the war these are the "must read" books, not the ones that are merely easier to get through or more alluring. There is plenty of entertainment here, but it's all to help you make sense of the biggest, bloodiest, most complex war in human history.

6. *The Second World War* by Winston Churchill. The inside story by one of the main players.

7. *A World at Arms: A Global History of World War II* by Gerhard L. Weinberg. A magnificent effort that fits all the essential material on the war into one volume.

8. *Brute Force* by John Ellis. Why bigger was better in winning World War II.

9. *Crusade in Europe* by Dwight D. Eisenhower. The inside story by one of the key military commanders. As much about politics as about military affairs.

10. *Eagle Against the Sun* by Ronald Spector. An excellent and comprehensive one-volume account of the war in the Pacific.

11. *Eisenhower's Lieutenants: The Campaigns of France and Germany, 1944–1945* by Russell Weigley. Eisenhower's war, without the politics, which makes it look like a different war entirely.

12. *Fighting Power: German and U.S. Army Performance, 1939–1945* by Martin Van Creveld. Detailed explanations of the reasons Germans were so hard to beat on the battlefield.

13. *Great Battles on the Eastern Front* by Trevor Dupuy and Paul Martell. All the key battles on the Russian front, and why these battles were so important.

14. *The Two-Ocean War* by Samuel Eliot Morison. The official history of the U.S. Navy in World War II, but so well written that you can't put it down.

15. *Guadalcanal* by Richard B. Frank. The definitive work on the campaign that broke the back of Japanese military power in the Pacific.

16. *Japan at War: An Oral History* by Haruko Taya Cook and Theodore F. Cook. What the Japanese really thought about World War II, told in their own words. You won't believe some of this stuff.

17. *Popski's Private Army* by Vladimir Peniakoff. Peniakoff, whose nickname was "Popski," was the ultimate World War II commando—and he could write, too.

18. *The Rise and Fall of the Third Reich* by William L. Shirer. The most comprehensive book on the origins of Nazism and how it nearly destroyed Europe.

19. *Silent Victory: The U.S. Submarine War Against Japan* by Clay Blair Jr. The only successful submarine campaign (against another nation's shipping) in history. This book tells how it was done.

20. *Soldiers of the Sun* by Meirion and Susie Harries. The Japanese army was very different from any other; the authors explain why and how.

21. *Stilwell and the American Experience in China 1911–45* by Barbara Tuchman. China was where most people were killed during the War in the Pacific, and Tuchman recounts both Japan's and the United States's failures there.

22. *The Good War* by Studs Terkel. Interviews with people who never made headlines, but did all the work during World War II.

23. *The Shadow Warriors: O.S.S. and the Origins of the C.I.A.* by Bradley Smith. The Office of Strategic Services (OSS) turned into the CIA after the war because it had developed a new form of war.

24. *War As I Knew It* by George Patton. In his own words, by the best combat commander America had during World War II.

25. *When Titans Clashed: How the Red Army Stopped Hitler* by David Glantz and Jonathan House. The Russians claim the most credit for winning World War II, and this book explains why.

26. *Why the Allies Won* by Richard Overy. More important, this book explains how the Allies could have lost.

27. *The Battle for History* by John Keegan. An illuminating discussion of the many types of books written about World War II, and why some are very good, and others are not.

28. *The Battle of Britain* by Richard Hough and Denis Richards. A very thorough and readable description of the 1940 air campaign that changed the history of warfare.

29. *A Battle History of the Imperial Japanese Navy* by Paul S. Dull. How the Japanese navy fought key battles during World War II, as described by Japanese navy officers.

30. *The World War II Databook* by John Ellis. All the data you'll ever need to make sense of the war.

31. *The Times Atlas of the Second World War* edited by John Keegan. All the maps you'll ever need to make sense of the war.

32. *Commandos and Rangers of World War II* by James Ladd. One of the lesser known innovations to come out of the war.

33. *Deception in World War II* by Charles Cruickshank. A technique that played a much larger role in the war than it is commonly realized.

34. *War in the Shadows* by Robert B. Asprey. World War II was also the largest guerrilla war in history, and some of those battles are still going on.

35. *Hitler's Last Weapons* by Jozef Garlinski. How the Germans came to invent cruise and ballistic missiles, and how the Allies, with the help of guerrillas in Nazi territory, learned about and fought these new super-weapons.

36. *The Wizard War* by R. V. Jones. The battle of wits between British and German scientists, as both developed new electronic warfare gadgets.

37. *The Pacific War* by Saburo Ienaga. How the war in the Pacific began in some political disputes in Japan, and what the war did to Japan.

38. *Jane's Fighting Ships of World War II*. It's all here. The ultimate record, in more ways than one, of World War II warships.

39. *Marching Orders* by Bruce Lee. How the allies got regular briefings from Hitler himself, and were able to use this remarkable source of information.

40. *Overlord: D-Day and the Battle for Normandy* by Max Hastings. The most ferocious battle the Western Allies fought in World War II, and how it was won.

41. *Russia at War: 1941–1945* by Alexander Werth. Mostly about the Russian people at war, Werth's book puts a human face on the brutal fighting in Russia.

42. *The American Magic* by Ronald Lewin. How American code breakers, independent of the British efforts, cracked several critical Japanese codes and changed the course of the entire war.

43. *The Historical Encyclopedia of World War II* by Marcel Baudot, et al. All those little details you never seem to find when you need them. Here they are.

44. *The Japanese Navy in World War II* by Former Japanese Naval Officers. The Japanese officers who led the fighting were remarkably candid about what worked and what didn't.

45. *There's a War to Be Won* by Geoffrey Perret. How the United States increased the size of its army more than thirty-fold between 1941 and 1945. (It wasn't easy.)

46. *Ultra in the West: The Normandy Campaign, 1944–45* by Ralph Bennett. How the code-breaking initiatives benefited commanders in battle, although they didn't know the information came from deciphered codes.

47. *War Plan Orange: The U.S. Strategy to Defeat Japan, 1897–1945* by Edward S. Miller. How American planners predicted the future in their prewar planning process.

48. *Winged Victory: The Army Air Forces in World War II* by Geoffrey Perret. Between 1941 and 1945, the U.S. Air Force grew from one of the smallest, to *the* largest air force.

49. *The Last 100 Days* by John Toland. World War II in Europe didn't end neatly, and Toland describes what was going on during the last hundred days.

50. *The World War II Almanac: 1931–1945* by Robert Goralski. A chronology of the war, plus many useful facts. Essential for keeping it all in perspective.

One

THE BIG PICTURE

---

*T*HE FOLLOWING BOOKS, in one way or another, cover the entire war. World War II is easier to grasp if first you get the big picture. Included here are what I consider the best of the general works on the war. Also included are an atlas, an almanac, and several other sources that provide all those bits of information sometimes missing elsewhere. The books in this section offer lots of numbers, for World War II was, more than any previous war in the past, a war of numbers—the largest war in history and the one most dependent on scientific breakthroughs and huge industrial production. It was also a war that featured the leadership of a few remarkable men. One of these, Winston Churchill, also happened to be an excellent writer and historian, and lived long enough to record his experiences. If you read nothing else in this section, read Churchill's history. He was there, he knew what he was talking about, and knew how to tell the story so others could understand it.

A World at Arms; A Global History of World War II

by Gerhard L. Weinberg

Cambridge University Press, 1995

It took nearly half a century, and many attempts, but someone finally wrote a one-volume history of the war that was equal to the challenge, and Weinberg did it in a complete and comprehensible fashion. No easy task, and after reading this book you'll realize why. Many critical issues haven't gotten the attention they deserve in other one-volume histories of the war—here they do.

For example, in 1940 the British government seriously discussed cutting a deal with the Germans, an arrangement that could have changed the course of the war. Another topic covered in detail was Germany's troublesome relationships with its allies. The Germans never had much confidence in the Italians, were let down continually by the Japanese, and other minor allies provided more headaches than advantages. The author contrasts this with the Allied Forces who were much more successful at working together.

Since *A World at Arms* covers the war from a strategic viewpoint, it's only natural that coverage of the battles should be brief. Battle and campaign descriptions always make reference to how each particular action influenced the strategic situation, a factor more interesting than you may have realized. We tend to forget that battles are part of a larger operation, and their impact on the greater scheme of things is more important.

Weinberg has taken advantage of documents that have been declassified since 1945 and has gone over previous research thoroughly. Surprising revelations abound. Many have to do with the Axis leaders who, much of the time, tended to be unrealistic in the extreme. The author's descriptions of German and Japanese war plans, and especially the internal debates that produced them, will change your thinking about just how much mature thinking the Axis forces gave to the war. The initial successes of the Germans and Japanese were largely the result of years of preparation, and some smaller wars gave their troops invaluable experience, but at the time, it seemed that Germany and Japan were facing such formidable opposition that they would not, as reasonable national leaders, undertake such a risky war. The author makes it clear that the Axis nations were led by very unreasonable and, quite often, illogical, men. More than a hundred million people had to die before this insight became clear to all.

The author's concentration on a strategic view of the war makes this one-volume history well focused, illustrating how a series of decisions, that could have gone either way, led to the war spreading globally. None of the Axis powers planned to carry their conquests as far as they did, which may explain how both Germany and Japan found themselves overextended and vulnerable to Allied counterattacks. While logic and practicality were to be found among the lower ranks of the Axis military machine, at the top there was illusion and pure fantasy. The racism of the senior German and Japanese commanders, who believed that Americans were weak and decadent "mongrels," probably did more to produce an Allied victory than any other factor. The Germans dismissed American industrial might as incapable of producing anything but consumer goods. Likewise the Japanese believed Americans unable to sustain a hard fight.

The Nazis were equally dismissive of their Slavic neighbors to the east and south. The genocidal attitude towards the Jews by

Germany (but not Japan, which provided sanctuary for many Jews) was another flaw in German thinking that cost them dearly. As strong as the Germans and Japanese were militarily, they were weak at strategic leadership, and this book makes the point that being able to see the big picture clearly helps you make the *best* decisions, rather than the ones that make you feel better. This was key to the Allies' victory. Early in the war, the Allies too made some bad decisions, and the Axis took advantage of them. But by late 1942, most of the bad-decision-makers were speaking German or Japanese, a curse from which the Axis was unable to recover. Yes, the Axis, especially Germany, showed signs of waking up by 1944. But it was too late. The Japanese never wised up.

The book also pays attention to the home front. Even during a World War, politics was still a local affair. Major powers on both sides each were faced with unique political and economic situations. By covering these, Weinberg makes the military decision-making and operations comprehensible. The Allies, for example, already had a tradition of liberated womanhood. In America and Britain, more and more women were holding jobs, so it was no great leap to fully mobilize women for the war effort through industrial and commercial employment. Although Germany and Japan began to mobilize women toward the end of the war, it was too late.

The author deftly blends into this history the economic issues the national leaders had to deal with, but never lets these economic discussions grow boring. They remain connected to all other crucial elements that drove the war. Military, political, diplomatic, and economic issues are covered in proportion, in their proper sequence, and with a clarity rarely seen in books of this scope. Perhaps most useful is the discussion, from each side's perspective, of the options that were available at key points in the war, giving the reader an almost you-are-there perspective. *A World at Arms* does manage to put you "there", as much as one can in so vast and sprawling a subject.

THE TIMES ATLAS OF THE SECOND WORLD WAR

edited by John Keegan

HARPERCOLLINS, 1989

World War II makes much more sense to a reader when he has some good maps. It's so easy to get lost in an explanation of some aspect of the war when an appropriate map isn't handy—you may end up finishing a book in something of a daze. There are dozens of World War II–related atlases, and picking one is tough. Although my personal favorite is the *West Point Military History Series Second World War Military Campaign Atlas,* that's a four volume set, and not always convenient. Thus my preference is for the one-volume *Times Atlas,* which succeeds at getting a lot of information into its maps, and keeping them clean.

This atlas covers the war chronologically, with each one- or two-page map covering operations that took place, on average, over several months, the time scale changing depending on various factors. In the Pacific, for example the war moved relatively slowly; in Russia, the pace was more lively. There's an index, and an abbreviated chronology in chart format (allowing for events in different theaters to be shown next to each other when they occurred at the same time). The 10 x 14-inch format allows for large maps, and prevents crowding. If a picture is worth a thousand words, a good map is worth a bit more.

Brief texts accompany each two-page spread of maps. When reading about unfamiliar aspects of World War II, you could easily absorb the basics from the maps. The identification of ground units is via the standard box with x's on top. Dates are clearly marked. Maps like these make a huge difference in understanding campaigns of World War II. Unlike during World War I, when armies barely moved for months, swift and far-reaching movement was the norm in World War II.

It's true that the gist of many World War II campaigns can be gotten using only text. For example: Germany invaded Norway in early 1940, during a three-month campaign between April and June. Okay, that's accurate and pretty much sums it up. But maps, like the ones here, show much, much more. This Norwegian campaign was quite complex, with air, naval and ground units moving simultaneously, from different directions, often towards the same objective. A map illustrates all these locations and how they relate to each other.

Many campaigns, on the other hand, were simple, straight-ahead affairs. Germany's quick conquest of France in 1940 was one of these. Here text can tell you more about this campaign than the maps. For example, the French were defeated by the Germans because of muddled thinking and poor planning. These things are difficult to represent on a map.

The *Times Atlas* devotes a good deal of coverage to the war in Russia, in recognition that more than 60 percent of German casualties were suffered there. To follow many of the campaigns in Russia maps are essential. Often the battles were confused affairs, even late in the war. Russian and German forces, for example, frequently got behind each other's lines simultaneously. Likewise, the 1941 invasion of Russia was not a simple matter. It was accomplished in a fairly complex series of maneuvers by the German armored and infantry divisions. One nice thing this atlas does is to orient its map of the initial German attack to show the German perspective. At the bottom of the map is Russia's western border. At the top are Leningrad, Moscow, and other cities. All in all, the maps here offer as much clarity as one would expect.

The naval campaigns in the Pacific were just as complex. This was more of a problem for the Japanese, as they tended towards elaborate operations. While their plans usually failed, they did so in interesting ways, and only a large-format atlas can really do the grandiose Japanese plans justice. The atlas displays clearly how, during their initial offensive in late 1941 and early 1942, the Japanese sent some of their forces literally halfway around the world.

Later in the war, even more complicated Japanese plans are rendered clearly and comprehensibly in the atlas' maps.

The charts included in the *Times Atlas* provide relevant statistical information, and are often accompanied by maps to best illustrate relationships such as the dispersal of populations, movements of refugees, economic factors, and military concerns such as air defense systems. No matter how good are the maps in the best World War II histories, they cannot equal the efficiency and clarity of those found here.

BRUTE FORCE

by John Ellis

VIKING, 1999

Many books discuss World War II strategy. Talking about whether commanders could have done this or that, however, usually is very sleep-inducing. *Brute Force* is different. The author takes the position, backed by easy-to-understand statistics, that the allies used their massive material superiority to bludgeon the Axis into submission, a point on which most historians tend to agree. Although the author lambastes Allied leaders for resorting to brute force, he tacitly admits that few Allied military leaders could have done otherwise.

World War II was a revolutionary moment in military history. It was not only the largest war in human history, it occurred at a time when warfare was undergoing momentous technological changes, and too few generals and admirals were quick enough to take full advantage of all this change. When the war began in 1939, the Germans knew more about making war successfully than their opponents. But these early German victories educated those who survived the initial German onslaught well enough to avoid being overrun again so easily. Such was the case in Russia where, as Ellis points out, most of World War II took place.

Even at the end, Germany never lost its edge at ground warfare, although its advantage diminished as the war went on and its opponents became more adept. The Germans and the Russians produced the largest number of outstanding generals, leaving the British and Americans to find their own ways to cope with the more capable German armies. The American answer was more weapons and firepower—the "brute force" of the title. There were only two American commanders as innovative and quick as their best German and Russian counterparts. George Patton was rightly feared by the Germans as the Western Allies' only real "Panzer [armor] General." By contrast, other British and American commanders relied on using lots of artillery. Patton preferred maneuver and aggressivness.

In the Pacific, the one commander who really knew what he was doing was General Douglas MacArthur, who used deception, mobility, and novel applications of technology to defeat the Japanese. And he did it with fewer American casualties than any other American commander. Ellis says what many American historians are reluctant to admit—that the U.S. Marine Corps battle across the central Pacific was a waste of men and resources. Better to do it MacArthur's way: come up from the south, cutting off Japan from its oil supply in the Dutch East Indies.

The author really has it in for the Allied strategy in the Mediterranean, where what Ellis refers to as the "soft underbelly of Europe" turned out to be a tough nut to crack. And that brings one round to the author's main point, that you can't always depend on a massive material superiority to win a war. The Allies did so but they could have won sooner, and at much less cost, if their leaders had been as well armed mentally as their troops were materially.

This book is a sobering lesson in how wars are really won, and nearly lost.

WAR IN THE SHADOWS

by Robert B. Asprey

MORROW, 1994

World War II provoked more widespread and diverse resistance to occupying enemy troops than any other war in history. *War in the Shadows* covers these movements in depth, explains where "partisan" or "guerrilla" fighters came from, and tells what happened to them after World War II. Some of these World War II era resistance movements are still going on. Actually, 220 pages of this 1277 page book are devoted to just the World War II–era guerilla wars. So you get a bonus in the form of information on how many pre–World War II resistance movements revived or expanded because of the war, and which ones kept going after the war officially ended (there were quite a few).

Many World War II buffs may be unaware of just how many countries hosted significant guerrilla operations during World War II. Here are the main ones.

- Although Albania was invaded and occupied by the Italians in 1939, a resistance movement did not get started until June 1941, when the Soviet Union was invaded by Germany. This was a common pattern in many nations, because the most effective underground groups in most countries were usually organized by Communists. In the 1930s, the Soviet Union encouraged the

11

formation of communist parties in other countries, the objective to come to power by means of a revolution. Thus, when these nations were invaded, the Communist cells were already prepared to form armed resistance groups.

- Belgium's population contained many Nazi sympathizers, many of whom joined the Waffen-SS (Nazi Party combat troops) to prove their loyalty. But the country also had an active anti-Nazi resistance, that lost over 17,000 Belgium freedom fighters to acts of savage German (and pro-German Belgian) retribution.

- Burma's population was largely indifferent to the war. Some Burmese actively collaborated with the Japanese, but several tribal groups, such as the Kachins, supported the British, who had been ruling Burma as a colony, and who treated the tribes better than the majority of Burmese. The tribes formed the core of a very active resistance. The armed resistance is still going on.

- Bulgaria was controlled by a pro-German government throughout the war, but as the Bulgarian people were traditionally pro-Russian, they did not declare war on the Soviet Union until 1944, at which point, local Communists formed a resistance movement that waited for the Red Army to arrive and support them.

- China probably had more guerrillas than the other occupied countries combined. Some were loyal to nationalist Chiang Kai-shek, some (the most effective) supported communist Mao Tse-tung, and some bandits and other political parties worked for themselves. The Japanese Army considered the partisans a nuisance, one that could not be ignored and would not go away. After the Japanese surrendered, most Chinese partisans regrouped and resumed fighting each other in the civil war that ended in a Communist victory.

- Czechoslovakia, already occupied by the Germans before the war began, assembled a well-organized resistance movement, but the partisans kept their heads down for most of the war. Nevertheless, the Germans were brutal anyway; more than 350,000 Czechs were sent to concentration camps, where 250,000 died, and many others died during anti-resistance campaigns. At the very end of the war, the Czechs rose up against the Nazis as the Red Army approached, and several thousand more Czechs perished.

- Denmark—not very large, not very defensible, and largely self-disarmed before the war—was conquered, in one day, by the Germans in early 1941. Organized resistance grew slowly, and plans were made for an armed uprising, but the war ended before these could be carried out.

- Resistance in Ethiopia, occupied by the Italians since 1936, was widespread and active from the very beginning. By the time the British arrived in 1941, the Italians were eager to surrender rather than face the continuing wrath of the tribal partisans.

- Resistance among Europe's Jewish partisans developed rapidly. Jewish fugitives formed guerrilla bands in forests throughout Europe, operating against German and other Axis troops, often in cooperation with local partisans but occasionally without their help. Jews in various ghettos armed themselves, and many joined nationalist resistance groups, such as the Yugoslav partisans.

- Partisan resistance in France, conquered in 1940, was active from the beginning. A Communist resistance cell only became active after the Soviet Union was invaded in June 1941 (before which time the French Communists collaborated with the Nazi occupiers and the Vichy government). By 1944, the resistance was more united, or at least better coordinated. The Germans were energetic in anti-partisan operations, particularly because the French resistance accounted for the principal espionage activity and was responsible for getting many downed allied pilots back to Britain. The resistance began active military operations (as opposed to sabotage, espionage, and assassinations) after the Allied invasion of Normandy in June 1944, and aided the Allies in driving the Germans out of France by the end of the year.

- Germany saw resistance to the Nazis crop up as early as 1933. Before war broke out in 1939, many senior German Army officers were actively trying to get rid of the Nazis. But the British and French were hesitant to cooperate and the Army became less of a source of resistance activity after war was under way. While resistance was widespread, and provided espionage services for the Allies, it was never organized on a large scale. The efficient Nazi secret police constantly arrested proven or suspected resistance members. When the war ended, many surviving resistance participants played roles in the rebuilding of the German government.

- Greece's many resistance movements emerged after the German invasion in 1941. Unfortunately, the partisans spent more time fighting each other that they did the Germans. Allied efforts to unite the various resistance groups were futile, something the Germans took advantage of, playing one partisan group against the other. When the Germans withdrew from Greece in 1944, the partisans were still engaged in a civil war continued until the late 1940s.

- Because Hungary had a pro-German government already in power when World War II broke out, Hungary became an active ally of Germany. The only resistance came initially from the Communists, who were ruthlessly hunted down by the secret police. As the war turned against the Axis, the Hungarian people lost their enthusiasm for the war, and the Germans. Strikes and demonstrations, often orchestrated by the Communists, led to Germany occupying the country in March 1944. At that point armed partisans became active, while parts of the Hungarian Army went over to the Russians. When the Red Army arrived in late 1944, the country was in chaos.

- Indonesia produced one of the strangest resistance movements. When the Japanese arrived in the Dutch East Indies, the leaders of the anti-Dutch independence movement agreed to bet on both sides. Some of them actively collaborated with the Japanese, even raising troops for their masters; others took to the hills and, with some Allied assistance, organized a moderately successful guerrilla movement. The Dutch returned in 1945 only to discover that both pro-Allied guerrillas and pro-Japanese collaborationists were lined up against them, aided by equipment the surrendering Japanese had abandoned. The result was a bloody post–World War II war for independence, which the Dutch lost.

- Italy experienced some low-level political resistance to Mussolini and his Fascist government before 1940, but afterward many Italians realized to their dismay that they had been dragged into World War II as a German ally. Mussolini's Fascists were not quite as bad as the Nazis, and some open opposition was tolerated. In fact, Mussolini was forced out of office in a July 1943 coup engineered by the king of Italy. Germany had by then occupied Italy north of Naples and proved to be far more ruthless in dealing with opposition. By this time armed resistance began in earnest, and there followed nearly two years of savage fighting between Italian anti-Fascist partisans and German troops assisted by armed pro-Fascist groups.

- The Netherlands was overrun in five days during early 1940. Many Dutch either sympathized with the Germans or simply considered the war over and the Germans the victors. As a result, there was little resistance during the first year of occupation. Afterward, however, increasing Allied successes caused many Dutch to change their minds, and a resistance movement grew. Because of the presence of many German combat and secret police units in a small country, armed resistance was never a practical option, but sabotage and espionage were common, coordinated by the government-in-exile in London. For a time, Prince Bernard, the husband of Queen Juliana (by birth a German), actually ran the resistance from inside the Netherlands.

- Norway was invaded and occupied by Germany in early 1940. A resistance movement was quickly organized. Unlike most others, the Norwegian resistance refrained from sabotage and armed activity in order to spare the civilian population reprisals (which usually included the taking and killing of hostages). The Norwegian resistance did engage in considerable espionage activity and assisted British commando operations within the country, actions that caused the Germans to suspect that one of the Allied invasions in 1944 would be in Norway. As a result, 17 German divisions were stationed in Norway during most of that year, tying up considerable forces in an area the Allies had no intention of invading, while making it even more difficult for the resistance to operate.
- Many American and Filipino troops fled to the mountains of the numerous Philippine islands even before the last regular U.S. and Philippine units surrendered on Bataan and Corregidor in mid-1942. Off in the bush, these soldiers organized resistance units that harassed the Japanese garrisons for the next two years. Cut off from aid because they were far from the nearest Allied bases, it wasn't until 1944 that regular contact was re-established, when US submarines and aircraft began to provide weapons and advisors. Most of the partisans were Philippine citizens, others were US officers and troops. Some radio contact was always maintained with the Allies, and the partisans were an invaluable source of information about the Japanese occupiers. When the Allies invaded the Philippines in late 1944, the tens of thousands of armed partisans were a major asset in quickly defeating the Japanese ground forces.
- Poland was invaded and carved up by Germany and the Soviets in 1939. A resistance movement, initially known as the Home Army, immediately sprang up. At first, only Britain offered assistance, but after the German invasion of the USSR in 1941, the local Communists (formerly active collaborators with the Nazis) got into the act too. In their efforts against the Polish resistance the Nazis were ruthless, and millions of Poles were killed. Because the Home Army was loyal to the government-in-exile in London, conflict flared with the Soviet-backed partisans who emerged after the Germans invaded the USSR. The two partisan armies did

not fight each other (at least not much), but the Home Army received little support from the Soviets (who were able to fly in arms and supplies for the Communist People's Army and refused to undertake operations that might aid their opponents). When the Germans were driven out in 1945, the Home Army began fighting Soviet troops and by the end of the decade the Home Army was exterminated and a Communist government established.

- Siam (Thailand) was the only independent nation in South East Asia at the start of World War II, and the Japanese leaned on the Thais to allow passage of Japanese troops on their way to invade British held Malaya and Burma. This was not popular with much of the population, but the Thai government thought it preferable to outright Japanese conquest. In the end, Japan occupied Thailand anyway, but still considered Thailand an "ally." A well-organized resistance movement, supported by many government officials, was active from 1942 on. The partisans provided invaluable espionage services for the Allies, as well as performing some sabotage, and thanks to that, Thailand was not treated as a former enemy nation after the war, even though technically it had been an ally of Japan.

- Partisan groups formed in the Soviet Union as soon as German units conquered Soviet territory. Many of these were composed of civilians, local Communists, or Soviet soldiers cut off in 1941 by the fast-moving Germans. Most partisans fled into the forests and swamps. Through 1941 and early 1942, partisan activity was largely uncoordinated and sometimes nationalist-oriented (pro-Ukrainian or anti-Communist, for example). By the end of 1942, the partisans came increasingly under the centralized control of the Soviet government. During 1943 and 1944, the Germans were hit with an increasing number of partisan attacks, and the resistance served as a valuable source of information for the Russians, a factor that became increasingly important as the Red Army took the offensive. By late 1944, the partisans were a major problem for the Germans, who often undertook multi-division operations in an attempt to clear resistance units from the German rear areas.

- Vietnam had been a French colony since the late 19th century. When the country was taken over by the Japanese, more or less peacefully, in late 1941, a resistance movement against the French was already in place, and it promptly shifted the focus of its operations to resist the Japanese. The Communist partisans were led by Ho Chi Minh, but included non-Communist groups as well. Armed attacks were made on the Japanese, and espionage missions were conducted for the Allies, who in return supplied weapons and supplies.

- Yugoslavia was invaded by the Nazis in early 1941, but until 1943 Germany's Italian allies comprised most of the occupation troops, aided by locally recruited Croat and Bosnian collaborators. Resistance formed immediately after the German invasion, but because of Yugoslavia's multicultural population, and the enmity between Communists and monarchists, more fighting was waged between partisans than with the occupying Italians. After Italy left the war in 1943, German troops took over the occupation. The partisans grabbed as many of the Italians' weapons as they could, and many anti-Fascist Italians joined them. Non-Communist partisans, most of whom were Croats, collaborated with the Italians, and then with the Germans, to gain an advantage over the largely Serbian Communist groups. Other ethnic groups tended to fight among each other rather than the occupying army. The Germans took advantage of this, to the extent that they recruited two SS divisions composed of Muslim Yugoslavs who were then turned loose on Christian civilians and partisans. By 1943, the Allies realized that, although they had been sending most of their aid to the non-Communist partisans, it was the Communist partisans led by Josep Broz (Marshal Tito), who were most energetically fighting the Germans. As a result, later that year, the Allies backed Tito and his partisans, who throughout 1944, became stronger and stronger and, eventually, earned the distinction of being the only partisan army to liberate their own country without the aid of Allied troops. The Yugoslav partisans were even able to keep the Red Army out of the country.

The amount of fighting done by the World War II guerrillas was enormous, and resulted in several million deaths to all involved. But because it was very difficult for the media to cover these operations, little attention was paid to one of the bloodiest and most savage aspects of the war.

THE BATTLE FOR HISTORY

by John Keegan

VINTAGE, 1996

This is a slim volume (128 pages) that delivers a masterful discussion of what is right, and what is wrong, about many of the most famous (if not always useful) books on the subject of World War II. The author has written extensively on military subjects, and his depth of experience supports his opinions on what has been written about World War II. In the book's six chapters, Keegan covers a different aspect of the war.

"Controversy and the Second World War" covers some of the better known, and still contentious, conspiracy theories, reasonable doubts and distaff interpretations of the war, from those who regarded Hitler as merely misguided and who insist that the Holocaust is a myth, to the endless arguments over what key leaders were really thinking when they made questionable decisions. Keegan's summary of these controversies in a mere twenty-one pages leaves one thinking that such conspiracies were, rather, simply the actions of people, some merely overwhelmed and perplexed, others downright evil, trying to make the best of desperate and confused situations.

"Histories of the Second World War" makes the point that no one has yet written a history of the war that satisfies the majority of the nations involved. Given the vastness of the war, and the fact that it was actually a number of separate, but interconnected conflicts, it's likely that no one ever will write such a history. Nevertheless, Keegan discusses which books he considers some of the better attempts, and suggests that the best way to understand what happened in World War II is to draw upon a number of different sources.

"Biographies" are another tough category. Dozens of major personalities participated in World War II, and biographers have made hundreds of attempts to unmask the real people by telling their stories. Part of the problem, as Keegan points out, is that World War II produced a bonanza of powerful men, able to lead nations, armies, and fleets, whereas World War I, by comparison, produced a slender fraction of the leadership talent that appeared two decades later. And, unfortunately, biographies of two of the most notorious of those leaders, Hitler and Stalin, have eluded a really thorough examination because so many of the key people to surround them throughout their careers did not survive the war or, in the case of Stalin, were silenced by fear of their leader even after his death and took their secrets to their graves. The best covered of the major figures was perhaps Churchill, because he was himself a prolific writer. Churchill's massive history of World War II is the work of a superb historian as well as the wartime leader of Great Britain, and is, in many ways, better than an autobiography.

In Keegan's opinion, biographies can better portray those second-stringers, just below the men at the very top. Mainly these were military commanders, whose activities were recorded in great detail. Regrettably, most of the Russian biographies have been edited to make sure they were "politically correct," and this often led to inaccuracies, falsehoods, and omissions.

"Campaigns" provides a host of good material, and Keegan gives due credit to some very good books. The only problem with books on campaigns and battles is that they show you only a narrow sliver of the war, a steaming jungle in the Pacific, a frozen battlefield in Russia, or a desert operation in North Africa. Among naval campaigns, frogmen planted explosives on the undersides of enemy battleships, individual submarines stalked their prey for months, and enormous fleet battles took place in the Pacific, in some cases involving more than a hundred aircraft carriers. Keegan cautions that many good accounts have been written about the same campaign, that the diligent readers can avail themselves of multiple, and illuminating, perspectives.

"The Brains and Sinews of War" covers espionage. This is one aspect of the war that is dominated by the ability of the Allies to read enemy secret codes ("Magic" in the Pacific and "Ultra" in Europe). Not much was written on this subject until the 1970s, because the Allies' code–breaking skills were still in use, deciphering other nations' secret messages. There were ample opportunities for conventional espionage during World War II, as well as "unconventional" (read guerrillas and commandos) warfare. This chapter also deals with books on industrial production, technology development, logistics, and economics, all of which was vital to winning World War II.

"Occupation and Resistance" treats some of the less pleasant, and less talked about, aspects of the war. Many nations were overrun and occupied by enemy forces for years. While much is made of the "heroic" resistance, far more people collaborated with the enemy. As more and more members of the generation that lived through occupation die off, it becomes easier to write books on this subject (without inciting a political firestorm).

THE HISTORICAL ENCYCLOPEDIA OF WORLD WAR II

edited by Marcel Baudot, Henri Bernard, and Hendrik Brugmans

FINE COMMUNICATIONS, 1997

People, places, things. They are all important, and many are mentioned in books without providing much context. You can easily get lost. This book, an encyclopedia of the entire war, with emphasis on people, battles, special events, and unique organizations, solves that problem. In other words, the little things you want to know. For example, you might be reading about Sweden's role during the war and encounter a casual reference to the "Iron Road." What do you do? Look it up in *The Historical Encyclopedia of World War II*. (It was a vital German route to ore mines in northern Sweden, and the reason Germany invaded Norway—to prevent the Allies from interfering with the transport of ore along this route to Germany.)

Hundreds of minor (but at times critical) personalities in the war are described. Take Kanji Ishiwara, a Japanese lieutenant general and rival of general Tojo, and a major player in the Japanese invasion of China in the 1930s. After losing out to Tojo in a struggle for leadership of Japan, Ishiwara retired and spent the war years running patriotic organizations. Another figure of minor importance was Ante Pavelich, who ran the pro-Nazi government of

Croatia. Croatia was the most enthusiastic of Germany's allies and had long wanted to be independent of the more numerous Serbs. The chance came during World War II, but many Croats paid for it after the war when the Serbs took revenge. Pavelich fled to Argentina, and continued to champion Croatian independence until his death in 1959.

You have probably just gotten used to mystery names coming up while reading something on World War II. Sure, most authors try to explain new personalities when they first show up, but who can keep track of who is who later in the book? Okay, some authors either continue to remind readers of who these guys are, or provide a cast of characters in the back of the book. If there's an index, you can always use that to refresh your memory. This encyclopedia solves the problem by providing descriptions of most of the important personalities you will come across, and can never remember when you need to.

Also useful are descriptions of important places, campaigns and battles. There's always some out-of-the-way place, like the Congo, that comes up in discussions about Charles de Gaulle and Free France. (Actually, some interesting events were transpiring down in the Congo in 1940, and you'll find it all here.) A wealth of otherwise hard-to-find information on the countries that played minor roles during the war is also included, as are other items that don't often receive much attention. Take "Peace Overtures." You get over five pages on that subject, and fascinating stuff it is. Another important topic covered in some depth is "Hygiene and Preventive Medicine." All those men crammed close together made a perfect breeding ground for epidemic diseases. Food turned out to be a critical "weapon" on the Russian front, where Russian troops were left to starve to death on "secondary fronts," while the men making a major attack at least got to die on a full stomach. The Russians figured out how to extract Vitamin C from pine needles, avoiding one critical vitamin deficiency from occurring among their troops.

Another topic covered here, and in a very handy fashion, is "Evacuation and Resettlement." In other words, refugees. Here the topic is restricted to refugees who fled during the war, an area all too rarely touched on in most books about World War II.

The Historical Encyclopedia was first published in France, compiled by French editors, written by largely European contributors, all of which gives it a different feel, while still being fair and accurate.

THE SECOND WORLD WAR

by *Winston S. Churchill*

MARINER BOOKS, 1986

Here's a history of the war from the ultimate insider. A six-volume work, published between 1948 and 1953, Winston Churchill's chronicle of World War II is unique because he was the only major leader to write such a history. His position as prime minister of wartime Britain and, along with Roosevelt and Stalin, one of the three key Allied leaders, placed him in a unique position. Churchill himself recognized this when he observed, "This is not history; this is my case." It's a pretty impressive case. The six volumes contain 5,000 pages of text, maps, and illustrations, are still in print, and are well worth reading.

The first volume, *The Gathering Storm*, covers two periods. The first is the two decades before 1939, as the aftermath of World War I mutated into the preliminaries of World War II, a time when Churchill was more observer than participant. But he was an astute observer, even as he was denounced often for alarmism over what was happening in Nazi Germany, and his predictions about the looming threat of another major war. The second period starts on September 3, 1939, with the German invasion of Poland, and ends on May 10, 1940, as the Germans are about to invade France. When war broke out, Churchill, then 64, was not yet prime minister, but was appointed head of the navy ("First Lord of the Admiralty"), a position he had held during World War I.

Churchill describes the war's early days from this particular vantage point, but by 1940 Churchill had become prime minister (or, as his opponents put it, the "War Prime Minister") and was seen by most Britons as the man for the job. Reading this, you can see why. Despite his age, Churchill was a whirlwind of activity. He could deal effectively with important details while never losing sight of the entire situation, a talent reflected in the 80-page appendix to this volume, giving statistics and other notes on operations during this period.

The second volume, *Their Finest Hour*, recounts how Churchill ran his part of the war. The first half covers the catastrophe in France during early 1940, when German armies conquered that country in six weeks. Churchill had long complained about France's lack of preparation for war with Germany, and he discusses the roots and results of those policies. The second half of the book covers the Battle of Britain, Germany's attempt to defeat the Royal Air Force using only their Luftwaffe. Churchill described Britain's response as its "finest hour" and, speaking of the few thousand British pilots that went up and defeated the more numerous, and equally determined, pilots of the Luftwaffe, famously remarked, "Never have so many owed so much to so few." This is a riveting account of a wartime leader facing a much more powerful opponent, but determined to resist to the end.

While British intelligence knew of Germany's preparations to invade Russia, Stalin was blind to any such evidence. Churchill's accounts of his attempts to convince Stalin that Russia was about to be attacked are another aspect of this wartime history that you will find in no other.

Churchill had a lifelong interest in military affairs, but he was not a conventional thinker. It was Churchill who supported the idea of the tank in World War I, and gave generals and admirals fits with his less practical ideas. During World War II, however, he was the top dog. If Churchill had an idea, the brass had to make it happen, or be prepared to face The Man himself and explain why. Churchill's big military innovation of 1940 was to create more commando units and make use of them throughout the war. The American Special Forces, Delta Force, Rangers, and Navy SEALs are all direct descendants of Churchill's wartime brainstorm.

The third volume, *The Grand Alliance*, shows Churchill's spirits on the rise as first Russia, then the United States, join the United Kingdom to combat Hitler. In both cases, Britain's new allies had to suffer attacks—Russia by Germany in June 1941, and America by Japan in December 1941—before entering the war. Churchill was the man in the middle of the "Big Three." A longtime anti-Communist, he quipped that after Germany invaded Russia he would put in a good word for Satan himself if the Nazis invaded hell. Britain began shipping military aid to Russia even before America entered the war, and Stalin appreciated this. There is much here about the close relationship Churchill developed with Franklin Roosevelt, and by the end of this volume, when the Germans and Japanese are at the peak of their powers Churchill knows that, with the United States in the war, the Axis will surely be beaten.

The fourth volume, *The Hinge of Fate*, carries the story from mid-1942 to the turning points at the end of the year. This volume opens with the Japanese rampage across the Pacific, seizing control from Britain of Hong Kong, Malaya, and the major naval base of Singapore, as well as the oil-rich Dutch East Indies from the Netherlands. Churchill was faced with Australia's fears that Japan would invade them, as well as the Japanese conquest of Burma and their advance into the mountainous jungles of eastern India. Churchill could depend on America to help defend Australia, but India was considered Britain's responsibility. The situation in North Africa was also growing desperate, as nothing seemed to be able to stop German General Rommel. In this volume, Churchill comments at length on the communications and conferences he had with Roosevelt and Stalin, as well as with other British politicians (Churchill was running Britain while he was also running the war). You can skip over these passages if you prefer to concentrate on the war, but bear in mind that the decisions made at these conferences played a large role in deciding how the war would be fought. This volume ends with the Germans defeated in North Africa, the Russians on the offensive, and the Japanese on the defensive.

The fifth volume, *Closing the Ring*, spends a lot of time describing the Italian campaign, fought largely at Churchill's insistence, which he pitched as an assault on the "soft underbelly of Europe." It turned out to be a brutal slog up the mountains of central Italy against determined German troops. This volume covers events from early 1943 to just before D-Day—June 6, 1944. It had been understood as early as 1942 that France would be invaded early in 1944. In the meantime, the Russians were screaming for help in pushing back the Germans.

Although Britain and the U.S. were sending huge amounts of aid to Russia, it was still a desperate fight on the "Russian Front" (for the British, the "Eastern Front"). Churchill had to cope with the Russians' constant demands that the Allies open a "Second Front" to assist them.

Churchill doesn't say much about the war in the Pacific, as it was largely an American war and, in Churchill's eyes, secondary to defeating Hitler. Pacific operations are mentioned mainly in discussions about the shortage of amphibious ships, which had to be massed in British ports in preparation for the D-Day invasion. Some American generals and admirals proposed that more amphibious ships be kept in the Pacific. Churchill discusses these behind-the-scene negotiations, which ended with most of the amphibious shipping used for D-Day sent off to the Pacific by the end of 1944, an action that explains the increasing number of amphibious operations in the Pacific during late 1944 and early 1945.

The last volume, *Triumph and Tragedy*, opens with the D-Day invasion of France in June, 1944. From there, the title of this volume becomes painfully accurate. For even as Germany and Japan are being defeated, the 45-year-long Cold War is beginning. Churchill is aware of this. Indeed, it was a speech he gave in March 5, 1946, in Missouri, where he coined the phrase "Iron Curtain." Much of this last volume is not about the string of victories in the closing months of the year, but about the diplomatic and political maneuvers Churchill conducted to try and avoid the Cold War. It was not to be, that is the "Tragedy" in the title.

Churchill's history of World War II holds up remarkably well. While many key items could not be covered, like the cracking of Ultra, the German secret communications codes, and Churchill only occasionally alludes to the "intelligence work," of Polish, British, and American code breakers, he never lets the reader lose sight of the critical logistical and political work that had to be done to bring about victory. Many key documents that Churchill consulted (and some he authored) in writing his history are still classified, and will not be available to the public for another 25 years or more. For now, this history of World War II is one of the most powerful and informative available. Plus, it's a damn good read.

(An abridged version of the six-volume set was published in 1959 and includes an additional essay in which Churchill discusses what happened during the ten years after the war.)

THE WORLD WAR II ALMANAC:
1931–1945

by Robert Goralski

PERIGEE, 1982; RANDOM HOUSE, 1985

The World War II Almanac: 1931–1945 is a chronological account of the war, taking the reader from the moment in 1931 when Japan invaded China (which many feel was the real start of the war), to September 2, 1945, when Japan signed a surrender agreement on an American battleship in Tokyo Bay. Interspersed among nearly 4,000 entries are maps, relevant pictures, and short items explaining such disparate matters as Arctic convoys, or women in the Soviet army, in detail. Keep this one by your side along with Baudot's *Historical Encyclopedia of World War II.*

Another useful feature of the almanac are its cross-references. Looking up the Battle of the Bulge, for example, you will find that, at the same time, heavy fighting was under way in Budapest, Burma, in the Philippines, and in Eastern France. Fifty pages of other reference material, cover such topics as comparative ranks, ship and personnel losses, equipment specifications and the like.

My well-thumbed copy of this book has been at my side for over twenty years, and I find myself going back to it again and again as I read new books on the war.

THE WORLD WAR II DATABOOK

by John Ellis and Michael Cox

AURUM PRESS, 2002

This book is an essential tool because World War II was a truly immense war. We're talking huge here, with lots of things going on at once. To truly understand the war you need access to the basic data about the war. Not the kind of material you find in an encyclopedia or almanac, but just plain old basic data. The details of any great event that hold it all together for those who want to understand what really went on.

This book contains the details of war: notable leaders, military formations, major ships, bases, production, and battles. Such information—and statistics—help put the war into perspective. The information in the *Databook* is organized in eight sections:

Maps. While most books on World War II include maps, the ones here are supplemented with dates and the locations of major units. These maps will often fill in gaps that less informative maps in other books do not.

Command Structures. Every nation has its key officials who make decisions and issue orders. History books often mention them in passing, leaving the reader to wonder, Who the hell was that? Here you have the answers for twenty-five nations involved in World War II. Senior civil and military leaders are listed, along with the dates when they began and ended their jobs. The names are presented in organization charts for the senior commands, so you know where everyone fits in. For the armies and fleets, there are simply lists.

Order of Battle. This is a vast subject, set forth in wire diagram form, showing which units were involved in battles or campaigns. Included are the formation date and combat record of all American combat divisions (there were less than a hundred), as well as similar coverage for units from Russia, The British Commonwealth, and several other European nations, but nothing on China, which had over 400 divisions (many only brigade size and poorly equipped). Good as far as it goes, and additional order-of-battle references are given in the bibliography, which also tracks changes in order-of-battle during selected campaigns. Excellent coverage on the Russian front and Europe. The section on campaigns includes diagrams that show how the divisions were organized during major campaigns, and an "ebb and flow" chart, that illustrates which divisions left the theater (or were destroyed) each month, and which new ones entered.

Tables of Organization and Equipment (also called TO/E). These tables show the most significant units in about two dozen nations and the major items of equipment (tanks, artillery, machine-guns, etc.) they used, data that can be useful when reading about a particular operation and reference is made to its weapons and equipment.

Strengths. Nearly fifty tables show comparative ground, air, and naval strength for all the major nations involved in the war. Items listed include manpower, tanks, warplanes, merchant ships, and warships, and interpret relatives values of such material as German versus Russian armored vehicle strength, or Axis versus Allied warplanes available for combat at specific campaigns. Bombing campaigns are covered, giving tonnages of bombs dropped, as are ship types and quantities for major naval battles.

Casualties and Losses. Tables in this section give overall casualties, followed by breakdowns of losses for armies, air forces, navies, and shipping. The information is organized by date and theater, including cumulative totals and comparisons between Allies and Axis for different periods.

Production. The underlying strength of each nation at war depended on the food, raw materials, steel, oil, and equipment they could produce. Such factors are mentioned briefly in other histories of the war, but the *Databook* furnishes important numbers for each category. One such item, aluminum, was critical because it's what most World War II aircraft were made of. Looking at American production statistics one notices huge aluminum production capacity—the reason the United States produced so many aircraft. Data are also provided for major weapons like tanks, artillery, mortars, and machine-guns, along with those for another critical component of World War II warfare—trucks. The tremendous production of trucks in the United States was a key factor in defeating the Germans, who used horses for hauling in their combat divisions. Warship and merchant shipping production is also included.

Hardware. This section lists the basic characteristics of hundreds of weapons, among them aircraft, tanks, warships, artillery, and anti-tank guns. Information includes armor thickness, speed, and types of guns carried by tanks; speed, radius, and range for artillery and bomb load, for aircraft. Also given are the dates each weapon entered service and how many were produced.

WHY THE ALLIES WON

by Richard Overy

W.W. NORTON, 1997

This book makes one point and makes it very well: an Allied victory was not inevitable. It has been fashionable since World War II to assume that no matter how much the Allies screwed up, no matter what the Axis did, the Allies would prevail eventually. Not so, says the author, who makes a compelling case why this is so.

One of the most critical reasons for the Allies' success is known, but rarely explored: the Germans did not mobilize for war until 1944, and their production of weapons peaked early in 1945. Given that, from 1941, Germany controlled most of the industrial capacity of Europe, an earlier mobilization would have made the German armed forces much more powerful. That alone could have changed the course of the war. The reason Hitler did not order the kind of mobilization going on in Russia, the United States, and Britain, was that he thought he didn't have to. Hitler believed he could increase his popularity in Germany by not upsetting the people, who felt that they were already winning and enjoyed the fact that German factories were still turning out lots of consumer and luxury goods.

Hitler also made a number of fundamental strategic errors. He was too slow to realize the critical role submarines would play, and refused to build more of them. Instead he ordered the construction of battleships and an aircraft carrier (that was never finished). It wasn't until 1943 that the Allies got the German U-Boats under control, mainly because the Germans had only a few dozen available for operations in the Atlantic. Had the Germans built three or four times more subs before war began, and put more money into developing new submarine equipment earlier, Britain would have been more vulnerable to a German invasion, and the landing at Normandy on D-Day, and the strategic bombing campaign against Germany would have been much more difficult. German battleships and an aircraft carrier were worthless to the Nazis. Had the resources used to build these big ships been diverted to construct a hundred Type-VII subs in the late 1930s, the outcome of the war might have been quite different.

Then there was the Battle of Britain in late 1940, where the Germans misunderstood the importance of radar and its use in fighting the first modern air campaign. There was no reason why the Germans couldn't have figured that out. Actually, some did, but, in a pattern repeated throughout the war, Nazi leaders boldly made wrong decisions in blatant disregard for the facts. Allied leaders made some dumb decisions, too, but they were a distant second to Nazi big shots.

It's long been thought that the United States development of the atomic bomb first would have cancelled any edge the Germans might have gained earlier in the war. That's true, except for a few key details. First, the bomb wasn't ready for use until the summer of 1945. Had the Germans won the submarine war, and conducted their Russian campaign in a more thoughtful manner, by 1945 Britain and Ireland would be occupied by German troops, as would most of Russia and the Middle East from Morocco to the Persian Gulf. If the U.S. had an atomic bomb, how were we going to deliver it? A B-29 base on Iceland was a possibility. But this problem was foreseen, and was the reason for the development of the B-36 bomber, which began in November 1941. The B-36 (which entered service in 1948), could fly from North America to Europe, drop an atomic bomb and fly back. What about enemy interceptors? No problem, the B-36 would fly at 40,000 feet, where in 1941 no fighter could reach it. By 1945, however, there were fighters that could. And there is the problem with atomic bombs and the "one bomber, one bomb, one city" argument. If the one bomber gets shot down, there goes your one bomb. Building an atomic bomb turned out to be more difficult than thought. (By 1949, we only had a hundred of them.) If, by the time the U.S. has a hundred bombs, the Germans might have caught up and have a few of their own, and the nuclear edge is lost. Without air superiority over part of Europe, you can't deliver your nuke to Berlin, or any other German city.

Put simply, the Allies were better at solving problems than their Axis opponents. And often the solutions hinged on seemingly simple things that had far-reaching consequences. For example, when American long-range bombers were being chewed up by German interceptors in late 1943, there suddenly appeared a simple solution: the addition of drop tanks for fighters, so bombers could be escorted all the way to their targets and back, a tactic that saved the bombers and destroyed the German fighter force, which was worn down trying to fight. Without those drop (fuel) tanks, carried where fighters usually slung a couple of bombs, and dropped after the fuel was used up, the bomber offensive would have been crippled, German weapons production would have been much higher and the war would have lasted longer. The Germans were aware of this innovation, and its usefulness in destroying the German air force. With American bombers wandering at will over Germany in daytime, Germans were forced to withdraw most of their fighters from the Russian front to defend German industry against bombing. This allowed the Russians to regain control of the air over Russia. After 1943 the Allies always had air superiority in Western Europe because Britain and the U.S. were out-producing Germany in aircraft and trained pilots. Without the drop tank, Allied air superiority could only extend as far as Allied fighters could fly, and beyond their range, elsewhere in Germany, factories and railroads would continue working unhindered. Something as simple as drop tanks accelerated the destruction of German air superiority.

No single innovation won the war for the Allies, but dozens of solutions, taken as a whole, did. For example, during the bloody fighting in the hedgerows country of Normandy after D-Day, Allied tanks were suffering tremendous losses because they exposed their soft underbellies to German fire as the tanks climbed over the hedgerows. An American army sergeant realized that by welding two knife like pieces of metal to the front of the tank, the hedgerows could be lifted up and tanks (as well as trucks) could move right through them. Another simple idea that reduced Allies losses and increased German losses. Then there was the use of long range bombers to hunt submarines, another innovation.

Throughout *Why the Allies Won*, Richard Overy makes a clear and convincing case for many alternative outcomes to the war. He also points out that there was something the Nazis could not change, the fact that they were bloody-minded tyrants who did not have the support of most Germans. The first people sent to concentration camps were political opponents of Hitler, and there were a lot of them, but the Nazis had the power to force obedience. Hitler found many willing collaborators in the nations he conquered; nevertheless, there was always a large number that continued to actively oppose the Nazis. The author makes clear that the Nazis had the means to compel cooperation, and had they immediately mobilized the industrial capacity of occupied nations for their war effort, the outcome of World War II could have been different.

Overy shows that World War II was not a matter of who was better, but who was worse. The Nazis and Japanese were worse at making strategic military and political decisions, worse at realizing the kind of situation they were in, worse at doing what had to be done and doing it quickly, and these failures gave Allied leaders opportunities that, for the most part, they seized.

The Allies, especially the U.S. and Russia, realized the potential for mass production and, as the Russians liked to put it, "quantity has a quality all its own." The Americans and the British also made the most of their abundance of scientists and engineers to devise more military innovations than their German and Japanese counterparts. The Germans came up with many good ideas first, but in attempting to "perfect" their novel ideas, they frequently ended up producing too few of a better weapon. Also, the Allies did a better job at managing their alliance. Germany resented the fact that the

Japanese never declared war on Russia, and that Italy betrayed them and switched sides in 1943. The Allies had no such problems.

You'll never look at World War II history the same way after reading this.

Two

THE WAR IN THE WEST
(EUROPE AND THE MIDDLE EAST)

---

*D*URING MUCH OF World War II, this is where the action *wasn't*. France had been conquered in six weeks in 1940. Until Italy was invaded in late 1943, there were long periods with no ground combat in the West. However, there was always something going on in the air. The dramatic Battle of Britain in late 1940 turned into a vigorous two-way bombing campaign by 1941. Increasingly, bombs fell on German military targets in France, French factories producing goods for the Germans, and French railroads moving German material. (The French resistance was insignificant until 1943.) From 1940 to 1943, the heavy action was in Russia, the Mediterranean, and North Africa. On June 6, 1944, the Allied amphibious invasion of France brought the ground war back to Western Europe in a major way, and led to the end of the war in less than a year.

CRUSADE IN EUROPE

by Dwight D. Eisenhower

JOHNS HOPKINS UNIVERSITY PRESS, 1997

This is the sort of book by a military commander that explains "what I did and how I did it." It's a classic of its type, especially in light of how much information was still classified when Eisenhower wrote the book right after the war. Not until the 1970s was anyone allowed to talk about code-breaking or the deception measures used during World War II.

Eisenhower covers a lot of ground, and in doing so gives an invaluable insider's account of what happened. Ever the diplomat, Eisenhower doesn't dish the dirt—he was hell for gossip columnists and those writers feeding off disasters and the acts of inept leaders. Eisenhower, though not flamboyant, was capable and dependable, which was why he got as far as he did as fast as he did.

Eisenhower was a general who never led troops in combat, yet managed to put together one of the largest military operations in history, and win the one campaign over which he did preside. Raised in Kansas, and graduating from West Point in 1915, he trained tank troops in the United States during World War I, preparing them for the "final battle" against Germany that never happened because Germany accepted an armistice in 1918.

Promoted to captain for these efforts, Eisenhower demonstrated early his capacity for getting things done.

He spent the 1920s in staff jobs and attending Army staff and command schools, finishing first in his class at the Command & Staff school. He later spent two years working with retired General John Pershing, who had commanded American forces in France during World War I. The work for Pershing involved taking care of the graves of Americans killed in France during World War I, and preparing educational materials for Americans who would visit those cemeteries. Eisenhower learned much from Pershing about the development of mobile warfare during the last year of World War I, which included masses of tanks and trucks on the battlefield, paratroopers, and extensive use of airpower.

In 1933, now a major, he joined the staff of Army Chief of Staff Douglas MacArthur. Eisenhower got along with MacArthur (which wasn't easy), who recognized in Eisenhower someone with military, administrative, and managerial talents. When MacArthur formed the Philippines army in 1935, he convinced Eisenhower to accompany him to help out. As usual, Eisenhower excelled, and was promoted to lieutenant colonel. MacArthur was heard to remark that Eisenhower was "the best clerk I ever had." Eisenhower learned that MacArthur was an officer given to original thinking and was interested in the rapid adoption of new technology and as a particular fan of air power, Eisenhower learned to fly while working with him in the Philippines.

After the war began in 1939, he returned home to assist in preparing the U.S. Army for possible involvement. In March 1941, he was promoted to colonel and became chief of staff of the Third Army. Eisenhower's administrative skills came to the attention of Army Chief of Staff George Marshall, who brought Eisenhower to army headquarters in Washington. At the end of that year, he was assigned to work on plans for a British-American invasion of Europe, which had been under discussion by President Roosevelt and Prime Minister Churchill.

Although the United States was not at war, Britain and Russia were taking a beating from the Germans. American military and economic aid for Britain and Russia was considered a stop-gap until the United States was dragged into the war. By December 1941, America was in the war. Unfortunately, the Germans were in the Moscow suburbs, Britain was being regularly bombed by German aircraft and Nazi submarines were sinking ships off the coast of the United States. But it was the job of staff officers, especially at the highest level, to plan ahead. Eisenhower's work during 1942 on an invasion of German-occupied Europe so impressed General Marshall that Eisenhower, who had been already promoted to brigadier (one-star) general in September 1941, was made a major (two-star) general in March 1942. Three months later, Marshall chose Eisenhower over 366 more senior generals to make him commander of U.S. forces in Europe, and in July, 1942, Eisenhower was promoted to lieutenant (three-star) general and given command of the American force that would land in western North Africa (Operation Torch).

Eisenhower handled such promotions well, even though he left most of the battlefield decisions to his subordinates. When one corps commander proved wanting, Eisenhower sent in George Patton, who quickly sorted out the situation. Eisenhower took a lot of heat for working with the Vichy officials in charge of Algeria, who had collaborated with the Germans, but the deal he worked out with them spared his men considerable fighting against French troops. In February 1943, Eisenhower was promoted to four-star general. He had gone from colonel to full general in only seventeen months.

After the Germans in North Africa surrendered in May, Eisenhower presided over the successful invasions of Sicily and Italy, which occurred before the end of the year. In late December, he was made supreme commander of the Allied Expeditionary Forces that were soon to invade France. He arrived in Britain in January 1944 to oversee the final preparations.

Eisenhower had been involved in planning for this operation for more than two years, and discovered early on that this would be no easy task. The Germans not only kept a large garrison in France, but had the ability to pounce quickly on any invasion from the sea and push it back.

Eisenhower was quick to appreciate how the Germans had

developed new mechanized warfare tactics. The original plan for an invasion of France in 1943 called for three divisions to come in over the beaches and two airborne brigades to land behind those beaches to delay German reinforcements. But as Eisenhower discovered in Italy, the Germans could be very, very quick. In late 1943, Eisenhower had three divisions landing near Salerno, in southern Italy. There was only one German division opposing this, the 16th Panzer division, which was covering over 30 kilometers of coastline. Eisenhower knew that additional German divisions would rapidly move towards his beachhead. He thought that he had enough air power to keep the German reinforcements away. But most of the Allied aircraft were still operating from North Africa and were unable to get enough aircraft over the roads the Germans were moving south on.

On September 14, five days after the Allied divisions landed, they were being attacked by two German Panzer Corps. When it looked like the German attack might push the Allies back into the sea, Eisenhower ordered everything that could fly to get up to Salerno and to go after the attacking Germans. That, and gunfire from Allied battleships, stopped the Germans about four kilometers from the beach. It was close, very close. Eisenhower remembered this near disaster as he went back to Britain to prepare for the 1944 invasion of France.

Eisenhower knew how fast the Germans could respond to an amphibious landing, and he saw to it that there was no shortage of airpower to keep the panzer divisions away from the beachhead in France. To do this he needed control of all the warplanes operating out of Britain for several months. Eisenhower had to threaten to resign to achieve this, because not everyone agreed that his plan to isolate Normandy, using only air power, would work.

But the plan was simple. Using thousands of fighters and bombers, all the railroad bridges and engines from Paris to Normandy would be constantly attacked for nearly two months before the D-Day invasion. Before the air attacks began, the Germans had been moving a hundred trains a day into Normandy. By the end of April, they were only moving forty-eight trains a day. By the end of May, fewer than twenty trains a day were getting in. By D-Day,

June 6, the Allies had cut every railway bridge over the Seine river and shot up any locomotive they could find south of Paris. No new trains were getting south of Paris.

Normandy was cut off. This meant supplies and combat divisions could not move by rail, the preferred mode of transportation. The panzer divisions would have to move by road, and the roads were covered by low flying fighter bombers all day. Movement by night was possible, but this meant crawling along at ten kilometers an hour, if that. For infantry units, night movement meant a speed of 3–4 kilometers an hour. And these were the shortest nights of the year, with the Summer Solstice approaching in late June. Three German panzer divisions were sent towards Normandy, it took them several days to get there, and all had lost over twenty percent of their vehicles in the process. This time, German armor never threatened the Normandy bridgehead as they had nine months earlier at Salerno. Eisenhower did not make the same mistake twice.

Eisenhower's strategy, which included a huge bombing raid on a panzer division to assist the breakout from the Normandy beachhead, did indeed work, and within months, on August 25, Paris was liberated. But after that the Allied armies continued moving towards Germany using Eisenhower's "broad-front" plan. This approach was considered more prudent than sending individual columns after the retreating Germans. Patton was the only Allied army commander that Eisenhower felt could handle the Germans in a mobile battle. And Eisenhower knew it was too risky to leave it up to just one army commander to tangle with some of Germany's best generals, even if the Germans were outnumbered. There was also the problem with the British, and their hero, General Montgomery. The British realized that Eisenhower was in charge because the majority of the troops were American, but did not go along with the idea that Patton was a better general than Montgomery. This, despite the fact that Patton had already demonstrated this in North Africa and Sicily. So Eisenhower did the prudent thing, which was what he was there for.

German resistance stiffened when the Allies reached the German border, and in December 1944 the Nazis launched a massive offensive (the Battle of the Bulge). That same month, Eisenhower was promoted to the special wartime rank of five-star general ("General of the Armies," equivalent to "field marshal" in other armies). The Allies crossed the Rhine on March 7 and the war in Europe ended two months later.

Despite criticism for the way he commanded the Allied forces in Europe, most of Eisenhower's decisions were made correctly. He was knocked for some of the officers he chose to lead armies, but people forget that there was only a small pool of Allied commanders who had successfully commanded armies in wartime, much less any with a track record against the still-formidable Germans. In retrospect, we see that Eisenhower made smart choices, and went the extra mile to keep his best general, George Patton, out of trouble and on the job.

One of the reasons Eisenhower was picked for the supreme commander job was because he was low key and got things done without a lot of fuss. Eisenhower had to deal with major personalities from several nations (the U.S., Britain, France and Russia), and many smaller ones. He could easily screw up and cause major diplomatic problems. But he never did. Eisenhower was something of a stealth general. This led some to believe that he wasn't really doing much and was just lucky. Well, he was lucky, a quality commanders like Napoleon, and many others, recognized and respected. But Eisenhower was also insightful, shrewd, and efficient. Both MacArthur and Marshall (and Roosevelt and Churchill) admired how Eisenhower always carried out what he was asked to do. No muss, no fuss, just results. The main part of Eisenhower's job as supreme commander was to, well, herd cats. He handled that, and anything else that was tossed in his direction. There's not much more you can ask of a supreme commander.

Crusade in Europe is more than just Eisenhower's account of his work as a senior American commander during World War II. The book shows a very smooth, decisive and diplomatic general at work.

DECEPTION IN WORLD WAR II

by Charles Cruickshank

OXFORD UNIVERSITY PRESS, 1985

You can't understand World War II without knowing something about the role deception played in more than fifty major operations deployed by the Allies in the European Theater, the many others used by the Germans, Russians and Japanese, and hundreds of additional minor deception operations developed by guerrilla movements in order to survive. Military deception is more than just camouflage and wearing green uniforms. Many different techniques are used: the sending of false radio messages, use of dummy buildings and vehicles, the work of spies, and much more. Deception became a formal part of World War II military operations.

Part of this was due to the large number of people (over a hundred million) who found themselves armed and in harm's way during that war. Over 90 percent of these troops were civilians before the war began, and they brought with them a degree of pragmatism and inventiveness rarely seen in wartime. Not wanting to get themselves killed, and casting about for ways to avoid that, new deception techniques was the natural result.

But professional soldiers were also open to new ideas to a greater degree than in any past war. World War I was still fresh in everyone's mind, and even the most tradition bound professional remembered that during that war, doing things, "the traditional way" almost always led to disaster. Thus it should come as no surprise that there were many new ideas enthusiastically embraced by military professionals during World War II.

Despite the fact that deception was practiced frequently and with great enthusiasm, little has been written about it, partly because there is nothing particularly sexy about deception. Impressive-looking weapons get plenty of attention. Heroic efforts by the troops are often praised. But deception? It might have something to do with the fact that deception is thought of as somewhat unsoldierly, almost cowardly. It can be hard to get steamed up over how soldiers stayed hidden and avoided contact with the enemy, or how commanders made up elaborate lies and false fronts to deceive their opponents.

There is another reason: many deception campaigns remained secret long after the war. *Deception in World War II* could be written only after Britain finally declassified its deception files in 1977. Most British World War II records were subject to the Thirty-Year Rule, and were declassified as early as 1969, but not those concerning deception, because many techniques and methods were still in use, and had to be kept from potential enemies. Military paranoia? Maybe.

Consider that the first widespread use of deception by the British occurred in late 1940, during the Battle of Britain. This air campaign between the R.A.F. and the Luftwaffe, was fought to prevent Germany from gaining control of the air over the English Channel. Had the Germans won, they could have invaded and conquered Britain. Deceptions used successfully against the Luftwaffe were still considered in the 1970s potentially effective against enemy aircraft in some future war.

Deception had long been used by hunters, and still is. But the military were not major users of it, if only because, for thousands of years, military operations concentrated on fighting battles to quickly decide who won, and lost, the war. There were still uses for deception, but it was rarely of the hide and seek variety used by hunters and primitive warriors. Large armies were difficult to hide, and generals learned to use light cavalry as scouts, and to chase away enemy scouts. Generals also played mind games on their opponents, trying to make them think they were somewhere else (which made surprise attacks possible) or more, or less, numerous than they actually were (which made all manner of devilish tricks possible).

Twentieth-century technology had an enormous impact on the art of deception. First came aircraft, initially used primarily for scouting. No longer could troops be hidden by keeping them behind a hill or in a forest. Ground camouflage was largely ineffective with enemy aircraft overhead. And not only combat troops worried about deceptions; aircraft and longer-range (and more accurate) artillery made deception a life-saving practice for troops normally out of sight of the enemy.

During World War II, it was a given that anyone in the "combat zone" (about thirty kilometers from the front line, where infantries were trading fire) had to hide themselves from aerial observation. This involved more than putting camouflage nets and foliage over positions and equipment. You had to literally hide your tracks. Trucks, armored vehicles, and horse-drawn wagons and weapons left track marks in the ground when they moved cross-country, on dirt roads, or when veering off roads to hide in a forest, and these tracks were visible from the air. Troops quickly discovered that covering their tracks could be a matter of life or death. This was a simple, but life-saving deception. So was faking tracks that were left uncovered, tracks leading to a patch of forest that was empty of troops and equipment. Let the enemy bomb and shell that all he wants, and waste lots of ammunition. Deception had many uses.

Deception in World War II mostly covers British deceptions because Britain had a tremendous incentive to develop convincing deceptions early on. At the end of June 1940, Great Britain was in big trouble. Germany had just conquered France, and the British, cut off and nearly surrounded, were forced to evacuate most of their troops from France and leave their weapons and equipment behind. Because Britain refused to negotiate with Germany, Germany prepared to invade. With most of the army's heavy weapons and equipment abandoned in France, it was up to the Royal Navy and RAF to stop the Germans, and victory in the Battle of Britain, in which the outnumbered RAF prevented the Germans from gaining air control over the Channel, was accomplished in no small part via deception.

The Germans knew they had more aircraft, and they knew that if they could destroy the British aircraft, air fields and aircraft factories, victory would be theirs. The British used deception to weaken the effectiveness of German bombing attacks and keep the RAF in the air. The principal deception was false airfields and, to a lesser extent, false aircraft factories and other prime targets. Two type of false airfields were used, one (the most common) for deceiving night bombing attacks, the other to deceive daylight attacks. Over a hundred of these "Q" sites (for deceiving night bombers) were built and were pummeled by twice as many bombs as the nearby real airfields they protected. "Q" sites didn't look anything like an airfield in daylight and used lights for their deception, which depended on the fact that an airfield at night would show only landing lights around the landing strip, along with the lights of landing aircraft and planes circling the landing strip. The "Q" sites rigged lights (using strung lines, pulleys and carriages) to simulate, as seen from the air, an airfield in action. Radar was effective in giving warning when German bombers were approaching, allowing time for the real airfield to extinguish its lights, while the "Q" site would turn its lights on. If the Germans were fooled (and eventually they did discover the existence of decoys), their bombers would hit the "Q" site, resulting in the odd situation whereby the "Q" site operators, safely in bunkers near their fake airbase, would cheer as the Germans bombed them.

When German recon aircraft often returned the next day to check on the damage, all they could find were bomb craters nearby, in an open area that in daylight was obviously not an airbase. Suspicions were raised, but never enough to render all the "Q" sites useless. At night, even with electronic navigation aids, German pilots could still be deceived into bombing the fake airfield a few miles from the real one.

Whenever the Germans were strong enough, they would make daylight raids, attempting to destroy as many enemy aircraft as possible and get a clear shot at British airfields. You might think it impossible to build fake airfields good enough to deceive enemy bombers in daylight. It was. The British built sixty "K," or dummy, airfields but they did not fool the Germans, who carefully examined any new airfield and soon determined whether it was a phony. The Russians were later more successful creating dummy airfields later in the war, but this was because the real Russian airfields were pretty primitive affairs to begin with, and the Russians were always building new airfields.

Aircraft factories were the other prime target for German bombers. The British built four fake aircraft factories, two of which managed to fool the Germans, who bombed the fakes instead of the real ones nearby. During 1940, the British also prepared extensive fake ground defenses, in expectation of the worst-case scenario of German troops storming ashore. Apparently the Germans were taken in by these deceptions, but never had occasion to act on them because their troops never entered Britain. Most of these British deceptions took place during the Battle of Britain, from August to October of 1940, after which Germany redirected most of its aircraft for the upcoming invasion of Russia. The Germans did learn from their experience with British deceptions, however, and used some of the same tricks against Allied bombers.

Germany never got any spies operating in Britain either, although they thought they did. Early on, Britain rounded up nearly all German spies and turned most of them into double agents, the famous (but also secret until the 1970s) XX ("Double Cross") System, an initiative so effective that the Germans never caught on to the fact that their spies in Britain were working for the other side.

One area of British deception the author does not examine is that of master of deception, Jasper Maskelyne, much of whose work during World War II is still classified. Maskelyne made his mark in late 1942, as the British and Germans faced each other in North Africa at El Alamein. The British were desperate for a victory, but knew from experience that having more men, guns, and tanks was not enough—they had to deceive the Germans into holding back their reserve force of armored divisions while the main British attack was chewing through the German defenses. They needed some magic, and got it from Jasper Maskelyne and his "Magic Gang." Maskelyne was a third-generation stage magician, the greatest in Britain, and a major celebrity. He joined the army when war broke out, and quickly impressed the British army with his ability to create militarily useful deceptions. The British commander in North Africa, General Montgomery, recognized Maskelyne's skills and put him in charge of deceiving the Germans. This Maskelyne did, building fake armored divisions, supply dumps, railroads, and staging areas to make it appear like the main attack would come in the south. The real attack would be in the north, but if the Germans were deceived, the British would be spared having to face the formidable panzers of the German reserve force.

Maskelyne made his deception work because he brought to the job techniques most practitioners of military deception lack: misdirection and lighting. A stage magician uses both to divert attention when a trick is being performed. Maskelyne examined aerial reconnaissance photos and went up himself to see what it really looked like from up there. One thing he discovered was that dummy tanks didn't have to be full-size in the desert. As long as there were no other visual reference points, the dummies could be two-thirds size and still be convincing, thus saving scarce materials and enabling the production of more dummy vehicles. Also a master in the use of light and shadow, he created deception techniques no one had ever thought of before. The Germans were thoroughly deceived.

Maskelyne later returned to Britain where he worked on some deceptions that were so sensitive they remain secret to this day. Partly because of the secrecy of his work, he never got the credit he deserved. When *Deception in World War II* was published, Maskelyne was considered a somewhat mysterious character, and he still is. Those who worked with him in North Africa were in awe of his skills, and it's from their glowing reports that we know of Maskelyne's deception efforts at all.

While the author doesn't say anything about Maskelyne, he does go into some detail about the excellent inflatable dummy tanks, trucks and guns, and how these were used. Maskelyne's technique of using smaller (than life size) dummies only really worked in the desert. Any place else, there would be objects that would show how out of scale the smaller fakes were.

Deception in World War II also covers several other imaginative deceptions, such as the rumor campaigns among British civilians. Actually, the Germans used this one as well. The basic idea was to have convincing intelligence agents go out to crowded places (pubs, markets, trains) and casually "plant" the desired rumors. While the German spies in Britain were all under British control, there was still unofficial communication between Britain and Germany via neutral countries (Switzerland, Portugal, Sweden) and rumors tended to travel pretty quickly along those routes. The author explores in detail the massive deception campaigns that led up to D-Day. This would be the most crucial deception of all: Would the Normandy invasion be the real one, or merely a deception? This was truly one of the most massive, and successful, deception campaigns in history. Too huge to keep entirely secret after the war, many of the technical details were nevertheless kept in the shadows until the 1970s.

The author gives only slight coverage to the Japanese, no great loss. All of their deception techniques were revealed and widely publicized after the war. The Japanese used effective strategic deceptions before launching their offensive against the U.S. and its Pacific allies in late 1941. The use of radio silence and false radio traffic, to hide the position of major portions of the Japanese fleet, worked quite well, and was, in fact, used successfully during World War II by many nations. This involved having a bunch of radio operators imitating a unit, or group of ships, that did not exist, or was actually somewhere else. If done correctly, meaning sending realistic messages, even though most were in code, it worked. It was, and still is, very hard to see through a false-radio-traffic deception.

The Japanese were also exceptionally imaginative at camouflage. For example, when small supply ships were sent to Guadalcanal during late 1942 to help Japanese troops retake the island and its airfield from the Americans, the ships tied up at night in coves of nearby islands, disguised to resemble the many small islets that dotted such coves. Once the Americans caught on, they had to send PT boats to inspect the coves regularly.

Even Japanese Kamikazes engaged in defective deceptions. One was seen off Okinawa in 1945. The American fleet was being constantly attacked by Kamikazes, and there it was that the "phony dogfight" ploy was first seen. Two Japanese aircraft would approach an American ship, usually one of the destroyers on the edge of the fleet, and just out of range of their anti-aircraft guns. The two aircraft would go through the movements of aircraft trying to shoot each other down. The American sailors manning the anti-aircraft guns would hold their fire, assuming that one of the dog fighting aircraft was American. When the two Japanese aircraft got so close that it was obvious they were both Japanese, they would both dive at the nearest American ships, thus receiving a lot less anti-aircraft fire than otherwise, and often succeed in their attack.

It's too bad that Cruikshank gives short shrift to the Russian deceptions, which were in a league of their own. Russian troops were, if anything, more imaginative and thorough than the Japanese, the British, and just about everyone else. Moreover, the Russians thought big, working out deception plans that involved their entire armed forces and the defense industries that supplied them. Partly this was to make it difficult for spies to gather useful information, a motive that persisted after World War II, when Russian deceptions during the Cold War grew more elaborate, impressive, and effective. For this reason, many Russian deceptions of World War II are still secret, and were not revealed until after the Soviet Union collapsed in 1991.

EISENHOWER'S LIEUTENANTS: THE CAMPAIGN OF FRANCE AND GERMANY, 1944–1945

by Russell Weigley

INDIANA UNIVERSITY PRESS, 1990

This book serves as something of a companion piece to Eisenhower's *Crusade in Europe*. Eisenhower, writing about people who were still alive, many of them holding high positions in the military, could not be as blunt as Russell Weigley, writing thirty-five years later. Comparing the two books, one can see how Eisenhower held the Allies together by not antagonizing a number of senior people, while at the same time, the compromises he made prolonged the war months longer, causing thousands of additional Allied casualties.

Eisenhower made his mark with his people skills. Generals are, by virtue of their powers of life and death, a pretty stubborn and arrogant bunch, and Eisenhower's job was complicated by an inexperienced American army and equally inexperienced generals. He also had to deal with more experienced British generals, who never hesitated to remind yanks that the United Kingdom had been in the war since September 1939, two years before America. But most of the troops invading France would be American. This meant an overall American commander. And that was Eisenhower. But senior positions had to be given to Brits, and it was considered more diplomatic trouble than it was worth to dump any of them if they proved incapable of doing their jobs well.

The problem was that, while the Germans had cleared out nearly all of their "old-fashioned" (think World War I and cautious, using very clumsy tactics) generals, the Western Allies had not. Eisenhower recognized that "blitzkrieg" was something new, and required new approaches to commanding troops and looking at the battlefield., but not all of his subordinates did. Some of Eisenhower's generals could do the blitzkrieg (especially Patton), most could not (especially British Field Marshal Montgomery).

Eisenhower's Lieutenants dishes the dirt on the personal relationships of Eisenhower and his colleagues, and discusses how often Eisenhower had to bow to pressure from Washington and the British when deciding who to promote and who could not be dismissed for low performance. Eisenhower had some very effective American Army and Air Force commanders (Collins, Eddy, Middleton, Patton, Quesada, Simpson, Spaatz, Truscott and Wood), certain others possessed better reputations than they deserved (Bradley, Clark, Lee, and Brits Alexander and Montgomery). Prime Minister Churchill was himself been a problem at times, for although Churchill often had good ideas, one had to deal with many less useful ones.

Crusade in Europe is written by a participant, who saw things as he experienced them, and felt that his decisions were the right ones. After all, the Allies defeated Germany. But reading *Crusade in Europe* and *Eisenhower's Lieutenants* makes you realize that, while Eisenhower may have been the right man for the job, he wasn't the best one. His orders were to win the war, and not aggravate relations with the United Kingdom (or with politicians back in Washington), while doing it. Eisenhower carried out his orders, but in doing so he missed many opportunities to shorten the war and save many lives.

Eisenhower's biggest problem was with Bernard Montgomery, a capable general and a genuine British hero who defeated the Germans at El Alamein in North Africa after all his predecessors had failed. Within months, Montgomery controlled all of North Africa and was poised to go after Sicily and Italy. To the average Briton, this was a remarkable achievement; Montgomery was their hero and he could do no wrong.

Unfortunately, Montgomery was not a first-class general. He was careful and steadfast, capable of inspiring his troops. His victory at El Alamein was largely a result of careful preparation, overwhelming force, and a foe that was at the end of a slender supply line. Montgomery did not pursue the fleeing German mechanized units because he knew the Germans were far better in a mobile battle. Montgomery's orders were to win, but more important, Churchill did not want him to get beaten up by the Germans.

Later, Montgomery was not a problem during the D-Day assault—that was the kind of set-piece operation he excelled at—but when the breakout from the beachhead began, and Patton took the lead and attempted to bag most of the German Seventh Army by cutting off their retreat through the town of Falaise, he was ordered to halt his troops and let Montgomery's lads do it. Montgomery proceeded too cautiously, and most of the Germans escaped. Patton was steamed, while Eisenhower was content that the Germans were on the run. Eisenhower then made another strategic mistake. Rather than turning his most aggressive general (Patton and his Third Army) loose, it was declared that everyone would advance together in a continuous front. To generals like Patton (and many others), who had studied the early German victories, this was insane. The blitzkrieg worked when you used speed. And when you didn't have sufficient fuel to let everyone go forward with all possible speed, you diverted fuel to your most aggressive general.

When the allied armies all moved across France to the German border, resistance became more intense. The slow advance gave the Germans time to get away, and bring up reinforcements. But the allies' supply situation had improved as well. Eisenhower knew his most aggressive general was Patton, and that there was only enough fuel and ammo available to support one army making a big push. Montgomery insisted that he get the gas, so he could undertake a complicated advance in Holland, using three airborne divisions and many more infantry and armored divisions, to break through the German lines. This was Operation Market

Garden, the "bridge too far" attack through Arnhem. It failed, and the British airborne division was practically wiped out.

Meanwhile, Patton scraped together what gas he could, moved into Germany and began to battle through the fortifications the Germans had built to defend their Western border. Then, in December, the Germans launched a surprise attack just north of Patton's area of responsibility. This was the Battle of the Bulge, and this time Eisenhower called on both Patton and Montgomery to stabilize the situation. Patton responded by turning his army around in forty-eight hours (an unprecedented feat) and attacking the Germans in the flank. Patton's troops bored into the German rear area, cutting off their supplies. Montgomery moved a few thousand troops to confront the oncoming Germans, but only a few German tanks were seen, as Patton had halted the rest by cutting off their fuel supplies. To everyone's consternation, Eisenhower showered Montgomery with praise for saving the situation. Even Winston Churchill was confounded by this and pointed out that the "Bulge" was almost entirely an American battle. And anyone who was there knew that Patton's remarkable leadership played a major role in defeating the Germans.

Eisenhower was determined to not lose, rather than do all he could to win as quickly as possible. Riding herd on a multinational coalition and closely scrutinized by superiors in Washington and London, he knew he had to keep many competing constituencies happy. Churchill was a particular pain in the butt, as he was close to President Roosevelt, as well as being responsible for keeping British voters behind the war effort. This often put Eisenhower on the spot, and keeping Winston happy took a lot of Eisenhower's time. And when he wrote *Crusade in Europe* right after the war, with Churchill still alive, Eisenhower was as diplomatic as ever. But Eisenhower was also a guy who got things done, although not always to everyone's satisfaction. He managed to keep the armies going in the right direction.

Eisenhower's Lieutenants also discusses how the Allied invasion of Europe actually worked. One of the most intense military operations of the war, the Western Allies dedicated 5.4 million troops,

970,000 vehicles, and 18.2 million tons of supplies into the effort between June 6, 1944, and May 7, 1945. Eisenhower put in a flawed performance, but a very successful one. When all is said and done, it's hard to think of anyone else who could have done a better job.

FIGHTING POWER: GERMAN AND U.S. ARMY PERFORMANCE, 1939–1945

by Martin Van Creveld

GREENWOOD, 1982

Fighting Power explains why the German army was so difficult to defeat.

For several decades after World War II, the conventional wisdom was that the methods and practices of the German army were inadequate because they lost two world wars. True, but as historians began to study the battles, it became clear that German soldiers were, man-for-man, generally more lethal than their opponents. Not until after the Vietnam war, when the U.S. Army went through a period of reform, did American officers began to appreciate what their fathers had told them about fighting Nazis—that it was a tough business. The Germans may have lost both world wars, but they were much better at giving GIs a hard time on the battlefield.

The reform-minded U.S. Army officers of the 1970s decided to take a closer look at German World War II practices to see what could be learned from them. As part of that process, various scholars were commissioned to do studies of the subject, and one of these studies turned into this book. The author, who already knew that the Israeli army had adopted many German practices (without giving it much publicity), studied the enormous amount of data available on American military operations and discovered not only that the Germans usually had an edge in combat, but why.

The reasons were simple, and based on practical experience. Germans took war very, very seriously. Unlike the United States, where a military career was not one of the most sought-after life-styles, the opposite was the case in Germany. For several generations, the German military had attracted more than their share of bright, energetic, and ambitious young men as career officers. Moreover, the military in Germany was a high-prestige outfit, and civilian experts, eager to do whatever they could when asked to help the military, developed some very sound and practical solutions for the combat problems all armies must face.

Most important, Germany paid close attention to training and leadership. The combat soldier underwent programs of physical conditioning, weapons training, and carefully designed battle drills. The Germans were very careful about who was selected for NCO or officer training. Even during the war, the Germans spent more time training men selected to be sergeants than did the United States for men selected to be officers. In peacetime, NCOs were given two years of training, which produced leaders superior to officers in most other armies. During wartime, they felt it better to have too few officers than to dilute the overall quality by skimping on standards and training. During wartime, officer candidates went through basic training, NCO school, and officer training, along with service at the front, a process that took twelve to fourteen months. In the American system, by contrast men selected to be officers had eight to nine months' training, and were sent straight to a unit. Thus it should come as no surprise that German soldiers had more confidence in their NCOs and officers, even if they didn't know them personally.

Germany went even further. After World War I, panels of officers and NCOs were convened to examine how the army had performed, which practices could be kept, and which needed improvement. Noted was the overreliance on aristocrats as officers, especially infantry officers. Standards were high even then, but as in many other European armies, to be a combat officer was seen as the preserve of young aristocrats. Commoners had to be admitted to keep the numbers up, and officers tended to adopt a stand-offish attitude towards the troops. This, the panel members (all combat veterans) concluded was a bad thing. Those officers who, later in the war, were promoted from the ranks, had a much healthier attitude towards their troops. Thus, before World War II, the German army adopted a policy that encouraged the commander to get to know personal details about his soldiers, including such mundane things as having the company commander congratulate each man on his birthday. The troops reciprocated, believing that the officers cared about their welfare, and extended that extra effort which often brings victory in battle. These pre-World War II reforms, which placed more emphasis on forging personal bonds among men in the smallest unit, the infantry squad, produced an army considerably more capable than it looked. The Allies soon came to realize this a little too late. In fact, they really didn't figure out why German soldiers were better led until after the war was over.

Germany also realized, again from World War I experience, that tactics, even at the lowest level, had to be carefully thought out, and meticulously taught to the troops. They also realized that battle plans needed to be flexible, because once the shooting started, the unexpected became the norm. So the Germans departed from standard practice and developed the concept of "mission orders," meaning that officers and troops were given the objective of the coming battle and were turned loose to get the job done any way they could. This went against the conventional wisdom among Americans that German soldiers were a bunch of robots. In actuality, German soldiers were given more flexibility, and called on to use more initiative, than any other World War II force. The official manual for combat leadership (*Truppenfuhrung*, nicknamed *Tante Frieda*—"Aunt Frieda") stressed "decisive action." This, and the insistence on initiative at all levels, created a tremendous amount of flexibility, imagination, and speed in German military operations.

A lot of these new practices originally came came from the Stosstruppen (storm, or "assault" troops), methods the Germans had developed in the last two years of World War I. Looking for a way to break the trench warfare deadlock, they revolutionized the way infantries were organized, equipped, and led. The basis of infantry organization became a squad of about ten troops. Each squad had at least one machine gun. Troops were trained to use hand grenades more frequently when fighting in trenches (other armies sent their troops to attack enemy trenches armed with a rifle and bayonet). NCOs were trained to get out in front and lead the troops. Anticipating that many sergeants would get killed or wounded being out front, several of the more promising soldiers in the squad were trained to take over should their sergeant be killed.

Trained to move fast, the Stosstruppen were equipped with more firepower than other World War I troops. In addition to new, lighter, portable machine-guns, the Germans also introduced the first infantry assault weapon. This was the MP 18, a weapon that would eventually evolve into the modern assault rifle. The MP 18 fired the standard 9mm pistol round and used a 32-round drum magazine and fired 6–7 bullets a second. But for the tactics the Stosstruppen used (sneaking up real close before attacking), the MP 18 was ideal. Several members of a Stosstruppen squad would have MP 18s.

The main reason for the success of the Stosstruppen tactics was that the troops did whatever they could to keep advancing. Once they broke, or sneaked, through enemy lines, the Stosstruppen kept going. Bypassed enemy troops, who were now cut off from supply and reinforcement, usually were taken prisoner by German infantry. Although only about 20,000 troops were trained in the Stosstruppen tactics in 1918, it was decided after World War I that all German soldiers should be trained to Stosstruppen standards. They also addressed the problem of why the Stosstruppen tactics worked in Russia in 1917 (forcing the Russians to quit the war), but not in the West in 1918. While the Stosstruppen blew away an entire British army in 1918, the German reinforcements were too slow advancing over the torn up (by shelling and trenches) battle-field to exploit the breach. The well developed railroads behind the Allied lines enabled the British, French and Americans to rush reinforcements in fast enough to stop the Germans. In the East, the Russians did not have as good a railroad system, or many divisions of fresh American troops to throw at the German breakthrough. So the Germans looked around and saw that the tanks, which the British had invented in 1915, could be improved and used in large numbers to rush through a hole in the enemy line created by their superb infantry.

Between the world wars, the Allies largely ignored these German military reforms and innovations, one of the reasons for the spectacular success of the German army early in World War II. While the media, and many military experts, were attributing the German success to their panzers (tanks), the real linchpin of the German blitzkrieg (lightning war) was its excellent infantry. Most German divisions used horse-drawn transport, and the infantry walked, advanced slowly, and caused foreign observers to think that these outfits were of lower quality. They were not. Once the unmotorized infantry reached the battlefield, they were quite effective. And the panzer divisions also had lots of infantry, trained to the same high standards of all German infantry. The only difference was that in Panzer divisions, the infantry had armored vehicles or trucks to ride in. It was the close cooperation of the infantry and the tanks, and the well trained leaders improvising new tactics and battle plans as they went that enabled the Germans to quickly defeat millions of enemy troops between 1939 and 1941.

Two factors eventually brought the Germans down. First, they were outnumbered by more than two to one; second, their foes eventually learned the secrets of their success.

Fighting Power is concerned mainly with comparing how the Germans did it right, and how the American army did not—something the author was criticized for, along with failing to point out how the Americans largely closed the gap by late 1944. How the U.S. prepared its fighting men to face the Germans is a long story in itself, but the bottom line was that the training bureaucracy in the United States was slow to implement improvements, whereas in Europe, several American division commanders did figure out the secrets of German success. These generals retrained their troops, were more careful in selecting NCOs and officers, adopted many German tactics, and outfought the Germans using the enemy's own methods.

Another factor in the American successes late in the war was that the Germans were running short of manpower. By late 1944, American troops often faced recent recruits (kids as young as fifteen) or older men who had last lifted a rifle in 1918. Even so, there was much yet to learn from how the Germans trained and led their combat troops during World War II. When American officers began to study the subject in the 1970s, they found many ideas worth adopting. However, realizing that there was still resistance to adopting anything the "damn Nazis used," the battle proven German techniques were passed around as just another bit of useful combat knowledge. No source was given, and this was pretty common with Army field manuals.

The introduction of so many new combat techniques all at once had some interesting side effects. For example, in the early 1980s, I was up at West Point and the subject of general Bill Dupuy (the first commander of TRADOC, the Training and Doctrine Command created in the mid 1970s) and his "Dupuy Foxhole" came up. This was a hole dug in the ground with a high berm in front, with the machinegun firing obliquely to catch the enemy in the flank. Some of the instructors found this rather amusing, although they noted usefulness in the ability to fire into the enemy flank without taking much fire in return. They were unsure of the practice actually working in combat, believing it to be just some bright idea by general Dupuy. Then I pointed out that this was an old, and highly successful German tactic first developed during World War I, and used successfully during World War II as well. To emphasize the point, I recounted an incident I had read about where a German general inspecting the front lines in Italy during World War II chewed out a company commander for not using this type of position. The technique required interlocking fire from several positions, so everyone's front was covered and the enemy would get hit in the flank before they even saw the enemy. This got a lot of allied troops killed and saved a lot of Germans. Using something like this is a real sign of professionalism and good training.

This idea, and many like it, have since been absorbed into the American battlefield playbook. It takes a professional to spot little touches like this, but they make an enormous difference in combat, and were a major reason American troops were so successful during the 1991 and 2003 wars with Iraq. During World War II, there were many times where the Germans were the well trained and led super troopers, and the Americans were the brave, but unskilled guys getting shot down in large numbers.

While the author makes much of the cultural differences that led to the German combat superiority, culture can change. German troops have seen little action since World War II, but those few incidents (the Balkans, Afghanistan) indicate they are still competent soldiers. But the military is not nearly as well respected in Germany today as it was before World War II. While in the United States, there has developed a professional military that is admired by the general public and has an excellent combat record over the last two decades.

The reasons for the initial poor showing of U.S. troops was largely the result of too-rapid expansion and general inexperience. The U.S. produced only ninety-five ground combat divisions (eighty-nine army and six marine) during World War II, and many of the army troops didn't see combat until 1944. Unlike the Germans, not enough combat-experienced troops (from the North African and Italian campaigns) were sent back to the United States to assist in training new recruits. By comparison, Germany typically ordered 20 percent of its troops assigned to front-line units to be sent home on leave or to participate in training duty with new recruits. This paid big dividends in terms of morale (the troops on leave) and combat capability (training given by experienced combat troops). American commanders allowed very little leave and were reluctant to let go of any combat-experienced men for training duty back in the United States.

Although most U.S. divisions got plenty of training, it didn't do a lot of good. The wrong things were being learned over and over again. Once in combat, a division could turn itself around very quickly if the division commander realized the problem and instituted a program of retraining. Some division commanders did this, and their units were more successful as a result. But too many American generals were new to the business of war. The Germans were not. When Americans closed the gap by the end of the war, thousands of American troops had died due to inexperience and lack of good training.

Fighting Power goes into a lot more detail, and the author makes a compelling case for the difference in combat power between American and German units. Van Creveld's observations upset some historians and veterans, but many of the points he made were taken up when the U.S. Army planned reforms in the 1970s and 1980s.

HITLER'S LAST WEAPONS

by Jozef Garlinski

J. FRIEDMANN, 1978

This book is about the largely secret war that went on between the Allies (and their secret agents inside Nazi controlled Europe) and the German "wonder weapons" projects. Think of it as a real life James Bond story. But this is all true and actually happened.

To the Allies, German technology was something to fear. Allied intelligence heard rumors about how quickly the Germans could develop new combat technology. It was known in the 1930s that Nazi scientists were working on jet engines and liquid fuel rockets, but so were British and American scientists. (It was, in fact, an American scientist who developed some of the basic ideas for the V-2.) But the Germans were excellent engineers, able to take the oddest concepts and make them work, and throughout World War II, the Allies had reason to fear that Germany would be first to make some critical breakthrough, and engineer it into a useful new weapon before the Allies could do anything about it.

World War II was famous for introducing a large number of "secret weapons" that suddenly appeared on the scene. The atomic bomb was the most prominent, but the Germans developed more than their share of new weapons. The list is impressive and includes the assault rifle, wire-guided missiles, smart bombs, cruise missiles, night-vision equipment, nerve gas, and ballistic missiles.

The German cruise and ballistic missiles are the subject of this book. The V-1 (or FZG-76) was a cruise missile developed by the Luftwaffe, and the V-2 (or A4) was a ballistic missile (the Russian postwar version was the SCUD) developed by the Wehrmacht (German army). The air attacks against Britain killed 60,595 Britons (29,890 in London), and wounded another 86,182 (50,507 in London). German missiles accounted for 8,588 (14 percent) of those killed. The missiles were used at the end of the war when Allied air power was so dominant that the German bombers could no longer reach British targets in any meaningful numbers. The "V Weapons" got through, however, and they were terrifying. The Germans were down, but not out, and here were the wonder weapons to prove it.

The appearance of such weapons did not come as a surprise to the British. An extensive intelligence network, extending into Nazi-occupied Europe and neutral nations like Sweden and Switzerland, gave advance warning that "Buzz Bombs" and "German rockets" were on their way. What makes *Hitler's Last Weapons* so useful is that it is the only one to cover the German effort to develop, perfect, and deploy these weapons, as well as the Allied efforts to learn about Germany's "wonder weapons" and how to stop them.

Development work on the V-1 cruise missile began in June 1942, and the first successful flight took place in December of that year. The V-1 was an air force project, rushed along to go into action before the army's V-2 was ready. The first German V-1 cruise missiles were launched against southeast England in June of 1944, and eventually some 10,492 V-1s targeted Britain. The V-1, however, was crude; only 7,488 reached Britain and only 2,448 hit their intended target (the largest number of cruise missiles that have ever hit military or civilian targets). The Germans also were the first to launch cruise missiles from the air, using some 1600 V-1s in this fashion. Basically a jet aircraft with a rudimentary guidance system, the V-1 was high-tech by World War II standards. It was cheap to make (each costing some $6,300 in current dollars) this largely due to the heavy use of slave labor.

The V-1 missile had to be launched directly at its target, as it flew in a straight line (via a simple guidance system to keep it on course), and at a constant speed (about 300 to 400 miles an hour) and altitude (3,000 to 4,000 feet). It used a simple pulse jet engine that shut down and plunged the missile to the ground after it had travelled a programmed distance. Only slightly faster than contemporary fighters, the V-1s could be shot down by anti-aircraft guns or intercepted by fighters. Relatively small, it was not always spotted by radar. In effect, it was "stealthy." Because the technology of the period did not allow for a very accurate guidance system, the V-1 attacked area targets, like cities, that were large enough so that wherever the V-1 landed it would do some damage. As such, it was not terribly efficient, but it was successful as a vengeance weapon, a means to lower the morale of British civilians. Despite this success, it had no effect on the war effort as a whole (other than the diversion of some anti-aircraft guns and fighters to deal with it).

The V-2 was a much more expensive proposition, each costing about $440,000, not counting the extensive development expenses. Some 6,000 V-2s were built, but only half were actually used in combat (300 were used for testing, another 250 were under construction and 2,100 had not yet been fired by the end of the war). Factor in the cost of construction, transportation, and development and the V-2 project easily cost Germany the equivalent of some $20 billion (in current dollars).

Some 31,000 V-1s were built, but only 20,000 were actually used. The total V-1 project costs were probably one-tenth that of the V-2. This naturally raises the question, why build V-2s when you can deliver the same payload for less? There were three reasons. First, the V-2 could not be intercepted—an enormous advantage. V-1s could be stopped, and as time went on, a higher percentage of them were shot down, but a weapon that could not be stopped was much more frightening. Second, the V-2 had a longer range than the V-1 (320 kilometers versus 200). The third reason was Germany's belief that "wonder weapons" would somehow cancel out all their other military disadvantages and reverse their slide into utter defeat. This never would have worked.

The V-2 was too expensive to deliver enough destruction to make a difference. But it *was* impressive.

If the Germans had successfully developed nuclear weapons (which would have cost at least as much to produce as the V-2 project), the V-2 could not have carried one. The two types of A-Bomb created by the United States weighed 4 tons (for the uranium bomb) and 4.5 tons (for the plutonium bomb). A scaled-up V-2 capable of carrying a mid-1940s A-Bomb would have been pushing the limits of the era's aeronautic technology. Moreover, the average reliability of the V-2 was only 81 percent, 90 percent at most. All in all, an atomic attack via V-2 was highly unlikely.

Even with a high explosive warhead, the V-2 was a terrifying weapon. It gave little warning, only the boom of the warhead breaking the sound barrier as it plunged to the earth, followed quickly by a second boom as the warhead hit and exploded. Even more unnerving was the fact that the V-2 was a mobile weapon. For example, during the last two weeks of September 1944, two V-2 missile regiments (each with about 3,100 troops and 800 vehicles) fired 127 V-2s from five different sites. That's about four to five missiles per regiment per day, launched regardless of the hundreds of Allied warplanes assigned to track down and destroy these missile regiments. The missile units did take casualties, and were slowed down. The Germans estimated that, without the constant harassment from Allied aircraft, these two regiments could have launched a maximum of one hundred missiles on a single day. On a sustained basis, they could launch about 350 a week.

In the great scheme of things, firing 350 one ton warheads at London or Amsterdam a week would not change the course of the war. Each successful missile launch would, on average, kill or wound about ten people. This would scare people, and since Britain was a democracy, the leadership would be (and was) under tremendous pressure to "do something." The British did do a lot, bombing the V-2 development sites deep inside of Germany even before the first V-2 was fired at an Allied city. Once the V-2s did start killing Allied civilians, Allied air and ground forces did go after the V-2 missile regiments, and eventually nailed them. *

So, why the V-2? Well, mainly because many German leaders

were obsessed with technology, and the potential ability of technology to change history. This scheme rarely works in wartime, and while the Nazi point of view was somewhat visionary, it was also bloody minded and evil.

The author, a Pole who spent much of World War II imprisoned in concentration camps, also recounts the truly heroic efforts by resistance organizations (particularly Polish and French) to gather information on the German efforts to build and use these weapons. This has rarely been told, and Garlinski makes it clear that their daring guerrilla missions were crucial in providing information about what was going on in Nazi-occupied Germany.

It's ironic that the Poles conducting such dangerous undercover work for the Allies did so partly because they believed, or at least hoped, that the Allies would prevent Russia from dominating Poland after the war, as they had for nearly two centuries. Unfortunately, the horse-trading between Churchill and Stalin over who would control what in postwar Europe left Poland as a Russian "satellite" state, and the country would not be free of Soviet rule until 1989.

This book details the largely untold and unknown story of how British researchers and Polish partisans and spies uncovered the secrets of the V-1 and V-2 before these weapons could be used, and discovered enough about the project so that Allied bombers could slow down development and deployment. It was the first time in history that there was such a technology race, and it probably won't be the last.

OVERLORD: D-DAY AND THE BATTLE FOR NORMANDY

by Max Hastings

SIMON & SCHUSTER, 1984

The D-Day assault on Normandy (June 6, 1944) was the largest amphibious operation in history. The first day of the operation alone put ashore 90,000 troops and 9,600 vehicles. The operation was so enormous, it was impossible to supply with only amphibious shipping. Two artificial harbors (called mulberries) were built, each capable of unloading 5,000 tons of cargo and 1,000 vehicles a day. Although the artificial harbors were soon wrecked by unexpected storms, 716,000 troops and 131,000 vehicles were put ashore within 30 days of the initial landing.

Until World War II, the tried-and-true method used to get troops ashore was to take control of merchant ships, which carried the men and weapons. When the enemy shore was in sight, barges and smaller boats were used to ferry the troops and their equipment from ship to shore. This procedure was slow, clumsy, and vulnerable to disaster if the enemy caught you while you were doing it.

During the 1920s and 1930s, new amphibious techniques were developed in America and Britain that provided an alternative to the flat-bottom boats used in the past, which were hard to handle in rough seas. The British invented the Landing Ship Tank (LST), a large ship (for the time), capable of carrying up to 5,000 tons, including 2,000 tons of cargo, that could run itself up on the beach and lower a ramp in the bow, down which fully loaded trucks and battle-ready armored vehicles could drive onto the beach and into combat. The LST was a tremendous advance in amphibious operations, and revolutionized warfare.

American Marine and Army officers developed new techniques for getting the troops ashore from these LST-type boats, and for quickly establishing the supply dumps and transportation arrangements necessary to support intense combat. In the past, troops in a beach assault took a long time to acquire enough supplies to enable them to wage a decisive campaign. No longer.

Amphibious assaults were managed differently in Europe than they were in the Pacific. Against the Germans and their fast-moving panzer divisions, you had to get the troops ashore very fast so you could defend yourself against quickly executed counterattacks. The Germans were known for meeting any threat with a quick and violent counterattack. Against an amphibious operation, it could be fatal if the force took too long getting troops and equipment ashore.

In the Pacific, the Japanese were defending dozens of islands so small that formidable fortifications had to be built right on the beach. Unlike Europe, where there were so many places to land that the option of hitting a more lightly defended shore was usually available, the many islands in the Pacific meant more places to be invaded. As a result Pacific operations were smaller, but more numerous than those in Europe.

The revolution in amphibious warfare was, like the development of the blitzkrieg, dependent on more mechanization, new equipment and new organization. To be more specific, there were three areas of new ideas and equipment that made 20th-century amphibious warfare possible.

First, there were ships that could run up onto the beach. In addition to the LST, similar, but smaller, ships carried vehicles and infantry. Then there were the amphibious vehicles, especially DUKWs and LVTs, and armored vehicles could be floated ashore. The Allies realized that the first wave of troops hitting the beach would need their support. You can't bring in the LSTs until the enemy had been cleared from the beach, and LSTs were too expensive, and too few in number, to risk losing to enemy fire.

Finally, logistical techniques were developed and perfected to maximize the effectiveness of such new equipment. It was an intense learning process. Two problems that arose early on were wear and tear. It was known from the beginning that running large ships, like the LST, onto a beach took a toll on the vehicle, but it turned out to be worse than anticipated. After about ten landings, the framework of an LST became so shaky that the ship was unstable at sea and ready for the scrap heap. Although nearly a thousand LSTs were built, few were considered seaworthy enough for postwar use.

An even more startling revelation was what beach duty did to army trucks. Normally these sturdy vehicles were good for at least 100,000 miles of duty, but send them ashore with an amphibious operation, and exposure to salt water and sand would reduce their longevity by 75 percent. A month of such use would reduce many trucks to inoperable wrecks. Beachmasters learned to use trucks for a week or two, and then send them inland for good, or risk losing them fast. In the Pacific, unfortunately, many of the islands were relatively small, and no matter where you landed fine sand and salt spray in the air did their damage.

While the troops were learning the details of amphibious warfare, the generals were arguing with each other over whose amphibious operations were the most important. More possible amphibious attacks needed to be made than there was amphibious shipping to support them. The question also arose on whether to deploy the scarce amphibious ships in the Pacific or Europe. It was agreed that Europe was the first priority, and until the invasion of France, in spring 1944, the Pacific had to get by on leftovers, as Europe had first dibs on most new construction. The first Pacific amphibious landing, at Guadalcanal, was done mainly with old-fashioned techniques and boats. Fortunately for the Marines going ashore, there was little opposition and the objective was not far inland. The Pacific began to receive some amphibious shipping in early 1943, but most of the amphibious assaults were relatively small affairs, and General MacArthur was good at landing where the enemy wasn't.

The first major amphibious operation of World War II was the American landing in North Africa in late 1943. This was also spectacular because many of the troops, and most of the ships, came straight across the Atlantic for the landings. In July, 1943, there was another major operation as Sicily was invaded, followed in September by Italy itself. Then the Normandy operation acted like a giant vacuum cleaner for amphibious shipping, taking all new production and anything else that was not involved in supporting a landing, or carefully hidden away. In September 1943, the Pacific had only 26 percent (400,000 tons) of what was available. By January 1944, the Pacific had 660,000 tons of amphibious shipping (42 percent of the world total), but by May 1944, the Pacific had only 710,000 tons (35 percent of the total). The Marines scrapped together enough amphibious shipping to get their cross Pacific campaign started at Tarawa in late 1943. But the Marines knew they could not do anything really spectacular until the Normandy operation was over during the summer of 1944.

Some four million tons of amphibious shipping (LSTs, LSMs, LCIs, LCTs, for the most part) were built during the war. About 35 percent of these ships were lost, mostly to wear and tear. Remember, it's not natural for a large ship to be run up on the beach, even if it's built for it.

Toward the end of the war, more than 90 percent of the Allies' amphibious shipping was positioned in the Pacific, getting ready for the expected, and dreaded, invasion of Japan. There was, however, no doubt that such an invasion would succeed. These operations, had they taken place, would have been bigger than D-Day at Normandy, and would have benefited from the three years of experience acquired in amphibious operations in Europe. That had provided sufficient time to form dozens of specialized units that made amphibious operations run smoothly. There were two important specialized units that were spectacularly successful during World War II. The most critical was the Army Engineer Amphibious Brigade, one of which was used to support each combat division engaging in an amphibious assault. The 7,400-man unit had two battalions operating over a hundred small amphibious craft and another two engineer battalions trained and equipped to get the supplies off the beach and to the right destination as quickly as possible. All the engineers were trained and equipped as infantry, but the brigade also had a small artillery detachment to assist in protecting the brigade operating area from any enemy attacks. In addition to the four engineer battalions, there were also two ordnance companies (to make repairs on weapons), a maintenance battalion (to keep all vehicles and other equipment running), a quartermaster battalion (to run the supply dumps), an amphibious vehicle (LVT or DUKW) company to help move supplies around on the beach and short distances over water. Finally, there was a medical battalion, to expedite medical care for troops wounded in the nearby fighting and to help get these patients off the beach and to a hospital ship offshore.

The Engineer Amphibious Brigade was such a splendid idea that the Navy and Marines promptly threw a fit at this blatant attempt by the Army to horn in on their amphibious warfare monopoly. The dispute got kicked all the way up to Washington, where it was recognized that the Army was going to be doing a lot of amphibious operations, and had enough ships under their own control to do it. But the Engineer Amphibious Brigades were handling a function that, before World War II, everyone agreed belonged to the Navy. However, the Engineer Amphibious Brigades were seen as so well thought out and effective, it seemed counterproductive to disband them. So there was a compromise. The army was allowed to keep the six Engineer Amphibious Brigades it had organized in 1942, but create no more. Meanwhile, the U.S. Navy and the British would carefully copy the Army concept, give it another name and make sure that there were enough Engineer Amphibious Brigades for the rest of the war.

The other big innovation was the Naval Construction Battalions (the SeaBees). These units actually predated World War II, but by the late 1930s there were new kinds of earthmoving and construction equipment available, and the SeaBee battalions equipped themselves with the new gear. To operate all this stuff, thousands of experienced construction workers volunteered for SeaBee duty after Pear Harbor. The Sea Bee battalions soon established a legendary (but largely accurate) reputation for spectacular construction feats in the Pacific. Building airfields in days, as well as logistical bases, roads and what have you was their job. Many of the SeaBees were a little old for military service (in their thirties and forties), but they had the experience needed to make the SeaBees so successful at building things. The Japanese quickly learned that once the American combat troops got ashore, the Engineer Amphibious Brigades and SeaBees made it impossible to throw the Americans out. In fact, the U.S. Marines have never been thrown off a beach, and during World War II that record was never seriously threatened. A lot of this had to do with the support the combat troops received.

Another thing that made Allied amphibious operations so successful was the careful planning applied to each assault. Problems were identified and quickly fixed, making an inherently unpredictable undertaking a lot more assured of success. For example, the newly developed scuba (underwater breathing gear) equipment was quickly adopted by newly formed UDT (Underwater Demolition Teams) that could check out beaches to be invaded, and destroy any manmade or natural obstacles encountered. Information collected by the UDT "beach jumpers" enabled the landing to be planned with a lot more predictability. Allied amphibious operations were also characterized by flexibility. With the confidence this approach built, and several successful operations behind them, amphibious operations were pushed with great vigor, and usually great success. But, let's face it, a lot of the success had to do with the greater capacity of the Allies to produce all the equipment needed. None of the Axis nations were able to produce the quantities of amphibious boats and equipment the Allies turned out.

A good example of this material advantage is not just the specialized amphibious shipping, but the smaller amphibious vehicles. For example, despite the ability to run LSTs (and similar, smaller, ships) up on a beach and have trucks drive off, there were often times when you needed a truck itself that could swim in from a ship offshore. This amphibious truck would then use its wheels to drive off to deliver something, or someone, inland as quickly as possible. Another angle that was forgotten, until troops encountered it, was the fact that amphibious operations often take place in marshy areas, crisscrossed with bodies of water and lots of mud. A truck that could swim was essential in areas like this. By late 1943, the problem was noted and addressed with the introduction of the DUKW (called "duck"). This amphibious vehicle was basically a standard Army 6 by 6 truck with a 5,000-pound carrying capacity, that was built to float. This was done by installing the truck's components inside a waterproof metal box, making the new vehicle a cross between a truck and a flat bottomed boat. A fully loaded DUKW weighed 8.8 tons and was 31 feet long, 8.3 feet wide and 7.1 feet high. Top speed on roads was 45 miles an hour, and about six miles an hour in the water. Maximum range with a full fuel tank was 220 miles on roads and 50 miles in water. A maximum of 25 troops could be carried. DUKWs spent most of their time ferrying supplies and troops from ships off shore to points within a few miles of the beach. Some 21,000 DUKWs were built. To take the strain off LSTs being run up on the beach, by 1944 several DUKWs were carried by LSTs and were used to ferry material to the beach, leaving the LST undamaged from running themselves up on a beach. Cargo ships also began carrying DUKWs for ferrying duty. The DUKW proved to be one of the more useful wartime inventions, making the delivery of supplies (especially badly needed ammunition) to troops fighting inland much quicker, and the evacuation of wounded troops equally swift.

About the same time the DUKW was invented, the U.S. Marine Corps noted a similar civilian vehicle; the "Alligator." This was a tracked (like a tank) amphibious vehicle developed for use in the marshlands of Florida. The marines ordered some militarized versions (with gun mounts) and called it the LVT (landing vehicle, tracked). The marines had the LVT in service by the end of 1942 and eventually bought ten thousand of them. The first ones were slow (12 mph on land and 3–4 in the water). This was remedied with the 1944 version, which could make 20 miles an hour on land and 5 in the water. While slower than the DUKW, the LVT was more mobile, being able to climb over just about anything. Starting in 1944, the marines also bought a thousand armored LVTs that mounted heavier guns (37mm and up).

Landing a division of troops required thirty to forty specially built amphibious ships (AGCs, APAs, AKAs, LSDs, LSTs, LCIs, LCTs) plus two dozen or more conventional transport ships and tankers. But the Allies built thousands of these larger amphibious ships, enabling them to launch dozens of amphibious operations at the same time, and absorb the high losses of amphibious ships from wear and tear.

By the end of the war, the Western Allies possessed an amphibious capability never equaled before or since. In recent years, there has been little call for such kinds of amphibious operations. In fact, the last World War II–style amphibious operation took place in 1951, at Inchon, Korea. Helicopters and air cushion vehicles have since replaced the World War II–era amphibious boats.

In size and complexity, the operation at Normandy on June 6, 1944, was in a class by itself. There will probably never be another like it. This book covers all the bases, focusing not only on the hard fighting after the landings, but describing how the vehicles and techniques that were unique to the Normandy operation, contributed to its success. The book also addresses several controversial issues. One of the more notable was the Allies' belief that their air superiority was decisive. The author having examined the German records, reveals that Germany quickly adapted to Allied control of the air, and that the damage stemming from Allied air power was much less than the Allies thought.

Overall, this is one book that eliminates the possibility of any future surprises because of something you didn't know about the Normandy campaign.

POPSKI'S PRIVATE ARMY

by Vladimir Peniakoff

STERLING, 2002

Every war produces its share of notable characters, and few were as unique as Vladimir Peniakoff, generally known as "Popski." He was the commander of the smallest independent unit in the British Army, a group of twenty-nine men that was distinguished by a most unusual designation: "Popski's Private Army." "Popski's Private Army" was but one name for his collection of oddball warriors formally known as the First Long Range Demolition Squadron. How do you top that? There are many ways. Consider the unit's unofficial (but widely used) recruiting slogan: "Join Popski's Private Army and Enjoy the War." Popski knew what kind of men he was looking for—men like himself, whose combination of daring, patience, and persistence was immediately recognizable to those few who shared such gifts.

Peniakoff did more than create and lead an exotic commando unit. He was an authority on many standard commando methods which have yet to be improved on. This book is his description of how he developed them, and personally executed some of the most daring and effective commando operations of the war.

Popski's story began when, at the outbreak of the war in North Africa, this Belgian-born, 43-year-old British officer convinced his superiors that he could do things out in the desert that the Germans would not believe possible. In short, he would penetrate deep into parts of the desert and raid enemy bases the Nazis believed were safe from attack.

Peniakoff already had a reputation as a man of the desert, a personality type made famous during World War I by T. E. Lawrence ("Lawrence of Arabia"). For over a century, a handful of Europeans had been drawn to the desert, and learned to master it, earning the respect of the desert nomads, be they Bedouin or Tuareg, who were impressed that foreigners could unlock the secrets of survival in their unforgiving land.

Peniakoff first saw the Sahara when, in the years after World War I, he found Europe dull, and went to Egypt to became a sugar manufacturer. While there, Popski gained knowledge of how to prevail in so inhospitable an environment. Like other Europeans attracted to the desert, he became addicted to life in these arid wastes. More important, he became expert at negotiating the vast expanses of sand and rock. Survival in the desert, he knew, is a matter of knowing where you are, where the nearest water is, and which terrain will provide the fastest way to the water before you dehydrate and die. Peniakoff wedded modern navigation techniques with the ancient ways of the desert people with enormous resourcefulness and organizational ability. He had a way of "reading" the desert, something that the natives recognized as a rare skill. He also learned how to do business with the desert tribes, and made note of who was likely to be trustworthy, and who was not.

As a second world war seemed imminent, he joined the British colonial forces in Egypt as an officer. The British had learned that in times of great danger some of the best officers for service in the colonies were the pro-British Europeans living there. Peniakoff took advantage of this when he was assigned to serve in the colonial Libyan Arab Forces. This organization was really a glorified paramilitary outfit intended to keep unruly elements from causing trouble among Libyans while British troops were fighting in the region.

Peniakoff found life in the Libyan Arab Force boring. He managed to get away and join the Long Range Desert Group (LRDG), a commando-type unit recently assembled in North Africa for deep desert patrols, to see what the Germans and Italians were up to and to raid enemy airfields and supply dumps. The LRDG was quite successful, but Peniakoff soon found even this too tame for his tastes. He felt that the "long" in Long Range Desert Group could be a lot longer. Recruiting 120 men, he formed the 1st Long Range Demolition Squadron. With them, he successfully went farther into the desert than the LRDG, and developed a reputation for boldness, innovation, and success.

Eventually, Popski was given his own unit to lead, and Popski's Private Army fought in North Africa until the Axis was driven out in early 1943, later saw combat in Italy, and was active in Austria at the war's end. Peniakoff succeeded in each location not only thanks to his talent and daring, but because the British army had a tradition of attracting, and tolerating, eccentric warriors, which usually paid off.

Popski's Private Army tells its tales matter-of-factly, but many of the events recounted are quite hair-raising. Peniakoff also describes in detail the many techniques and tactics he used. Peniakoff's favorite form of transportation was the jeep. He usually operated in a "patrol" consisting of five jeeps, each equipped with a .30 caliber and .50 caliber machine-gun. Each of the dozen men in the patrol was also armed with a .45 caliber pistol and a .30 caliber carbine or 9mm submachine gun. The patrol also carried a light machine-gun, a 76mm mortar, two long range radios, landmines, explosives and water and food for the trip. For really long trips, one or two trucks would be used. Peniakoff planned carefully and was adaptable. American Special Forces and British SAS commandos still use techniques Popski pioneered. (Self-contained commando truck patrols deployed recently in western Iraq are right out of Popski's playbook.) Peniakoff planned carefully and remained adaptable to circumstances. His book shows how highly personal his commando operations were, and offers proof that a few good men could make a big difference.

THE RISE AND FALL OF THE THIRD REICH

by William L. Shirer

SIMON & SCHUSTER, 1990

This is one book that will get you through all the sordid events that defined the Nazi Party, and the "Third Reich" that Adolf Hitler put together and inflicted on Europe. About 70 percent of the book gets you to the end of 1941, when the United States finally entered the war. There is much detail on how the "National Socialist Party of Germany" became one of the most evil organizations ever. But they were not alone.

Germany's National Socialist Party, better known as the Nazis, was one of two new forms of tyranny to develop in the twentieth century. The other was the Communists who, by dint of a better sense of public relations, have come off as the lesser of two evils in the last century. Actually, it was the communists who killed more people, and in the end you were just as dead whether you were killed for who you were (the Nazis) or what you believed (the Communists).

When the Nazis took over Germany in 1933, they declared their regime the "Third Reich" (meaning "empire"), the first having been established by Charlemagne in the 8th century, the second the German Empire that lasted from 1871 to 1919. The Nazi reich was supposed to last a thousand years, but made it only to eleven.

William Shirer's book examines where the Nazis came from, how they got to the top, and why they fell, and is one of the better treatments of the subject. Much speculation has been voiced about how the Germans, of all people, could have produced such a murderous crew as the Nazis. In my opinion, the reasons aren't mysterious at all. In post–World War I Germany, a new political order was much in demand. People wanted a strong state, one that would take care of them, and they wanted a strong leader to make it happen. The Nazis sought to unite all Germans in one German-dominated world.

The Nazis faced oppositions from communists and democrats, and were always a minority. But they were the most ruthless minority, and throughout the 1920s managed to intimidate the majority of Germans into backing down. Bad decision on the part of the German people. The Nazis were typical of the "Fascist" movements that were present in most European countries during the 1920s and '30s. Fascism was a combination of socialism, extreme nationalism and a desire to wear scary, military style uniforms and beat up people who weren't like you. The Nazis were the most extreme and ruthless Fascist movement, which is probably why they managed to take power in Germany.

Not all Fascists were alike. The ones that took over in Italy were, compared to the Nazis, "Fascist Lite," and pretty much considered as such by their German counterparts. The Falange that took over in Spain, after a bloody civil war with the communists and socialists, weren't Fascist at all, but mainly Catholic traditionalists and anti-communists. The Fascists among them were sent off to Russia to fight for the Germans, or given government jobs and encouraged to behave.

The author describes clearly how the Nazis established a police state and became caught up in their own rhetoric of racial superiority and military invincibility. The Nazis promised economic growth and elimination of unemployment. They achieved this by starting an arms race in Europe and renouncing (by expansion of their armed forces) the terms of their World War I peace agreement. This commercial activity lowered the unemployment rate quite a bit, and stimulated the German economy. Exports boomed during the 1930s. Many of the pipes used in the construction of New York's Rockefeller Center, for example, came from Germany, where the manufacturer marked them with a swastika before shipping them abroad. (If you are in one of the stairwells in Rockefeller Center, look at the side of the pipes that faces the wall and you will still see the swastikas.)

Could the Nazis have taken control without Adolf Hitler leading them. That's one of the great what-ifs of history. Certainly, Hitler was considerably more charismatic and persuasive than any of his associates, gaining strength through his speeches decrying Germany's defeat during World War I, the Draconian treaty that ended the war, the international economic collapse caused by the Great Depression, and the threat to business owners and religious minded Germans of communism.

Most Germans liked the economic turnaround the Nazis engineered. Those who opposed the Nazis, along with Jews, Gypsies, and homosexuals, were rounded up and sent to newly established concentration camps. Hitler knew he needed internal and external enemies to distract Germany from its real enemy—the Nazis themselves—and revived the anti-Semitism that had long existed in Germany. This was a dramatic turn of events, because for the past century anti-Semitism in Germany had been on the wane, partly due to a reform and assimilation movement among Jews. When the Second Reich was founded in 1871, it was relatively liberal; Jews were considered equal to other Germans, served in the armed forces and the civil service, and a few even made it into the aristocracy.

After the highly destructive religious wars of the seventeenth century, most Germans stayed away from religious discrimination. Thus German anti-Semitism took on a racial aspect. The concept of "race" was nothing new to Germans, or most Europeans, either. Most Americans think there is a lot of racism in the United States. Not compared to the rest of the world.

Germany, however, based citizenship on "blood," not on whether you were born in the country. Jews had been in Germany for more than a thousand years, and the population had absorbed centuries of intermarriage. By the 20th century, you needed a good geneal-ogist to figure out who was really Jewish. When the Nazis decided to rid Germany of Jews, they found that many senior members of the armed forces were, technically, Jewish, and they were shocked at how many Jews had served with distinction during World War I. Chasing out the Jews, and killing those who would not flee, de-prived Germany of much of its native talent (including many of its most capable scientists), but for the Nazis, political power was more important than anything else. The Jews were an ideal scape-goat, even if most of them were good Germans and many of them were hard to identify.

The Nazi treatment of the Jews was typical of the muddle-headed thinking which extended to diplomacy and economic pol-icy (the Nazis didn't mobilize German industry for total war until 1943). However, communism was a more dangerous tyranny be-cause it was more rational. Hitler, for example, would not put Germany on a wartime footing at the start of the war because he knew the war was unpopular with most Germans. Hitler was, to the end, a dictator with democratic sensibilities. This is not un-usual. Even dictators know that if they tick off too many of their subjects, there could be unrest and an end to the current dicta-torship. *The Rise and Fall of the Third Reich* treats the bizarre inner workings of the Nazi state in some detail, making clear that the Nazis were, to a great extent, the cause of their own demise. And even when making war, and preaching the need for sacrifice, they were careful to take the edge off it as much as possible. Rev-olutionary and ruthless political organizations like the Nazis are always aware that some one even more ruthless then them might be around the corner. While the Nazis used a lot of terror to keep people in line, they also tried not to antagonize any more Germans than they thought they had to.

After Hitler's quick conquest of France in 1940, he saw no need for economic mobilization. At this point, Hitler knew that many Germans believed he was a "Great Leader," and that it would be disgraceful for such a leader to cut back on the produc-tion of consumer goods just because he was planning to invade

Russia in 1941. The Nazis kept plans for the Russian invasion as secret as possible. Not mobilizing the economy was considered a good cover, and it was.

Russia, however, had been ready for war since the 1920s, and had kept this a secret, setting the Germans up for some nasty surprises in late 1941. While the initial German invasion of Russia in June 1941 went spectacularly well at first, the Russians never seemed to run out of soldiers or weapons. Where were they coming from? At this point, the Nazis realized that the Soviets were running a more effective dictatorship. It wasn't until the disastrous defeat at Stalingrad at the end of 1942 that Hitler faced the fact that he had dragged Germany into *total* war, requiring *total* mobilization, but it was too late to catch up.

Despite the terror of the Gestapo and the concentration camps, the Nazi police state faced considerable opposition. Hitler took advantage of the German tendency to blindly obey orders and respect authority, and compelled government officials and military officers to swear an oath of loyalty to him. Even Germans who opposed the Nazis were restrained from action by that oath. But this did not fully satisfy Hitler, and he kept looking for disloyalty, especially in the army, which brought about the dismissal of many able officers from active service, a policy that hurt the German war effort.

There were also some notable senior German officials who appear to have been sympathetic to the Allies. One such individual was Admiral Wilhelm Canaris, the head of the Abwehr (combined military intelligence) from 1935 to 1944. The Abwehr had been founded in 1925, as one of the post–World War I German military reforms. The Nazis never trusted Canaris (his family was of Greek origin) but Canaris was smart enough to work out cooperation arrangements with the Nazis, who sought to control all police and intelligence agencies in Germany. Canaris was a mysterious fellow who eluded all attempts to dislodge him until June 1, 1944, when Nazi investigators found his secret diaries, which revealed that he had been conspiring against Hitler since 1938. He was executed on April 9, 1945. Canaris was not an Allied agent per se—he was a very clever and intelligent officer who was opposed to

Hitler—but he did help the Allied cause on many occasions, and his widow was taken care of financially by the Allies after the war.

Some anti-Nazi Germans defected to Britain, including a number of Luftwaffe pilots, who brought their aircraft with them, or worked for the British within Germany. The Nazis knew that there were gaps in the loyalty of their population and throughout the war, the Gestapo and other security agencies spent much of their time looking for Allied spies. That they did not find many was proof that the Allies had managed to set up a very effective espionage organization within the Reich. (One benefit of this was the obtaining of secret information about Ultra, which allowed the Allies to crack German communication codes.)

Even before World War II began, everyone realized that a Germany controlled by this great evil was the most dangerous threat to the rest of the world. The Japanese were evil, but much less capable militarily than the Germans. The Soviets were evil, but they were also less capable than the Germans. It was only the Germans who built special facilities just for murdering people by the millions. The Third Reich was one of those really, really malignant organizations, staffed by technically advanced and well organized men with mass murder on their mind. The Nazis and their Third Reich were a scary development, one that may show up again.

Shirer recounts the details of these and many other aspects of the Third Reich, and does so in an easy-to-follow narrative. There's no way to put a pleasant face on so much relentless evil, but Shirer tells the story as grippingly as possible.

THE BATTLE OF BRITAIN

by Richard Hough and Denis Richards

W.W. NORTON, 1989

From July through October 1940, the first modern air war campaign was fought. The Battle of Britain was unique in that all the combat was in the air, and that the stakes were very, very high. Had Britain lost, German warplanes would have been able to fly unhindered over the English Channel and Britain's coastal areas, and Germany could have invaded and conquered the country. Although the Royal Navy would have certainly put up a fierce resistance, later events in the Mediterranean and Pacific showed that warships were dead meat against air power.

The Battle of Britain was a highly complex affair. Since the British were outnumbered, they had to rely on radical new technology to even the odds. The Germans were coming at them with 2,700 fighters, and Britain had only 800 fighters with which to fight back.

The British found an edge in the form of radar, which had recently been developed, and was still rather crude. The radar allowed British commanders to sit in a control room and, by moving markers across a large map, to keep track of enemy aircraft, sending their outnumbered fighters where they would do the most good. At the same time, the British increased their production of new fighters and trained as many new pilots as possible.

But it was a close call. The Germans had caught on to what the British were doing, and concentrated their attacks on British airfields and radar stations. By August 21, Britain had 941 fighters available, at the end of the month they were down to 867, and on September 15 their fighter strength was down to 728. During this time, Hitler and his Luftwaffe commander decided to shift the bombing attacks to cities. (Did this seemingly irrational decision save the British? This unresolved question is covered by the authors quite well.) The heaviest part of the fighting was over by October 12, when Hitler called off preparations for the amphibious attack, because the Luftwaffe had not been able to take control of the air. In the end, the Luftwaffe lost 1,733 aircraft, the British Royal Air Force 915.

The book also points out an interesting question: How many enemy aircraft did each side destroy? The Germans thought they had shot down many more British aircraft than they did. The inability to get reliable numbers about British losses played a role in confusing and confounding the German leadership and the chaos of battle led to double and triple counting. The British should have had less of a problem counting downed Germans, because the fighting was taking place over British territory, and if a German plane was shot down, the wreckage could be found (unless it limped off towards the Channel, where it may have entered the water, or made it back to a German air base). Yet the British overestimated the destroyed German aircraft by nearly a thousand. Far fewer German aircraft wrecks were located under the waters of the English Channel than was originally thought. For the Germans, it was the usual chaos. Gun cameras didn't come into use until later in the war, so the Battle of Britain was not only the first major air campaign in history, but one of the most haphazardly photographed.

The authors provide a comfortable blend of the technical and human sides of the campaign. While technology, superior organization, and solid leadership played a large part, it all came down to the bravery and skills of a couple of thousand pilots.

Read this history of the Battle of Britain and decide for yourself why the British won. That's not the main purpose of this history of the battle, as it is one of more comprehensive and clearly written accounts of this critical campaign. The book artfully managed to deal with the technology, innovations, human drama and military strategy and tactics all at once. One can make a career out of studying only the Battle of Britain, and this book is a good place to start, but if you don't want to make this campaign an obsession, Hough and Richards's book is a good way to learn all you need to know about it.

THE LAST 100 DAYS

by John Toland

RANDOM HOUSE, 1966

The last hundred days of war in Europe were a hectic time. The author sorts out the tumult of this time by tracking down many of the surviving key players and recording their stories. This was easy to do in the early 1960s, as most of those who had survived the war were still alive and in shape to talk. The author interviewed more than 600 people, including a few Nazis previously thought missing.

From February to the first week of May 1945, the Allies were crossing the Rhine and the Russians were advancing through Eastern Europe. The Germans still had some fight left in them, but as the Nazi empire was falling apart, it was fading fast.

In the east, 3 million Russian troops faced 750,000 battered German soldiers along a 400-mile front. Five million German civilians were fleeing the Russians as well. It was a mess. And the Russians were out for revenge as well as victory. Over the course of four years, Germany had killed 18 percent of the Russian population, mostly civilians, and many of them women and children. Because of this, the Germans knew that the Russians were out for blood.

A straight forward account of these hundred days could make

pretty dull reading. The Allies kept closing in, the Germans kept retreating, people were killed, things were blown up. Monotony is avoided by exploring the stories of a wide array of different personalities—Allies and Germans, troops and civilians.

All the essential elements are well covered, including the Allied prisoners fleeing east (either under guard by Germans, or free and trying to avoid the fighting between Russians and Germans while reaching the safety of troops who spoke their language). There are several flavors of civilian refugees (Germans, and non-Germans like former concentration camp prisoners and non-German slave laborers). And while it's the end of the Third Reich, a hundred days out, the Reich still covers a lot of territory (France, Italy, Hungary, Poland, Yugoslavia) and a lot of different people.

Toland's book concludes with an account of the horrific battle for Berlin, and an epilogue that ties up loose ends. Great history, educational, revealing and well told.

THE WIZARD WAR

by R. V. Jones

CLARA-MCCANN & GEOGHEGAN, 1978

World War II was the first war in which battles were won or lost according to how fast one side could create more innovative, more lethal technology. *The Wizard War* is the story of the "techno-commandos" (my term, not theirs) of the British Royal Air Force (RAF) who kept abreast of German technical developments, and devised countermeasures, and produced new weapons to use against the Germans.

In general, the Germans were more adept at producing new weapons. In addition to cruise and ballistic missiles, they developed the first smart bombs, wire-guided missiles and night-vision devices. Among the Allies, America developed nuclear weapons, and Britain took the lead in developing radar. The British were the first to miniaturize radar equipment sufficiently to carry it on aircraft, an advantage that made life much more difficult for night bombers and submarines (which spent most of their time on the surface).

R.V. Jones was a young scientist when, at the start of the war, he was recruited to join an elite RAF scientific intelligence organization. This outfit sought to discover what new German weapons, especially electronic ones, were in the works, and find out how they worked.

The bombing campaign against Germany cost many lives. Most men who flew the bombers did not survive the experience. It was estimated that an RAF man had about a 17 percent chance of surviving 30 missions (after which he was guaranteed a non-combat job). Superior German technology was what was killing these British airmen, so the RAF took the lead in high-tech weapons development, and the author found himself in the middle of a technology race with Germany. The efforts of the author and his colleagues helped Allied scientists to develop devices equal or better than German equipment. Detecting new enemy electronics was not always easy.

For example, the Germans developed several electronic navigation aids for their night bombers, and the first inkling the British had that something like this was being used was an unusual increase in German bombing accuracy. Bombing at night wasn't that accurate to begin with, even if you could find the target. The frequent rain in Britain meant that there was often cloud cover, making it difficult, or even impossible, to find a target. German bombers had secondary targets to go after if the primary one was clouded over. But often the secondary targets were also obscured, and then the German bombers would just drop the bombs anywhere (usually hitting nothing of any value) and go home frustrated. If the weather was clear, the bombers could follow the coast or a large river to a blacked out city or industrial area and drop their load to some effect. When the British saw few or no bombs dropped in out-of-the-way areas they knew the Germans must have some new electronic navigation aid. To investigate this possibility, the author and his crew examined the wreckage of shot-down German bombers. The interrogators who questioned captured German air crews would be briefed about the situation and would try to get information from them, but German engineers knew that some of their bombers carrying the new device would be brought down, and tried to conceal the gadgets so that, even after the bomber crashed, it would be difficult to find. Nazi bomber crews were warned how important it was to keep the navigation device a secret for as long as possible.

Fortunately, the British technology detectives had an excellent network of electronic listening stations. Any new German navigation system needed some type of electronic signal to work, and these stations were able to help detect such signals. The British also had airborne monitoring stations, in the form of large aircraft equipped with electronic gear for picking up signals.

Some of the technological problems that arose revolved around more than the deployment of new electronic warfare gadgetry. There was real fear that a new invention for evading radar detection would be discovered by the enemy and used against the Allies. The best example of this was "chaff," a simple method for blinding enemy radar. Chaff was nothing more than strips of aluminum foil or wire cut to the right length to reflect radar waves of a certain frequency. The British developed chaff in 1942, but did not use it right away because senior scientific and Royal Air Force officials believed the Germans could then turn around and use chaff to get more of their bombers into Britain. (At that time, Germans were still running bombing raids on British cities.) One of the reasons for at last using chaff in 1943 was that the decrypted German radio messages hinted that the Germans already knew about it, and refrained from using it for the same reasons as the British.

Jones and his teammates used a combination of methods to uncover German secrets, and this makes for an exciting book about a little-known but vital aspect of the war. The competition was so fierce in the European air war that electronic warfare as we know it today, was in full flower by 1944. With a few exceptions (like lasers), most of the electronic weapons that were so popular at the end of the twentieth century, were already developed and in use during World War II. The Japanese were at an enormous disadvantage because they were much less capable of dealing with the many new electronic items developed because of the hot house atmosphere of the European air war.

But the author dealt with more than electronic military equipment. There were also new weapons like missiles, aircraft (the Germans put the first jet fighters into action) and the possibility of Germany building a nuclear weapon before the Allies could. This book makes it clear that technology was a major factor in World War II, and that it took some exceptional people to make it happen.

ULTRA IN THE WEST:
THE NORMANDY CAMPAIGN, 1944–45

by Ralph Francis Bennett

SCRIBNER, 1980

Perhaps the most powerful "secret weapon" of World War II was the Allies' ability to decipher and read enemy military messages, a secret kept for twenty-five years after the war because countries were still using similar methods to encrypt their communications and the United States and Britain wanted to continue reading them covertly. Thus, all histories of World War II until the 1970s were missing a vital component. *Ultra in the West* shows how efforts to read secret enemy communications—the intelligence program codenamed Ultra—played a direct and decisive role in liberating France and ending World War II in Europe in early 1945.

For obvious reasons, military messages have used secret codes for thousands of years. The most common type of code was, and still is, substitution, which simply substitutes the letters of the alphabet with other letters or symbols. If you have the list of all substitutions, you can decode the secret message, but even without such a list, if you are good at solving puzzles, you can crack the enemy code. This weakness of substitution codes was overcome by using groups of numbers or letters for each letter of the alphabet, making messages more difficult, but not impossible, to decipher. In the 1920s, a more powerful approach was invented. The

Enigma machine (and other similar devices), initially developed for the business market, was soon adopted for military and government use by the Germans. Enigma used several rotors, each with its own substitution code, to produce a much larger number of substitutions. The Germans and Japanese thought it was impossible to crack their machine-generated codes, but a few years before World War II, Polish scientists developed methods that made it possible to decipher Enigma messages.

When war with Germany loomed in 1939, the Poles got their Enigma machine and notes out of the country to Britain, where their work was recognized immediately as a major breakthrough. One major problem, however, was never overcome. Various services in the German armed forces, as well as parts of the government, used slightly different versions of Enigma, as well as different settings for the rotors (and these too were changed from time to time). It was not possible to read all messages quickly. Weeks or months sometimes went by before a new Enigma set-up was figured out. Enigma codes were cracked, and much useful information was obtained, but not always on time.

Meanwhile, American cryptanalysts (as code breakers were called) had, independently of the Poles, figured out how to decipher the Japanese "Purple" machine. The Japanese used a somewhat different version of the coding machine, and were sloppier in their use of it. For example, Japanese messages would usually start with the same salutation. Very formal and respectful, those Japanese, even when sending secret military and diplomatic messages. This made it much easier to deal with a new setting, as a previous decoded message could be used to see what codes were used by comparing the salutation part of the older, known message, with the new, unknown, one. Between late 1939, when World War II began, and late 1941, when Japan's attack on Pearl Harbor forced America into the war, the British and American code breaking efforts became aware of each other, and began to cooperate.

Both the Germans and the Japanese never figured out that their codes were being read. This was partly due to their arrogance and blind faith in the Enigma type technology and their older code book based systems. But it was also due to measures taken by the Allies to make it look like they were getting their inside information from spies or other methods (like traffic analysis, counting the number of messages coming from all enemy transmitters).

Ralph Bennett was part of Ultra. Bennett was an academic brought in to turn decoded messages into messages that looked as if they came from an imaginary British spy network in Germany. There *was* no British spy network in Germany; it was a ruse created to make it seem that accurate and timely information about German military operations the Allies obtained was coming from British spies and not because Enigma had been deciphered. It was thought likely that the Germans would believe the fiction of a British spy network, and the deception succeeded. Throughout the war, the Germans searched in vain for the nonexistent British spies, and the truth, that Enigma had been (mostly) cracked, was not suspected.

Ultra in the West shows how difficult it was, at times, to convince generals that information obtained from Ultra was accurate and reliable enough to act on. Reports from spies had been known to vary considerably in reliability, and generals wanted reliable information above all else. Few generals knew that Ultra even existed; most of the senior military commanders who got Ultra information were told the cover story that it was from the mythical British spy network in Germany. Despite constant assertions that the information was indeed reliable, the most senior people who knew about Ultra could do little to convince subordinates who scoffed at the critical data presented to them, considering it reports from spies who might be blowing smoke. However, by the time of D-Day, a track record had been established, and more generals were accepting as rather more accurate these mysterious "intelligence reports."

As the war progressed, the efficiency of the British code-breaking was increased by automated techniques, including the use of some of the first working computers. Between June 1944 and May 1945, 45,000 messages were decoded. Wireless communications were used only when there was no other way. Ships at sea, or combat units in action where there were no telephone lines, had to send messages by wireless, and had to use Enigma, because anyone could pick up a radio message, and everybody knew that. However, there were cases where none of the relevant messages for an operation were sent by radio, the most famous of which was the Battle of the Bulge. On December 16, 1944, the Germans shocked the Allies with a massive surprise offensive in Belgium. Ultra missed this completely because this offensive was planned without the use of wireless messages. This was done not because the Germans suspected the Allies, but because the operation was planned from inside Germany and radio was unnecessary. Allied intelligence officers didn't anticipate this (though they should have) and, thus, the complete surprise at the Bulge.

Another item to consider is that many military decisions are often obvious; what staff officers call, "the correct solution." Thus the majority of the Ultra messages were mundane, telling the Allies things they already knew. But often the situation was ambiguous. In those cases, messages told you something you didn't know, and wanted to know, and this saved lives. The Battle of Midway, in June 1942, crippled the Japanese carrier fleet, and it was made possible due to decoded Japanese messages. That same year, in North Africa, the British were able to defeat a German attack (the battle of Alam Halfa) that would otherwise have led to the loss of Egypt, all because of a decoded German message (actually, several, just like at Midway).

On the other hand, the D-Day invasion succeeded largely because the Germans fell for a deception plan, which made Hitler believe that the Normandy landings would be merely a diversion, and that the main Allied invasion would take place farther north. The Allied deception made the Germans also think that the Allies had more divisions than they actually did. These deceptions were made possible because Ultra told the Allies what the Germans were falling for, and what they were dubious of.

In *Ultra in the West*, Ralph Bennett manages to show exactly how this worked. The importance of this is that when Ultra was declassified in the 1970s, no one bothered to get into the detail of exactly how the decoded messages were used by the combat commanders. Some examples were given, but Bennett knew that until more detail was provided, there would always be those who would try to discredit Ultra. That's exactly what happened, and Bennett makes it clear that Ultra worked, and shows exactly how.

No matter how many books I've read about Ultra (and its Pacific cousin Purple), I still can't get over how effective the intelligence community was at keeping it secret for a quarter-century. Information did leak out—Poles talked about their Enigma work, and the Russians apparently figured it out early on—but the general public was in the dark for nearly three decades. The story of keeping Ultra secret deserves a book of its own some day.

WAR AS I KNEW IT

by George S. Patton

MARINER, 1995

George Patton was the American general Germans feared most. The reason was simple: Patton was a superb combat leader. Although most people know of Patton through the blood-and-guts image he projected, he was actually a very thoughtful, organized, and opportunistic leader, who picked exceptionally competent people to work with him. All of this can be seen in the *Third Army After Action Report*. This large-format, two-volume work was printed in limited quantities in Germany after the war. To anyone familiar with military affairs, it reveals a military organization of exceptional professionalism and ability. Patton was primarily a supremely efficient manager, but he was also a combat commander, which required a different kind of performance. As he said, "The leader must be an actor."

Patton died in an automobile accident in Germany six months after the war ended, so he had no time to write a book himself. But he did keep a journal—had done so for most of his life—and, with the help of his wife and one of his staff officers, *War as I Knew It* was cobbled together from those journal entries. The "voice" of the book is unmistakably Patton's.

Born in 1885, Patton grew up in California wanting to be a soldier. He found out early on that his ancestors had fought in every American war, and he felt an unquenchable urge to follow in their footsteps. While an excellent athlete, Patton was also dyslexic and had to work very hard to deal with written material. He just looked at it as another challenge and overcame it. He graduated from West Point in 1909, and in 1912 represented the United States in the Olympics, placing fifth in the Pentathlon. In 1915 he found himself in Mexico with General Pershing's army, chasing Mexican revolutionaries who had raided into the United States.

Patton distinguished himself by using automobiles to chase down and kill or capture some key rebel leaders. This caught the attention of General Pershing, who promoted Patton to captain and put him on his staff. Two years later, Pershing was leading the American army sent to France. Patton had already noticed the introduction of tanks in 1915, and later commented, "Tanks are new and special weapons; newer than, as special, and certainly as valuable as the airplane." Pershing agreed, and turned Patton loose on the establishment of the United States Tank Corps. He remained with this organization until it was abolished in 1920. Patton, despite his junior rank (he was rapidly promoted from captain to lieutenant colonel), took charge in the Tank Corps and showed himself to be an innovative and effective organizer. He supervised, and often conducted, the training of the first five hundred American tank crewmen. He even designed a new uniform for tank crews, something other armies eventually did as well. Patton was out front in the first major battle for the Tank Corps, at St. Mihiel, where his fearless conduct and energetic leadership won him a Silver Star for bravery.

Although not the commander of the Tank Corps, he took charge of many aspects of the organization, coming up with, and implementing new ideas and procedures. Along with the British tankers, he and his men achieved victory at Cambrai, France, during the world's first major tank battle in 1917. In 1918, during the Meuse-Argonne Offensive, Patton had 345 tanks and crews ready for action. He was once more in the thick of it, and was wounded by machine-gun fire while up front, keeping the tanks moving. For his actions during the Meuse-Argonne battle, Patton received several awards (Purple Heart, Distinguished Service Cross) and was promoted to colonel. Before Patton recovered from his wounds, the war ended. But when he returned to service, it was as commander of the U.S. Army Tank Corps.

Patton saw tanks as the future of warfare, and before the Tank Corps was abolished in 1920 (because Congress cut the defense budget to the bone), he led the way in developing radios for tanks and the coaxial machine-gun/main gun arrangement that are still standards in tanks to this day. The cutbacks also meant he lost his "temporary" wartime promotions and he went right back to captain. But Patton was seen as a future general, and was promptly promoted to major. But with the Tank Corps gone, he went back to the cavalry. His tanks were given to infantry units.

Patton continued to push for more tanks, and research and experiments on tank warfare. He also learned how to fly and piloted his own sail boat from the West Coast to Hawaii. He graduated from the Army War College in 1932 at the top of his class. In 1934 he was promoted to lieutenant colonel. Patton kept active by writing articles and giving speeches. He was a serious student of military history and widely respected by other army officers as well as key people in Washington.

An outspoken advocate for tanks, Patton saw them as the future of modern combat. Congress, however, was not willing to appropriate funds to build a large armored force. Even so, Patton studied, wrote extensively and carried out experiments to improve radio communications between tanks.

When World War II broke out in September 1939, Patton's ideas about the use of tanks (he saw them as the future of modern combat) became suddenly very welcome in Washington. He was soon promoted to brigadier general and sent off to organize and lead an armored brigade. He was so successful with this that by 1941 the brigade had been expanded to form the 2nd Armored Division. Patton, as always, was an outstanding leader. During this period he became famous for showing up at all hours while his troops were training or out in the field. The troops appreciated seeing their commanding general appearing at 3 A.M. while they were getting ready to move out at dawn. It was great for morale. And Patton understood the importance of training for combat. He kept his troops out in the field a lot, at one point keeping the division in the field for seventeen straight weeks. This was hard on men and equipment, but most of the troops understood that they were better prepared for combat because of it. Also during this time, Patton began giving his famous "Blood and Guts" speech. He built an outdoor auditorium that could hold the entire division (nearly fifteen thousand troops) and regularly gave inspirational speeches (along the lines of "we are going to toughen up and kick some ass"). The troops ate it up. Here was a general who was a real warrior, a real kick ass son-of-a-bitch who would fight to win.

Patton used all this time in the field to develop new tactics and techniques for running an armored division. Patton often flew his own light aircraft over the division during training, to get a better idea of how everyone was doing. This was noted by others in the army and led to the widespread use of light aircraft for commanders to get around in, and keep an eye on things, during World War II. Patton was a constant innovator and problem solver, and attracted like minded officers to whatever organization he was running.

By April 1941, he was promoted to major general. During large-scale wargames held just before America entered the war, Patton distinguished himself by defeating all his opponents. In late 1942, as preparations were made to send American forces to North Africa to engage the Germans and Italians, Patton was the obvious choice to lead the armored units, and was later promoted to lieutenant general.

By March 1943, his troops were regularly defeating any Germans they ran into, victories so impressive that he was given command of the newly formed Seventh Army in April 1943 and assigned to capture Sicily. This he did rapidly, using innovative tactics and embarrassing the British forces that were also taking part in the operation. Here Patton got it trouble with the media and politicians back home when, while visiting a field hospital full of wounded troops, he slapped a soldier suffering from combat fatigue and called the man a coward. Patton had never studied this particular aspect of combat, although "shell shock" (as it was called in World

War I) was well known. Modern combat, because of the prolonged violence and stress, tended to cause mental breakdowns in many men. Patton made a public apology for his actions, but General Eisenhower, the commander of all American forces in Europe, was forced to sideline Patton for the rest of 1943.

In January 1944, Patton was sent to England to organize and train the Third Army. This would be the exploitation force for the invasion of France. Once the amphibious attack on France took place in June, and the Germans were worn down, Patton's army would go to France, punch a hole in the German lines, and sprint for Germany itself. It was hoped that Patton would quickly overrun France and, with any luck, get his troops inside Germany before the end of the year.

On July 28, Patton and his Third Army were turned loose. They did all that was expected of them and more. Over the next ten months, the army liberated 81,522 square miles of territory, captured 765,483 enemy troops, killed 144,500 enemy troops, and wounded 386,200. By contrast, the Third Army lost 16,596 dead, 96,241 wounded, and 26,809 missing—that is, for every soldier the Third Army lost, the Germans lost nearly eight.

Patton accomplished all this by applying lessons he had learned over the years. During the war, he frequently invented, and constantly used, catchy phrases that summed up his philosophy of combat leadership, preparation for combat and leading men in combat. His ideas about leadership and training can be summed up in his own words:

"Lead me, follow me, or get out of my way."

"Live for something rather than die for nothing."

"A good plan, violently executed now, is better than a perfect plan next week."

"A pint of sweat will save a gallon of blood."

"An Army is a team; lives, sleeps, eats, fights as a team. This individual heroic stuff is a lot of crap."

"Never tell people how to do things. Tell them what to do and they will surprise you with their ingenuity."

"No sane man is unafraid in battle, but discipline produces in him a form of vicarious courage."

"Untutored courage is useless in the face of educated bullets."

"Wars might be fought with weapons, but they are won by men. It is the spirit of the men who lead that gains the victory."

In combat, Patton advocated an aggressive style of operations that scared the Germans. This was because Patton, while aggressive, was also a careful planner. He surrounded himself with skilled staff officers and competent combat commanders, a fact perhaps nowhere more evident than during the Battle of the Bulge in December 1944. Patton's Third Army was positioned just south of the area the Germans attacked. When it became obvious that it was a major, and unexpected, German attack, Patton was asked how long it would take to turn his army around and move north to attack the Germans in the flank. Forty-eight hours, he said. Coming from any other army commander, it would have sounded foolish. But Patton always delivered. The Germans didn't think even Patton could turn the Third Army around that quickly, and when he did, the Germans were lost. Again, it was solid preparation that made feats like this possible. Patton got his staff working on the complexities of the task at hand as soon as he heard of the German attack in the north. When he was called to the meeting with Eisenhower and other senior generals, he told his chief of staff that he would call right after the meeting, and would use a code word to indicate that the "48-hour turnaround" was to be started immediately. That was an example of preparation and aggressiveness.

Throughout his combat career, Patton followed his own advice, and he expressed his thoughts succinctly:

"I am a soldier, I fight where I am told, and I win where I fight."

"War is simple, direct, and ruthless."

"May God have mercy upon my enemies, because I won't."

"You shouldn't underestimate an enemy, but it is just as fatal to overestimate him."

"You're never beaten until you admit it."

"America loves a winner, and will not tolerate a loser. This is why America has never, and will never, lose a war."

"Grab the enemy by the nose and kick them in the ass."

"Attack rapidly, ruthlessly, viciously, without rest. However tired and hungry you may be, the enemy will be more tired, more hungry. Just keep punching."

"In case of doubt, attack."

"A good solution applied with vigor now is better than a perfect solution applied ten minutes later."

"Never let the enemy pick the battle site."

"Fixed fortifications are monuments to man's stupidity."

"In war the only sure defense is offense, and the efficiency of the offense depends on the warlike souls of those conducting it."

Patton also had other, still useful, rules that he never turned into sound bites. He believed that troops on the defense should not put up barbed wire and plant mines, which would give them a false sense of security, sap their aggressive spirit, and make it more difficult to go on the offensive again. He also believed that, once his troops began a major offensive, and had not made much progress after four hours, something was wrong and the general had better identify the problem and get it fixed. Patton practiced what he preached, and his subordinates knew that if things got bogged down, they could expect to find him among their front-line units looking for answers. This motivated subordinate commanders to do the same, and do it before Patton got there.

To Patton, a key component of victory has always been logistics, and he was one of the most energetic practitioners and innovators in this arcane (to most civilians) area. In one instance, as his troops dashed across France in the summer of 1944, Patton sometimes obtained fuel for his tanks and trucks in colorful, quasi-illegal ways. He told anyone who would listen that he learned about logistics by studying how the great military commanders of the past won their campaigns.

Early in his career, Patton seized on motorization as a powerful new military tool. He saw that trucks and aircraft could be just as potent carrying supplies as they were carrying troops and guns. Patton knew that in battle, fuel was speed, ammunition was combat power, and fresh clothing and hot meals made men more willing to go the extra mile for victory. All of this required an exceptional attention to logistics. Patton recruited an exceptional bunch of logistics and transportation officers, and lavished praised on them when they, literally, delivered the goods. Truck drivers, mechanics, and supply handlers rarely got this kind of attention, and they responded enthusiastically. Patton's logistical support was the envy of all other armies in France that summer.

Patton, obviously, was a good communicator, a talent illustrated in a notice he wrote and had distributed to all the troops in the Third Army right after Germany surrendered:

HEADQUARTERS
THIRD UNITED STATES ARMY
APO 403
GENERAL ORDERS 9 May 1945
NUMBER 98
SOLDIERS OF THE THIRD ARMY, PAST AND
    PRESENT

During the 281 days of incessant and victorious combat, your penetrations have advanced farther in less time than any other army in history. You have fought your way across 24 major rivers and innumerable lesser streams. You have liberated or conquered more than

82,000 square miles of territory, including 1,500 cities and towns, and some 12,000 inhabited places. Prior to the termination of active hostilities, you had captured in battle 956,000 enemy soldiers and killed or wounded at least 500,000 others. France, Belgium, Luxembourg, Germany, Austria, and Czechoslovakia bear witness to your exploits.

All men and women of the six corps and thirty-nine divisions that have at different times been members of this Army have done their duty. Each deserves credit. The enduring valor of the combat troops has been paralleled and made possible by the often unpublicized activities of the supply, administrative, and medical services of this Army and of the Communications Zone troops supporting it. Nor should we forget our comrades of the other armies and of the Air Force, particularly of the XIX Tactical Air Command, by whose side or under whose wings we have had the honor to fight.

In proudly contemplating our achievements, let us never forget our heroic dead whose graves mark the course of our victorious advances, nor our wounded whose sacrifices aided so much in our success.

I should be both ungrateful and wanting in candor if I failed to acknowledge the debt we owe to our Chiefs of Staff, Generals Gaffey and Gay, and to the officers and men of the General and Special Staff Sections of Army Headquarters. Without their loyalty, intelligence, and unremitting labors, success would have been impossible.

The termination of fighting in Europe does not remove the opportunities for other outstanding and equally difficult achievements in the days which are to come. In some ways the immediate future will demand of you more fortitude than has the past because, without the inspiration of combat, you must maintain—by your dress, deportment, and efficiency—not only the prestige of the Third Army but also the honor of the United States. I have complete confidence that you will not fail.

During the course of this war I have received promotions and decorations far above and beyond my individual merit. You won them; I as your representative wear them. The one honor which is mine and mine alone is that of having commanded such an incomparable group of Americans, the record of whose fortitude, audacity, and valor will endure as long as history lasts.

G. S. PATTON, JR.,
General

And then there was "the speech." Patton developed a "Blood and Guts" speech he gave at every opportunity. Developed in the year before Pearl Harbor, it went through many minor changes and variations as Patton delivered it hundreds of times throughout the war. In the movie, *Patton*, George C. Scott, playing George Patton, opens the movie with a shortened (and rather less profane) version of the "Blood and Guts" speech.

Patton believed in the ancient tradition of a commander inspiring his men with a rousing speech. In Patton's case, it worked. This was the version of "the speech" that Patton gave when he spoke to some of his troops before the invasion of France in June, 1944. The speech was recorded by a court stenographer who was there.

Men, this stuff that some sources sling around about America wanting out of this war, not wanting to fight, is a crock of bullshit. Americans love to fight, traditionally. All real Americans love the sting and clash of battle. You are here today for three reasons. First, because you are here to defend your homes and your loved ones. Second, you are here for your own self respect, because you would not want to be anywhere else. Third, you are here because you are real men and all real men like to fight. When you, here, everyone of you, were kids, you all admired the champion marble player, the fastest runner, the toughest boxer, the big league ball players, and the All-American football players. Americans love a winner. Americans will not tolerate a loser. Americans despise cowards. Americans play to win all of the time. I wouldn't give a hoot in hell for a man who lost and laughed. That's why Americans have never lost nor will ever lose a war; for the very idea of losing is hateful to an American.

You are not all going to die. Only two percent of you right here today would die in a major battle. Death must not be feared. Death, in time, comes to all men. Yes, every man is scared in his first battle. If he says he's not, he's a liar. Some men are cowards but they fight the same as the brave men or they get the hell slammed out of them watching men fight who are just as scared as they are. The real hero is the man who fights even though he is scared. Some men get over their fright in a minute under fire. For some, it takes an hour. For some, it takes days. But a real man will never let his fear of death overpower his honor, his sense of duty to his country, and his innate manhood. Battle is the most magnificent competition in which a human being can indulge. It brings out all that is best and it removes all that is base. Americans pride themselves on being He Men and they ARE He Men. Remember that the enemy is just as frightened as you are, and probably more so. They are not supermen. All through your Army careers, you men have bitched about what you call "chicken shit drilling." That, like everything else in this Army, has a definite purpose. That purpose is alertness. Alertness must be bred into every soldier. I don't give a fuck for a man who's not always on his toes. You men are veterans or you wouldn't be here. You are ready for what's to come.

A man must be alert at all times if he expects to stay alive. If you're not alert, sometime, a German son-of-an-asshole-bitch is going to sneak up behind you and beat you to death with a sockful of shit! There are four hundred neatly marked graves somewhere in Sicily, all because one man went to sleep on the job. But they are German graves, because we caught the bastard asleep before they did. An Army is a team. It lives, sleeps, eats, and fights as a team. This individual heroic stuff is pure horse shit. The bilious bastards who write that kind of stuff for the *Saturday Evening Post* don't know any more about real fighting under fire than they know about fucking! We have the finest food, the finest equipment, the best spirit, and the best men in the world. Why, by God, I actually pity those poor sons-of-bitches we're going up against. By God, I do.

My men don't surrender. I don't want to hear of any soldier under my command being captured unless he has been hit. Even if you are hit, you can still fight back. That's not just bull shit either. The kind of man that I want in my command is just like the lieutenant in Libya, who, with a Luger against his chest, jerked off his helmet, swept the gun aside with one hand, and busted the hell out of the Kraut with his helmet. Then he jumped on the gun and went out and killed another German before they knew what the hell was coming off. And, all of that time, this man had a bullet through a lung. There was a real man! All of the real heroes are not storybook combat fighters, either. Every single man in this Army plays a vital role. Don't ever let up. Don't ever think that your job is unimportant. Every man has a job to do and he must do it. Every man is a vital link in the great chain. What if every truck driver suddenly decided that he didn't like the whine of those shells overhead, turned yellow, and jumped headlong into a ditch? The cowardly bastard could say, "Hell, they won't miss me, just one man in thousands." But, what if every man thought that way? Where in the hell would we be now? What would our country, our loved ones, our homes, even the world, be like? No, Goddamnit, Americans don't think like that. Every man does his job. Every man serves the whole. Every department, every unit, is important in the vast scheme of this war. The ordnance men are needed to supply the guns and machinery of war to keep us rolling. The Quartermaster is needed to bring up food and clothes because where we are going there isn't a hell of a lot to steal. Every last man on K.P. has a job to do, even the one who heats our water to keep us from getting the "G.I. Shits."

Each man must not think only of himself, but also of his buddy fighting beside him. We don't want yellow cowards in this Army. They should be killed off like rats. If not, they will go home after this war and breed more cowards. The brave men will breed more brave men. Kill off the Goddamned cowards and we will have a nation of brave men. One of the bravest men that I ever saw was a fellow on top of a telegraph pole in the midst of a furious fire fight in Tunisia. I stopped and asked what the hell he was doing up there at a time like that. He answered, "Fixing the wire, Sir." I asked, "Isn't that a little unhealthy right about now?" He answered, "Yes, Sir, but the Goddamned wire has to be fixed." I asked, "Don't those planes strafing the road bother you?" And he answered, "No, Sir, but you sure as hell do!" Now, there was a real man. A real soldier. There was a man who devoted all he had to his duty, no matter how seemingly insignificant his duty might appear at the time, no matter how great the odds. And you should have seen those trucks on the rode to Tunisia. Those drivers were magnificent. All day and all night they rolled over those son-of-a-bitching roads, never stopping, never faltering from their course, with shells bursting all around them all of the time. We got through on good old American guts. Many of those men drove for over forty consecutive hours. These men weren't combat men, but they were soldiers with a job to do. They did it, and in one hell of a way they did it. They were part of a team. Without team effort, without them, the fight would have been lost. All of the links in the chain pulled together and the chain became unbreakable.

Don't forget, you men don't know that I'm here. No mention of that fact is to be made in any letters. The world is not supposed to know what the hell happened to me. I'm not supposed to be commanding this Army. I'm not even supposed to be here in England. Let the first bastards to find out be the Goddamned Germans. Some day I want to see them raise up on their piss-soaked hind legs and howl, "Jesus Christ, it's the Goddamned Third Army again and that son-of-a-fucking-bitch Patton." We want to get the hell over there. The quicker we clean up this Goddamned mess, the quicker we can take a little jaunt against the purple pissing Japs and clean out their nest, too. Before the Goddamned Marines get all of the credit. Sure, we want to go home. We want this war over with. The quickest way to get it over with is to go get the bastards who started it. The quicker they are whipped, the quicker we can go home. The shortest way home is through Berlin and Tokyo. And when we get to Berlin, I am personally going to shoot that paper hanging son-of-a-bitch Hitler. Just like I'd shoot a snake!

When a man is lying in a shell hole, if he just stays there all day, a German will get to him eventually. The hell with that idea. The hell with taking it. My men don't dig foxholes. I don't want them to. Foxholes only slow up an offensive. Keep moving. And don't give the enemy time to dig one either. We'll win this war, but we'll win it only by fighting and by showing the Germans that we've got more guts than they have; or ever will have. We're not going to just shoot the sons-of-bitches, we're going to rip out their living God-damned guts and use them to grease the treads of our tanks. We're going to murder those lousy Hun cocksuckers by the bushel-fuck-ing-basket. War is a bloody, killing business. You've got to spill their blood, or they will spill yours. Rip them up the belly. Shoot them in the guts. When shells are hitting all around you and you wipe the dirt off your face and realize that instead of dirt it's the blood and guts of what once was your best friend beside you, you'll know what to do!

I don't want to get any messages saying, "I am holding my posi-tion." We are not holding a Goddamned thing. Let the Germans do that. We are advancing constantly and we are not interested in holding onto anything, except the enemy's balls. We are going to twist his balls and kick the living shit out of him all of the time. Our basic plan of operation is to advance and to keep on advanc-ing regardless of whether we have to go over, under, or through the enemy. We are going to go through him like crap through a goose; like shit through a tin horn! From time to time there will be some complaints that we are pushing our people too hard. I don't give a good Goddamn about such complaints. I believe in the old and sound rule that an ounce of sweat will save a gallon of blood. The harder we push, the more Germans we will kill. The more Germans we kill, the fewer of our men will be killed. Pushing means fewer casualties. I want you all to remember that. There is one great thing that you men will all be able to say after this war is over and you are home once again. You may be thankful that twenty years from now when you are sitting by the fireplace with your grandson on your knee and he asks you what you did in the great World War II, you WON'T have to cough, shift him to the other knee and say, "Well, your Granddaddy shoveled shit in Louisiana." No, Sir, you can look him straight in the eye and say, "Son, your Granddaddy rode with the Great Third Army and a Son-of-a-Goddamned-Bitch named Georgie Patton!"

War As I Knew It is not an autobiography, nor is it a detailed account of the battles Patton was in. It's better than that. It recounts the experiences of an exceptional combat commander, written while the events were unfolding. Patton was unique; in peacetime many would call him a "character," but in wartime, as many of his fellow generals recognized, he was a priceless asset. This book is proof of that.

Patton and the accomplishments of the Third Army will continue to be a testament to the bravery and adaptability of the American soldier. Their performance during the European fighting of 1944–45 highlights the central role logistics plays in any military operation. In addition, Patton's knowledge of military history, understanding and incorporating the latest technology, employment of combined arms, and his genuine concern for the troops provides logisticians and leaders alike a worthy example to study and emulate. His adage: "Gentlemen, the officer who doesn't know his communications and supply, as well as his tactics, is totally useless" is still applicable today, and is valuable advice to all who will fight America's wars in the twenty-first century.

Three

THE WAR IN RUSSIA

USSIA IS WHERE the German army was defeated, where German military power was broken. Much to the dismay of Russians, this fact is usually played down, or outright ignored, outside of Russia. Part of the reason for this is the Russians themselves. Until 1991, Russia was controlled by the Communist Party, an extremely secretive organization that kept information hidden even when spreading it around would have helped them. For decades, details of what transpired on the Russian Front during World War II were sealed in Soviet archives. Those archives are now open, but the moment has passed. There's no great rush to write the many books that doubtless would have been written earlier had there been access to the Russian people and the wartime records of the Red Army. While much of the color and nuance of the war in Russia has gone unrecorded, the basics can still be covered. The war in Russia was an old-fashioned toe-to-toe slugging match. There was nothing very high-tech about it, and nearly 40 million people died in the process. It was ugly, it was brutal, and it will take several generations before the Russian people really get over it.

The books covered in this section were selected for their ability to show what really happened on the Russian front. The war fought there was unique, and so are some of the books about it.

119

GREAT BATTLES ON THE EASTERN FRONT

by *Trevor Dupuy and Paul Martell*

BOBBS-MERRILL, 1982

Dupuy and Martell's book describes the seventeen major campaigns on the Russian front, from 1941 to 1945, as the Russians preferred to view them. No, it hasn't been written with a pro-Russian bias, but with an emphasis on the "correlation of forces" and numbers in general. The presentation is unique. Two or more pages of text describe each campaign, accompanied by a dozen or more pages of data tables and a map. The number of divisions and independent brigades are provided, as well as the number of weapons per kilometer of front, the density of troops and weapons in the area where a main attack is made, and data on the rates of advance. Such details were the sort of things the Russian (and German) staff officers and generals looked at when planning and carrying out their battle plans, and the data explains (in a rather blunt fashion) why a battle turned out as it did.

Great Battles on the Eastern Front makes clear that Russia defeated German troops by avoiding fighting under conditions that favored the Germans. This meant avoiding mobile battle, where the Russians never developed the leadership or tactics that would have enabled them to operate on the same level as the Germans. The Russians lost so badly during the first year of the war because they tried to fight the way the Germans did. Later, the Russians adopted tactics that exploited their strengths—quantity and steadfastness.

During the 1930s, Germany and Russia had been allies of sorts, and when Germany invaded Poland in 1939, Russia supported them as per an earlier agreement with the Germans to divide Poland between them. But the Russians were appalled at how much more efficiently the Germans went about combat in western Poland. The Russians rather bumbled in the east. The next year, the Russians attacked their much smaller neighbor, Finland, and got a bloody nose as the heavily outnumbered Finns stopped them cold. But the Russians poured it on and got the Finns to cut a deal, but it was obvious to the entire world that something was seriously wrong with the mighty Red Army.

Stalin was alarmed, and ordered more studies and wargames. There had been some of this after the sloppy performance in Poland during the fall of 1939, but Stalin had ordered his troops into Finland on November 30, 1939. There was no time to make any changes. The 460,000 Russian troops, and 2,000 tanks, sent against Finland were thought sufficient to get the job done with simple, brute force. At that time, the population of Finland was only 3.6 million. The Finnish army was only 160,000 troops. The war should have been over quickly. But after three months of fighting, the Russians had made no progress, but had suffered 800,000 casualties (including 700 aircraft and 1600 tanks lost).

The Russians didn't know that the Finns were short of ammunition, and troops as well, after suffering 65,000 casualties. So Stalin had ordered peace negotiations, as sending in more reinforcements did not seem likely to achieve anything. Moreover, the war was becoming a major embarrassment, with media, and governments, worldwide wondering what was wrong with the Russians. On a more practical level, the spring thaw was approaching. This was a major factor, as most of the Russian troops had originally advanced through marshy territory, which in warm weather protects much of Finland from invasion. That's why the Russians attacked in winter. But when the marshes thaw, movement and supply would become a nightmare. So terms were offered to the Finns (surrender ten percent of your territory and move 12 percent of your population), the offer was accepted, and the Russians pulled out their battered armies.

The Russians spent the next year trying to figure out what was wrong. No one dared tell Stalin that a major part of the problem was Stalin. In 1937, Stalin had purged the armed forces of "disloyal" officers. This included half the officers (30,000 men in all were executed). The losses among senior officers was worst of all; 3 of the 5 marshals of the army, all the admirals, 14 of the 16 army commanders, 60 of the 67 corps commanders, 136 of the 199 division commanders, and 221 of the 397 brigade commanders. Worse, the officers killed were those who showed the most initiative and energy. Stalin's secret police, in fact, were still arresting and executing "suspicious" Red Army officers into early 1941. Then, apparently, Stalin realized what he had done, and gave his generals a free hand to repair the damage as quickly as possible. This meant setting up schools to train new officers, while reorganizing combat units, and forming new ones, to deal with the organizational and leadership problems encountered in Finland.

The Russians were well aware of how the German blitzkrieg worked, but no one had the guts to tell Stalin it would take years to train Russian recruits to match the standards of current German soldiers. In 1940, most Russian officers were more concerned with not saying or doing anything that would attract the lethal attention of Stalin's secret police than with pointing out Stalins errors. Officers were much more concerned with "looking good" than in doing the right thing to get their troops in shape for another war.

But in 1940 and 1941, when Russia realized that the Nazis would invade *them*, they desperately worked to mobilize their population for war. In addition to millions of men on active duty, nearly ten million men in the reserves were checked to make sure they were still available for service. Their preparations were made more urgent by the German conquest of France in June 1940, which prompted the Russians to reconsider how they were to organize their armor units. But there was no time to train their tank divisions properly before June 1941, when the German invasion arrived.

The Germans stormed into Russia with 3.5 million troops. The Russians had 5 million troops, but these soldiers were poorly trained, led by officers who (because of Stalin's purges and the mobilization) had been bumped up two or more levels of command. This meant that many divisions were led by officers with little experience at commanding battalions. The 176 regiment and brigade commanders who survived the purges now had to occupy most of the senior command positions. Their German counterparts had twice as many years in service, and sufficient time to attend proper command and staff schools, along with useful field experience in Poland and France.

The authors point out, however, that Russia had twice the military-age population of Germany. And Russia was far more effective at getting their soldiers into uniform, armed, and off to the front. A year after they were invaded, the Russians had five million troops facing 3.1 million Germans, despite having lost nearly as many men in combat the previous year. By mid-1943, there were 6.2 million Russians facing 2.9 million Germans and by mid-1944, there were 6.8 Russians going after 3.1 million Germans.

The Russians also were improving their combat skills at a much faster rate than the Germans, especially among their officers. This had to do with the fact that the Germans took longer to train their troops. By 1941, the German army was full of men who had fought successfully in Poland and France, but when they were killed they were hard to replace, so as each year went by, the proportion of experienced Germans to experienced Russians grew less. The Russians lost four soldiers for every German soldier who died in combat, but the Russians who survived became very good at their job.

Senior Russian commanders also were very smart and perceptive. They knew that Russian troops were good at digging and building fortifications. As Russian tank units were good at adapting during fast-changing, fast-moving battles, Russian armored tactics emphasized the "point and shoot" technique. This was crude, but it could be very effective.

The German army that invaded Russia had over 750,000 horse-drawn guns and wagons. Horses were a logistical nightmare. For every hundred horses hauling guns and wagons, another sixty-five were needed to carry the feed and fodder. Horses and mules also were more prone to "breakdown" than cars and trucks. During the war in Russia, the Germans lost an average of 1,000 horses a day. Some 75 percent of the losses were due to combat, as horses were not as resistant to rifle fire or shell fragments as a truck. Another 17 percent of the losses were the result of overwork. You could force horses to work harder, but eventually they would simply collapse. The Germans were never able to completely replace horses with trucks during World War II, as did the U.S. and British armies. All in all, they lost about 2.7 million horses throughout the war, nearly double those lost during World War I.

One advantage of horses was that you could eat them. Most of those that died were used for food, and sometimes horses were killed for food when there was no alternative. The Russian experience with horses was similar, although they used fewer for pulling and more for cavalry (as many as 200,000 mounted troops in 50 divisions); they were quite useful in swampy and mountainous areas. The Germans also had seven cavalry divisions, staffed largely by Russian turncoats. Russia also continued to use horses throughout the war, not able end using horse drawn vehicles and cavalry until the late 1950s.

Thus *Great Battles On The Eastern Front* demonstrates how the Russians took advantage of the fact that most German divisions used horses and could often move no faster than a man could walk. As the charts in the book make clear, the Russians learned to concentrate enormous quantities of troops, tanks and artillery on a few kilometers of front, literally blast a hole in the German lines, and then rush tank units through and into the German rear area. If the Germans lacked tank units of their own to defeat these breakthroughs (and as the war went on, they more often did not), the slow-moving German infantry units would be cut off from supply and reinforcement and bludgeoned to death, or forced to surrender, by more numerous Russian infantry.

Russian generals realized that they could achieve quantitative superiority over the Germans faster than they could gain a qualitative edge. This was to be a crucial factor in the Russian victory. Before the German invasion, many Russian leaders believed that the Germans did not have a huge edge in the quality of their training and equipment. The 1941 invasion put paid to that theory. The Germans possessed greater artillery (7,200 guns to Russia's 5,900), but the Russians had more aircraft (about 10,000 to Germany's 2,800). However, the Germans managed to catch most Russian aircraft on the ground in their surprise offensive. After a month, the Russians had about as many warplanes as the Germans, but most Russian aircraft was of older, much less capable, design. Same situation with tanks. The Russians had some 12,000 tanks in Western Russia, but the vast majority were small, obsolete, and only recently organized into tank divisions.

What saved the Russians in the opening battles of the war were the sheer distances that had to be covered. German tanks were not built to travel hundreds of kilometers without adequate maintenance. By December, only 1650 German tanks remained in working order, half what they started with the previous June. Then came winter; weather weakened the Germans more than Russian resistance.

Russia also had a mobilization system, an important component of their very efficient police state, that enabled them to quickly take over five million civilians, who had previously served in their conscript army, and put them back into uniform. The mobilization system used the extensive records kept on every Russian, and restrictions on free travel, to quickly locate military age men and get them into uniform. This system performed well throughout the war.

The Germans went on the rampage again in 1942, this time heading for the Caucasus and the Russian oil supply near the Iranian border. A lot of military and industrial aid was coming in via Iran. The Russians managed to make a stand at Stalingrad, and repulsed the Germans in an offensive that took advantage of

Germany's less capable allies (who guarded the German flanks while the Germans fought in Stalingrad itself).

Then something else happened that does not get a lot of publicity. The United States sent Russia more than a hundred billion dollars' worth (in current dollars) of military and industrial material. After 1991, when the Soviet Union World War II archives were opened, Russian and Western scholars were able to examine the wartime data and find out to what extent U.S. aid influenced Russia's military activities. There was already anecdotal evidence about the influence of such aid. It was known that the Russians admired the American P-39 fighter. Although considered obsolete in the U.S., this aircraft, with its 37mm cannon, was prized by the Russians as a good ground attack aircraft.

Most appreciated was the nearly half-million trucks that enabled the Russians to create the truly mechanized combat units that made possible their rapid advances in 1944 and 1945. When the Russians realized how many trucks the United States was willing to provide, they turned over nearly all their automotive industry to the production of tanks. By the end of the war, Russia had produced only 281,000 trucks in its own factories. The Russians trusted us to keep the trucks coming. Russia had long admired American made trucks, and had established their own automotive industry using American technology as a model. To the Russians, and most of the world, American trucks were the best designed and most reliable.

There were other items that, until the 1990s, were underappreciated in the West for their usefulness on the Russian Front fighting. To the Russian air force generals, the large quantities of 100 octane aviation fuel made an enormous difference. Unknown to most Westerners, wartime Russia was unable to produce much fuel of this type. Having large quantities of American high octane gas allowed the Russians to get the most performance out of aircraft engines. Russian fighters were not as maneuverable as German aircraft, nor did the Russians have as many skilled pilots. But they quickly realized that faster aircraft made up, more than anything else, for the lack of maneuverability and pilot skill. With faster aircraft, Russian fighters had a better chance of getting into position to make one run at German fighters. If the Russian gunfire missed, the higher speed enabled the Russian pilot to get away. The best the Russian refineries could do was produce lower quality fuel, a problem the Russians considered a state secret. Thus something as mundane as higher octane fuel became a military weapon. The U.S. sent 476,000 tons of this fuel.

Russia was also very dependent on American communications equipment. The U.S. sent them over 340,000 radios, and it was American made sets that provided most of the equipment available to Russian combat units during the war. The reason for this was simple: the Russian electronics industry never really got going before the war, and most of what they did have was overrun by the initial German advance in 1941. Moreover, the American radios were more reliable.

Waterproof telephone wire required high quality manufacturing standards. Telephone wire is either waterproof or it isn't, and Russian manufacturing standards were such that their own wire always had a leak somewhere. The Western product was much more reliable and the Russians received over two million feet of it from the United States. As the Russians preferred wire communications to wireless (so the Germans couldn't listen in), this was a particularly valuable item for them.

One of the authors of *Great Battles on the Eastern Front*, Trevor Dupuy, was a retired army colonel with World War II combat experience in Burma. This experience gave him a firm grounding in how military operations work—and don't work—in the real world. What fascinated him more than anything else were the differences in troop quality between the various armies fighting in World War II, as well as the differences in troop quality within armies. Many other active participants in World War II noticed this too, but Dupuy did something about it. He collected numerous statistics available on World War II battles—troop strengths, losses for units of both sides, etc.—who fought each other. World War II was a very well documented war, more so than any in the past. Dupuy operated in the Washington, DC, area, where a lot of this material already was (American records and captured material as well). He built an enormous database from this material, and came up with a way to analyze it. This he called Quantified Judgment Method (QJM)—a mathematical analysis of battles that takes into account manpower, weapons, attack and defense posture, and even difficult-to-quantify items such as morale and leadership. The database included information on over two hundred 20th-century battles, mostly World War II and the 1967 and 1973 Arab-Israeli Wars. By using historical data, the QJM could be used to examine the likely outcome of future battles.

Without going into the math and data (which would fill another book), Dupuy came up with the average Combat Effectiveness Value (CEV) for World War II armies. Overall, the Germans had a 1.3 advantage over the Allies (U.S. and Britain). More to the point, the Germans had a 1.57 advantage over the Russians. (Just to round out the stats, the Allies had a 1.3 advantage over the Japanese.) What this reveals is what many Allied combat soldiers already knew: man for man, the German troops were more efficient. Fortunately for the Allies, the Germans were outnumbered. Quality is nice, but quantity can defeat it.

Russians, especially the Soviets, were fond of things like the QJM, and had their own variety which they called the "Correlation of Forces." *Great Battles on the Eastern Front* presents the battles of the Eastern Front in a style Russian military historians would be comfortable with. While the human element is critical, it usually comes down to numbers. Even seemingly ephemeral things like morale and leadership can be quantified, and when you do that, it *is* all about numbers.

RUSSIA AT WAR: 1941–1945

by Alexander Werth

CARROLL & GRAF, 1999

Alexander Werth's book is one of the few that covers the role of the Russian civilian, and Russian society as a whole, in defeating the German invasion. He has been accused of being an apologist for Communist dictator Josef Stalin and his murderous secret police and concentration camp thugs. This is true, but it doesn't detract from the book. Werth portrays Stalin as seeking peace while invading eastern Poland and the Baltic States and Finland in 1939. This was absurd when the book was published (in 1964) and even more absurd now that the Soviet Union has disintegrated and more documents about those events are now out in the open. We now know that Stalin outranked Hitler when it came to mass murder. But Hitler declared war on the United States in 1941, Russia didn't. So the "enemy of my enemy is my friend" rule applies.

Werth does an excellent job describing what the war meant to the average Russian. Nearly one in five Russians died during the war and hardly anyone was left untouched by death or destruction. World War II defined Russian attitudes for the rest of the century. Called at the time the "Great Patriotic War," the struggle encouraged collective sacrifice to repel the German invader. Throughout the Cold War, the average Russian lived in fear of another invasion as destructive as that of 1941. Americans tended to be blind to this fear, and mistook Russian defensiveness and paranoia as the sole result of communist propaganda. Westerners who lived in Russia for any length of time, such as journalists, learned better, but this cultural malaise was never easy to explain to outsiders.

This excellent book has one flaw, which readers may easily miss. Werth omits from his account the damage done to Russian military readiness by Stalin's execution of most of the senior military leadership in the late 1930s for suspected disloyalty. It's still open to debate whether having those officers on duty would have made much difference. Soviet society was based on "scientific socialism," which led to many strange ideas. Russian generals and scientists came up with weapons and tactics that simply didn't work, but because science was involved, and Communist Party leaders liked what they saw, silly policies were adopted, under the umbrella name of "Scientific Socialism" and everyone in Russia agreed it was good (to do otherwise was to risk arrest by the secret police and a trip to a labor camp, or execution). While there were tangible benefits, like the construction of factories and expansion of the railroads, many of the new weapons, produced in huge quantities, were obsolete or ineffective when it came time to use them against the Germans. Another truism is that Russia had a long tradition of being ill-prepared at the start of a war. Training and organization always seemed to be in disarray. This is a tradition that persists right up to the present, except now it is regularly reported in the Russian media.

This should have been no surprise to anyone who saw the Russian army stumble into Poland and the Baltic States in 1939. That "advance" (against minor opposition) was obviously the effort of an ill-prepared army. Actually, the Russians didn't even begin their advance into eastern Poland until September 17, after the Germans had been fighting, and chewing up, the Polish army since September 1st. Rather than risk the same embarrassment in the

Baltic States, Stalin threatened each in turn with massive destruction. This was a fearsome threat, as all three of the Baltic States were tiny compared to Russia (Estonia had a population of 1.1 million, Latvia 1.9 million and Lithuania 2.5 million). By October, all three had agreed to allow Russian troops, warships and aircraft to be stationed in their countries. But Stalin was still afraid of retribution from France and Britain, which, along with the Soviet Union, had been allies of Poland. Until Russia signed a non-aggression pact with Germany in late August, 1939, Germany dared not attack Poland. Once Russia had agreed to carve up Poland in cooperation with Germany, however, World War II was off and running. Even so, Russia did not completely take over the Baltic States until France fell. The Germans took Paris on June 14, 1940. Russian troops swarmed into the Baltic States on June 17. Stalin was not about to risk yet another military embarrassment.

It's interesting also to watch the author skate over Russia's collusion with Germany in the invasion of Poland. The official Soviet reason for Russia's 1939 treaty with Germany was to gain additional defensive space in eastern Poland and the Baltic States for use against an eventual German invasion. But by mid-1941, Russia hadn't done anything to fortify this additional territory. The inept training of Russian troops and their ineffective organization and distribution in western Russia was the real reason for the rapid German advance in 1941.

The Russian high command knew there were problems. The clumsy advance into Poland was no secret. And the combat performance of Soviet troops later that year in Finland was a major embarrassment. Stalin knew he was in trouble, and he could not bring his ace commanders back from the graves he had put them in. Some of those who had been imprisoned, instead of being shot, were released and put back on duty. The upper strata of Communist Party officials and military officers could see that war with Germany was getting closer. The Germans had knocked the French off in six weeks, after failing to do that after four years of trying in World War I. The rules of war had changed, and the

Russians weren't sure they knew what the new ones were. Moreover, one had to be careful what one said to Stalin. This guy was not only a mass murderer and very, very paranoid, but was quick to "shoot the messenger" who brought him any bad news.

What had been going on in the Russian armed forces for years was very bad news. The hot shot officers who had dreamed up the new weapons (like the T-34 tank) and new tactics, were now largely dead. Their replacements were both afraid to do anything, and, even if they did feel like showing a little initiative, didn't really know what to do. Officers who had been commanding companies (a hundred or so troops) a few years ago were now commanding regiments (over 1500 troops) and had not had time to attend any schools on how to do it, much less gain any practical experience. There was always the damn Zampolit—the "political officer," who represented the Communist Party, and could countermand any of his orders, or even have him shot, "for treason against the Communist Party and the people." Training wasn't being done, or done properly. Because of the poor showing in Poland and Finland, several reorganizations were ordered. This meant shuffling around officers, troops and equipment.

When the Germans swarmed into Russia on June 22, 1941, Russian troops were willing to fight, but they were led by a lot of officers who didn't know how to. Needless to say, this particular chapter in Russian military history is not covered in Werth's book in much detail. What is mentioned is that a lot of officers stood around waiting for orders that never came. That's because orders came from the top, and Stalin had convinced himself that the Germans would not attack, at least not just yet. When Stalin did get word of the German invasion, he dithered for several days. This despite the fact that he had ordered Russian forces on a high level of alert days earlier. Millions of German troops assembling on Russians borders was kind of hard to miss, although the Germans told Stalin that it was just a deception for their invasion of Britain. When the attack did come, commanders asked for orders to do just about anything, including firing back.

Stalin's persecution of the army leadership in the late 1930s had come back to cause fatal command and control problems. Most of the Russian aircraft along the border were destroyed on the ground, mainly because there were no explicit orders to take off and fight, or attack advancing German troops. The Germans, even their infantry divisions and their horse drawn equipment, moved faster than the Russians, and moved with more deliberation and purpose. Millions of Russian soldiers were surrounded and captured, making for a catastrophe of huge proportions. The author treats these events more thoroughly than most books; he speaks Russian and was able to talk to many who survived the event. While the author describes the chaos of the German advance and Russian collapse, he does not go into all those things that Stalin did to bring it about. Still, the eye-witnesses make it clear that those in charge on the Russian side were rather slow off their marks in June and July of 1941.

Despite its length (nearly 1100 pages), *Russia at War* is very well written and organized (lots of small chapters, few over 20 pages). The writer, although raised in Britain, was born in St. Petersburg, which may account for his pro-Stalin outlook and how he avoided living under the brutal Stalinist rule. You get an excellent feel for how life was for the average Russian, and for the major events of the war. Two in particular, the Siege of Leningrad and the Battle of Stalingrad, are covered in the kind of detail, and with a degree of realism not found elsewhere. Most of the major battles are discussed, although you may not notice that many Russian defeats, or disasters, are quickly passed over. The author did not have access to all the Russian archives, especially those listing the Russian death toll for the war (some 40 million casualties, half of them civilians, a fact not released until the early 1990s). But it doesn't matter that much. You read this book for the atmosphere, for stories about what ordinary Russians had to face and how they coped. *Russia at War* lets dozens of ordinary Russians tell, in their own words of the starvation, hard work, terror of Nazis and, of course, fear of Communist officials and the secret police. The Russians explain how they will resist the invaders, even if they don't agree with the communists. Stalin understood this, and during the war the communists switched their propaganda to stress nationalist and religious angles.

Some twenty million Russian civilians died during the war, and their story needed to be told.

SOVIET CASUALTIES AND COMBAT LOSSES IN THE TWENTIETH CENTURY

edited by G. F. Krivosheev

GREENHILL, 1997

For decades after World War II, Russia's losses were considered a state secret, and the records were locked up in government archives. When the Soviet Union disintegrated in 1991, these archives were opened. The author, a retired four-star Colonel-General in the Soviet Army, supervised the team of researchers that put this essential work together. Not only are all the numbers here (losses for all campaigns, and most battles, broken down by dead, wounded, and missing), but also included are brief descriptions of the battles and campaigns. He also provides summaries of the entire war and analysis explaining some of the "mysteries" of the Russian Front. One of those concerns how many Russian troops were taken prisoner. When Germany reported millions of Russians captured in the first six months of the war, many analysts in Allied nations thought the data was fake, just more German propaganda. It turns out to have been true—and most of the 4 million Russian POWs did not survive captivity. Only 1.8 million Russian POWs were alive at the end of the war, some 672,000 of them in captivity since 1941.

But there's more. Also included in *Soviet Casualties and Combat Losses in the Twentieth Century* are specifications for Soviet weapons, as well as quantities produced and available at different points in the war. Comparative German data is also provided. One fact that the tables do not reveal is how Russian tank building was influenced by foreign technology, and eventually produced some of the most effective tanks of the period.

When the Germans invaded in 1941, the Russians had some 20,000 tanks in service. But these were largely a mishmash of failed ideas, and by the end of 1941, only 3,000 of them were still in service. The rest were either destroyed by the Germans, or abandoned by their Russian crews. But three designs had been successful. One was the BT (Bystrokhdnii Tank, or "Fast Tank"), which used an innovative track mechanism (the "Christie suspension") invented by American J. Walter Christie. While this design had been rejected by the American army, it was eagerly adopted by the Russians. It meant putting more powerful engines in tanks (often these were modified aircraft engines), but the Russians planned to create brigades (a hundred or more vehicles each) of these tanks, and turn them lose once the enemy front had been broken. Unfortunately, Stalin's Great Purge put an end to that and the BT tanks were assigned to infantry divisions. Thousands of BT tanks were used during the war with Finland in the winter of 1939–40. The thin armor of these tanks, and their inability to use much speed in all that snow, led to most of the BTs being destroyed. The most common tank of the BT series was the BT-5. This was a 12 ton tank, with a crew of three and maximum armor of 13mm (half an inch). The 45mm gun was powerful for its time, but the BT-5's armor really only provided protection from bullets and shell fragments. Before the debacle in Finland, BT-5s (and the slightly heavier and better armored BT-7s) were used with great success in the Spanish Civil War and several border battles with Japan in China.

Despite the Great Purge, work had gone on with the "Christie suspension" (that made fast tanks possible). This work was combined with the development of another series of tanks, the KVs (Kliment Voroshilov). These tanks stressed very thick armor, but were slow. The KV-1 weighed 44 tons (making it huge by 1939 standards), had 90mm (3.5 inches) armor and a top speed of 30 kilometers an hour (compared to 50 for the BTs). Only a hundred of these tanks were built from 1939 to 1940, some used successfully against the Finns in 1940. At the time, there was no anti-tank gun (except the German 88mm anti-aircraft gun firing armor piercing shells) that could penetrate its armor. However, the KV series was seen as a dead end because of its slow speed and troublesome transmission.

In the year before the Germans invaded, Russian tank designers realized that they could combine the mobility of the BTs with the armor and firepower of the KVs. This resulted in the T-34 tank. The first version weighed 26 tons, had maximum frontal armor of 45mm (nearly two inches) and carried a 76mm gun. Most important, it used the same "Christie suspension" as the BT tanks, giving the T-34 a top speed of 50 kilometers an hour. This was an unheard of speed for such a large tank, and was a major reason for its success. Actually, the combination of thick armor, large gun and high speed was what made the T-34 such a lethal, and legendary, tank on the battlefield. The speed angle has continued to be a key factor in the success of heavy tanks. Even the current M-1, which weighs more than twice as much as the original T-34, is as fast and agile. In 1941, the Germans were astonished when they encountered the KV and T-34 tanks. The Russians, as was their custom, had managed to keep the development of these tanks a secret. In fact, some aspects of Russian World War II tank technology are still considered military secrets, and details (of certain types of anti-tank shells at least) remain hidden away.

Russian losses are also broken out by officers, NCOs, and troops. Notice that there weren't as many NCO casualties as one might expect in a Western army. This is because one of the casualties of communism was the demise of the NCO corps in the Russian army. Before the 1917 revolution, Russia had an NCO corps on a par with those of other European nations. After the Communists introduced universal conscription on May 29, 1918, men were taken at age 21, later reduced to 19 and, soon after, 18; length of service was increased from two to four years.

Before the revolution, a much smaller number of men were

conscripted for twenty years, allowing the more capable among them to graduate into very effective sergeants. But the Communists did not provide any encouragement to stay in the army and develop into a professional NCO. Instead, the Soviets selected and trained more men to be officers. This turned out to be a big mistake, one that the Russians are still struggling to solve. During World War II, many capable soldiers were promoted to NCO rank, but most of these left at the end of the war, except for the large number of them who were promoted to officer rank. Without a good NCO corps, it was difficult to supervise the troops in their barracks and when they were working. As a result, the bigger and nastier soldiers would exploit the younger ones, through beatings, theft, and goldbricking, making them do more of the work. Officers would not notice, and thus would not intervene, unless things really got out of hand. There weren't many problems during World War II, because most of the Red Army was in the field, where the officers lived in close proximity to their troops. But the problems were there before the war, and played a part in the inability of the Russian army to provide much opposition to the Germans in 1941. And after the war, the problems returned, and their destructive effect was seen any time the Red Army was called out (Hungary in 1956, Czechoslovakia in 1968 and Afghanistan in the 1980s).

As something of a bonus, *Soviet Casualties and Combat Losses in the Twentieth Century* provides casualty data from other 20th-century wars in which the Soviet Union was involved, starting with the Russian Revolution.

Krivosheev's book probably will not appeal to the casual reader. Nevertheless, it is a key source of information about Russia's role in World War II.

WHEN TITANS CLASHED: HOW THE RED ARMY STOPPED HITLER

by David M. Glantz and Jonathan M. House

UNIVERSITY PRESS OF KANSAS, 1998

Two things distinguish this account of the fighting in Russia during World War II, written with the benefit of access to the Russian archives. David Glantz has written extensively on the Russian Front for decades, and Jonathan House is a younger army officer who writes well and knows how armies work. This history of the "War in the East" is more balanced than previous accounts, which were heavily influenced by German accounts of what happened out there. Many of the German records were captured at the end of the war and were available to historians, as were many German generals and veterans of the fighting. Naturally, the Germans put their own spin on what they experienced in Russia, and one could only guess at exactly what the Russians were up to. The Germans tended to imply that the Russians were basically stupid, but there were a lot of them and the more capable German troops were simply overwhelmed. This book confirms what many have suspected: despite massive defeats in 1941, and a foe who would usually outmaneuver them and win, the Russians learned fast, exploiting their strengths and avoiding situations where the Germans had the upper hand. This book, told from the Russian point of view makes for a compelling story.

While both Germany and Russia were led by homicidal maniacs during the war, the Russians found themselves in a more desperate situation. Communism in Russia, as we now know, was always unpopular with many Russians. The German invasion was seen as liberation by Soviet subjects who were not Russian. Fortunately for Russia, and the Allied cause, the conquering Germans treated their new Russian subjects like "subhumans." This, and other military and political mistakes, were used by the Russians to their advantage.

After being invaded in 1941, Russia was quick to learn from its mistakes, quicker than the Germans learned from theirs. Russia reorganized its units, changed and upgraded its training constantly, and gradually closed the performance gap between German and Russian soldiers. Part of this was accomplished by simple attrition: less capable officers and troops were killed off, more capable ones survived. But there was also feedback from the front. Divisions were left in action until fewer than half the troops remained alive and fit for action. The division was then withdrawn and fresh troops added to replace casualties and bring it back to strength. The veterans knew that everyone's prospects of survival increased according to how much of their combat experience could be transferred to the new recruits. Weeks, or months, of training then followed and the reinvigorated division went back into action. By the end of the war, the quality gap still existed between German and Russian units, but some Russian outfits easily surpassed most German divisions in combat ability.

The Russians developed more practical weapons, such as rocket launchers, and while some German weapons may have been superior, the Russian ones were good enough and they had far more of them. However, *When Titans Clashed* is most revealing in its discussion of how the Russian military leadership adapted. The battles looked different from the Russian side, often quite a bit different. How? The Russians, on their guard for those rapid and well executed counterattacks the Germans were capable of up until the end of the war, used overwhelming force on several parts of the front line to break through, and followed up with their armored divisions (or "Tank Corps" as they called them) dashing forward to obliterate the German support units and supplies. These attacks became more and more devastating as the war progressed, and the Germans never came up with a countermeasure. Glantz and House show how the Russians became the masters of defensive warfare, and stopped the Germans at Moscow in 1941, Stalingrad in 1942, and Kursk in 1943, after which time the Russians took the offensive, and devised new ideas faster than the Germans.

When Titans Clashed also makes clear that the Russians knew that victory would go, as Napoleon liked to put it, to the "bigger battalions." The Russians used their larger population to replace losses faster than the Germans could replace theirs. More than 60 percent of the German armed forces were engaged in Russia from June 1941 through the end of 1944. The majority of German losses also were suffered in there. It was Russia that defeated the German army, in the East, something the Allies took advantage of when in 1944 they fought their way across France and into Germany against a much weakened German army in the West.

Glantz and House also point out that, because the Russians lost 30 million dead (18 percent of the entire population), the after-effects of the war have been more intense than in the United States (which lost 400,000 dead, or 0.3 percent of the population). This became an issue because, during World War II and then throughout the Cold War, most Americans had no idea how paranoid and fearful the Russians had become because of their World War II losses. The Russians didn't even call it "World War II," but the "Great Patriotic War." Part of the problem with the Western nations not appreciating Russia's sacrifices during World War II has to do with the communist dictatorship that ruled the country for seventy years (from the early 1920s to the early 1990s). The communists were keen to keep everything regarding how they ran things a secret. This made sense, in a way, because the main governing techniques of the communists were mass murder and terror. But even details on how they defeated the Germans during World War II were kept secret. After the Soviet Union fell, and communist officials could speak freely, they admitted that the main reason for keeping details on Russian performance, and losses, during World War II a secret was to prevent the world from knowing how screwed up the communist government was before, and early in the war. It was thought that admitting that 30 million Russians died in the war would reflect badly on how the communists ran things. That's probably an accurate assessment.

But Stalin was more ruthless and effective than Hitler in mobilizing the Russian economy and population for the war effort.

Given that most books on the war in Russia written during the past half-century have been, so to speak, from the outside looking in, it is revealing to see it from the winners' point of view.

Four

THE WAR IN THE PACIFIC

---

*I*N GEOGRAPHIC TERMS, the War in the Pacific was
the largest part of World War II. It was also the
most complex culturally, involving many quite different Asian nationalities. It was also a very varied war,
featuring numerous naval battles, amphibious operations, enormous land campaigns, huge guerrilla armies,
suicide attacks, and hopeless defensive battles. The only
five carrier-to-carrier battles ever fought occurred in
the Pacific. There's much to be said on the subject, more
than many people realize. Because the War in the Pacific
was so "alien," there was always less interest in it relative to the War in Europe. This has been taken into account when selecting books for this section.

A BATTLE HISTORY OF THE IMPERIAL JAPANESE NAVY, 1941–1945

by Paul S. Dull

U.S. NAVAL INSTITUTE, 1978

To understand how the Japanese navy swept all before it from December 1941 (Pearl Harbor) to June 1942 (Midway), you have to look at it from the Japanese point of view. *A Battle History of the Imperial Japanese Navy* does that, drawing readers into the distinctive mindset of the men who served in the Imperial Japanese Navy. The book is basically what its title implies, a history of the battles of the Japanese navy during World War II as seen by Japanese naval commanders. Japanese sources were used to document all the major battles of the Japanese navy during the war. The author was a Marine officer during World War II, was at Pearl Harbor the day of the attack, and speaks Japanese.

The Japanese navy was a unique organization. Begun in 1868 as part of Japan's efforts to bring itself in line with the modern world, in less than four decades it had managed to defeat the Chinese and, more important, the Russian fleets. Even though the Russians had the sorriest naval track record of all the Western powers, their defeat by the Japanese in 1905 was the first time an East Asian nation had beaten a European power. This was significant but Western powers, including the United States, tended to believe that the Japanese had done it the "Western" way. Big

mistake. The Japanese were a very un-Western combination of dili-
gence, discipline, and willingness to borrow freely from the West, but
in doing that they created a navy that looked Western but "thought
Eastern." Japanese sailors were better trained than their Western
counterparts, and Japanese naval commanders were more eager to
seek a "decisive battle" and, importantly, were inclined to ignore
supply problems. To the Japanese, a warrior did not bother with
something as mundane as making sure there were sufficient supplies
of fuel, food, and transports. This was the major flaw in Japanese
naval operations. The Japanese were not the first to make this mistake, but it cost them big time when they engaged the United States,
which did pay careful attention to keeping their troops supplied.

From the start, Japan recognized that Britain was the preemi-
nent naval power in the world. British naval officers were, therefore, hired to help train the new Japanese navy, while British
shipyards received many orders for warships and merchant ships,
all of the most modern design. By the end of the 19th century,
Japanese shipyards were themselves turning out equally sophisti-
cated vessels. This created the idea in the West that all the
Japanese could do was copy. Another big mistake. Of course the
Japanese had to copy others, but few noticed that they were also
making numerous little improvements in the methods and technology they acquired.

By 1941, the Japanese navy was one of the best trained and
best led on the planet. Japanese sailors tolerated training sched-
ules that would have caused mutiny in any Western navy. They
went out in the worst weather and at night, training with their
ships and their weapons. Japanese lookouts, in the years before
radar on ships became common, were peerless at the art of seeing
before being seen.

But as this book makes clear, the higher up the chain of command you go, the worse things get. In the Japanese navy, little
things were done extremely well, while larger matters of strategy
were often developed in strange, often disastrous ways. Japanese
naval commanders were frequently bold, but made some really
dumb decisions, some of which were not seen as mistakes in

Japanese eyes. For example, the Japanese recognized that submarines were crucial naval weapons, but could not accept the fact that the best use of submarines was against non-warships (freighters and tankers). An important part of being a Japanese officer, naval or army, was being a warrior, someone who went out and fought enemy warriors. There was no shortage of raw courage among Japanese naval officers, but this otherwise commendable quality crippled the Japanese submarine force, which throughout the war, spent nearly all its time looking for warships. It was considered shameful and wasteful to use a torpedo on a merchant ship—while American submarines were systematically destroying the Japanese merchant fleet. At the same time, American transports and tankers were pouring troops and supplies into the war against Japan, largely unhindered by Japanese submarine attacks.

While Japanese naval officers were often resourceful in unexpected situations, they just as often kept using the same ineffective tactics over again. There was a mitigating circumstance, however. The superb naval force with which Japan began the war could not replace its losses, or expand its forces, as the Americans could. Japan's industrial might was less than 15 percent the size of America's. Even though the U.S. was devoting more than half its resources for the fight against Germany, there was plenty left to use against the Japanese. The Japanese compounded the problem by refusing to change their painstaking and time-consuming training methods to adjust to wartime conditions and demands. Japanese ships and naval aircraft grew short of crews as the war went on.

Another major problem was the constant squabbling and lack of cooperation at the top between the army and navy. This was not unique to Japan, but it was more intense and destructive in Japan. In the United States, the leaders at the very top developed ways to keep the interservice rivalry from getting in the way of beating the enemy. In World War II Japan, a combination of warrior spirit and loyalty to one's service, led the army and navy to actually do things that greatly hampered each other's effectiveness. Typical of this was the refusal of each service to pool their shipping.

Cooperation in planning combat operations was often inefficient and ineffective. *A Battle History of the Imperial Japanese Navy* provides numerous examples.

In 1941, the Japanese navy was a potent combat force. But it was not able to replace the losses incurred once the American fleet piled on and dragged the Japanese into a war of attrition. America could replace its losses, and knew the Japanese could not. Moreover, American sailors learned on the job, even though it cost sailors and ships.

By 1943, most of Japan's edge was gone. From then on the Japanese knew that this was a war they could not win—a war where the largest fleet would prevail. They had known this in 1941, but it hadn't made any difference. Japanese sailors had their own peculiar sense of what was real and what was right. This book makes clear how that different mind-set influenced the outcome of the naval war in the Pacific.

EAGLE AGAINST THE SUN

by Ronald H. Spector

RANDOM HOUSE, 1985

If you're looking for a comprehensive history of the war in the Pacific in one volume, this is it. The only flaw in *Eagle Against the Sun* is that it does not pay much attention to the uniquely Japanese decision-making process, which emphasized consensus and tradition. This is relatively unimportant if you're looking for a readable and reasonably thorough description of how the war in the Pacific played out.

Making use of documents declassified in the 1980s, Spector takes a penetrating look at the debates over strategy and tactics that bedeviled both sides. Because it played such a significant role in Japan's defeat, the disruptive effect of the constant arguing of Japanese generals and admirals has long been known. Equally bitter disputes between American and Allied military commanders never got as much coverage. That is rectified here. Spector reveals that General Douglas MacArthur was not the only argumentative commander on the Allied side. It's taken decades for the dirt to come out, and some of it apparently is still buried in archives that have not yet been declassified.

Since the Allied code-breaking efforts were made public in the 1970s and 1980s, debates between World War II commanders have come to make more sense. For example, the credit MacArthur got for bypassing the major Japanese base at Rabaul (north of New Guinea) and instead landing his forces on less well-defended areas to the north (and closer to the Philippines) is now contradicted by the revelations that, for a long time, MacArthur *wanted* to attack Rabaul. Decoded Japanese messages to and from Rabaul indicated that supplies were very short there. The decoded messages made it clear that the Japanese on Rabaul were more concerned about starvation than an enemy attack, and indicated that Japanese bases to the northwest, on the New Guinea coast, were not only low on supplies and combat troops, but coping with malaria and other tropical diseases. The brass back in Washington used this information to convince MacArthur to bypass Rabaul and go after distant Hollandia, on the New Guinea coast, which put Allied forces closer to the Philippines and cut off Japanese access to their oil supplies in Indonesia.

By the way, MacArthur was quite keen on code-breaking, and set up his own "signals intelligence" shop in the Philippines before the war, and later expanded it when he evacuated his key code breakers to Australia. MacArthur's code breakers proceeded to make some major contributions to the Allied code-breaking effort. But MacArthur had such a high opinion of his own code-breaking operation, that he often ignored the deciphered messages available to him because his people had not done the work.

Disputes between MacArthur and the generals in Washington over strategy and the use of decoded information was common during the war. Not all senior generals were informed of the full extent of the code-breaking, and some of the debates were conducted with one side unable to use its most powerful argument, that the intelligence gathered came directly from a decoded enemy message. Reading about the often contentious decision making on both sides allows you to know the commanders better, and see why things were done the way they were.

Spector also takes advantage of the fact that the war in the Pacific was characterized by long periods of relative inactivity, punctuated by short periods of intense naval activity and land combat. He effectively weaves in political motives, which were torn between the American people's intense anger at Japan, and the U.S. government's decision to shift most resources to Europe and to secure the defeat of Germany first. What Spector makes especially clear is that the war in the Pacific was run on a shoestring compared to the materiel and manpower used to defeat the Nazis. To make matters worse, for a year after the Battle of Midway (June 1942), a third of the resources sent to the Pacific were used to mobilize forces seeking to dislodge the small Japanese garrisons that occupied two barren islands off the Alaskan coast. The Japanese saw this coming and withdrew most of their troops before the American and Canadian troops landed. But this was a major issue, as the Japanese had managed to occupy "American territory" (although the islands were uninhabited).

Spector also provides clear descriptions of the struggle over strategy between MacArthur, who led his forces northward from New Guinea and the Solomon Islands, and the Marines, who had created a huge amphibious force and insisted on using it to attack the Japanese from a completely different direction (straight across the central Pacific, north of the Equator, starting with Tarawa in November 1943 and ending at Okinawa in June 1945). The Navy had long advocated a central Pacific strategy, and all prewar planning and war games had concentrated on these islands. MacArthur's strategy, which could be accomplished with fewer American casualties, called for continuing his advance toward the Philippines and then to Okinawa, but the Navy was reluctant to risk its growing carrier force near all those Japanese bases on south Pacific islands.

In the central Pacific, the Navy could use their carriers to isolate the island groups one at a time, and send in the Marines to capture just enough of them to provide air bases and anchorages for the next jump. MacArthur was miffed, because there would be a shortage of amphibious shipping in the Pacific until after D-Day. He had to hold back until late 1944, while the Navy and Marines blasted their way across the central Pacific. The author covers this strategic conflict expertly, and brings in the Japanese side of the equation as well. The Japanese feared MacArthur the most, as it was his force that could most easily cut Japan off from their oil supplies in the Dutch East Indies. The U.S. Navy, however, had that covered as well, with an increasingly effective submarine campaign against Japanese shipping.

The key battles are all described. Preliminary maneuvers for these battles are also clearly described, not an easy feat in the Pacific war. All in all, *Eagle Against the Sun* offers readers a pretty comfortable way to get a grasp of the entire war in the Pacific without getting lost.

GUADALCANAL

by Richard B. Frank

PENGUIN, 1992

Guadalcanal was one of the more decisive and instructive battles of World War II. Not nearly as large as some others, Guadalcanal was most notable because it was history's first three-dimensional battle, combining intense action at sea, on land, and in the air. It was also the one campaign where American and Japanese forces were evenly matched in terms of numbers, and it was where the Japanese found out that, despite an even playing field, they would lose.

This particular book is important because it's well written, covers everything and leaves you knowing a lot more than you thought you'd ever know about one of the key battles of World War II.

Guadalcanal was a desperate fight for the control of an airfield. On land, the Japanese dedicated more than 30,000 troops to reclaiming the island from the Allies, but because they did so in small groups, they never managed to outnumber the defending Americans. As a result, the Japanese lost over 30,000 men, compared to 1,769 Americans.

The air battle also went against the Japanese, even though Japanese aircraft were built for maneuverability and distance. This, plus the skillful flying of their pilots, made them appear invincible. The Americans examined the situation carefully and found certain key Japanese weaknesses. A few bullets in the numerous fuel tanks of Japanese aircraft would bring them down. Unlike American warplanes, the Japanese saved weight by not equipping their planes with self-sealing fuel tanks. The lack of armor for fighter pilots also increased their losses. Most of the American aircraft stationed on Guadalcanal were fighters, and their main job was to shoot down Japanese aircraft. By the end of the campaign, America had lost 420 aircrew, compared to 1,200 Japanese. This hit the Japanese hard, because it had taken them several years to train each of those airmen.

At sea, it was a somewhat different story. Losses to both the American and Japanese navies were heavy. America lost 4,911 sailors, Japan 3,543. There were some forty naval engagements related to Guadalcanal, including two carrier battles and most of the battleship action in the Pacific war. In all, the U.S. lost two carriers, five heavy cruisers (plus an Australian cruiser), as well as two light cruisers and fourteen destroyers—a total of 24 major warships. The Japanese also lost twenty-four major warships, but with a much smaller economy, Japan could not afford these losses. They could not be replaced. Such was not the case with the United States.

On the island itself, there were eight land battles and some thirty air, or air-versus-ship battles. There were thousands of ground patrols and air raids. American ships prevented the Japanese from landing more troops on the island, and from bombarding into rubble the American airfields and support base. The inability of the Japanese to get enough supplies to the island on a regular basis led to over half the Japanese losses being from starvation and disease. The battle went on for six months until the Japanese accepted at last that they could not win, and could not afford the losses incurred by trying.

This 800 page book (including 180 pages of appendices and notes, many of which are useful in themselves) covers the campaign in splendid, but readable, detail. The entire affair has the air of an epic saga about it. But you won't see any movies made about the Guadalcanal campaign because there was too much going on. The battles on the ground, air and sea intersected at key moments, but otherwise went their own way. The U.S. Navy was running the show, and when they put an understrength 1st Marine Division ashore on Guadalcanal in early August, 1942, they knew they were asking for trouble. At this point in the war, the Japanese had more troops, warships and aircraft in the western Pacific. The only thing that made the landing on Guadalcanal possible at all was the battle of Midway, two months earlier. Four Japanese aircraft carriers had been sunk, so now the odds were rather more even in the carrier aviation department. The Japanese blamed Midway on bad luck, which was partially true. The Japanese didn't know the Americans were reading their secret messages, which played a large role in the "luck" the Americans had at Midway. Reading Japanese messages was not as important during the Guadalcanal fighting. It was more a matter of the Americans holding out, as Japanese ships, aircraft and troops kept coming south, until the Japanese gave up or the Americans withdrew.

What followed was four months of desperate fighting, which is vividly described in the book, and in sufficient detail that you can understand what each side was trying to do.

The basic problem during the Guadalcanal campaign was one of math. The American fighters, and a few light bombers on Guadalcanal had sufficient range to spot and bomb Japanese transport ships before they could get to the island. The Japanese responded by using destroyers to move supplies. But as fast as they were, the destroyers sometimes got caught during daylight and, worst of all, they couldn't carry enough to keep the Japanese troops supplied. Thousands of Japanese literally starved to death, and many more died of disease. The Japanese sent in battleships and cruisers to shell the airfield, but American warships were always available to meet the Japanese, and save the airfield from a fatal pounding. The Japanese tried to maneuver aircraft carriers and battleships to take out the airfield, but this just resulted in more naval battles the Japanese could not win, or win decisively. Japanese submarines swarmed around Guadalcanal, resulting in some patches of the South Pacific being nicknamed "torpedo alley." American warships were torpedoed, but there were always just enough left to parry the next Japanese attack.

The Japanese lost, but it was a close call. It's been said that the Japanese could have shut down the American airfield early on by bringing in their battleships, and moving them south until American aircraft could no longer operate off the Guadalcanal air base. This would have given the Japanese the opportunity to heavily reinforce their troops on the island and drive the Americans away. That they didn't try this sure-fire strategy has to do with two factors most people overlook. First, the Japanese didn't have enough fuel to dispatch their battleships to Guadalcanal night after night. Nor did they have enough troops handy to overwhelm the Americans on the island. These two facts may come as a shock to many, but they are well known to World War II historians.

Japan went to war in the first place because the United States, Britain and the Netherlands (which controlled the oil fields in the Dutch East Indies), cut off their oil supplies. There were no other suppliers, and without it, the Japanese armed forces would be out of fuel in less than a year. So Japan attacked, and seized the Dutch oil fields. But the Dutch were more thorough in blowing up their oil fields and pumping facilities than the Japanese expected. That would not have been an insurmountable problem, except that a Japanese transport, steaming south full of oil equipment and technicians to repair the oil fields, was sunk by the Allies. This was pure luck, for the Allies had no idea that this particular ship carried such a valuable cargo. But the Japanese were in a hurry to get the oil fields producing again, and sent that ship south while Allied warships were still in the area.

In the last three months of 1942, Japan had managed to pump only 1.2 million tons of oil out of its conquered oil fields. And only 643,000 tons made it to Japan (where most of the refineries were) because of a shortage of tankers. American submarines were starting to go after Japanese tankers, a process that would eventually reduce the flow of oil to Japan to a mere trickle. Meanwhile, the Japanese Navy was using about 305,000 tons a month. Some of that could be picked up at the oil fields, because most ships ran on oil that did not need to be refined. But most of the Japanese navy was still stationed in Japan or the Central Pacific. They could not run all the way down to Sumatra just to top off their tanks. So the problem was mainly one of fuel.

Japan had plenty of battleships available for action, but not the fuel oil to send them down to Guadalcanal night after night until the airfield was destroyed and American troops driven from the island. Japanese battleships carried 5,000–10,000 tons of oil each. They did not travel alone, needing destroyer escorts to take care of enemy submarines. Six or eight battleships would be needed to guarantee success, and take care of the newly built American battleships known to be in the South Pacific. The Japanese battleship force would need to operate around Guadalcanal for at least a month, and they would burn up several hundred thousand tons of oil doing so. This would make a serious dent in Japanese oil supplies, limiting aircraft and ship operations elsewhere. The Japanese admirals did the math and decided the cost was not worth the potential payoff. They were probably influenced by the disastrous Midway campaign earlier in the year, where they used more oil in that one operation than the entire Japanese navy used, before the war, in an entire year.

The United States could have survived being chased out of Guadalcanal, but the Japanese could not survive long without reclaiming it. Their reputation of invincibility was shattered, as was their confidence. The Americans proved to be far more formidable opponents than the Japanese expected. Not only were the Americans clever and determined fighters, their ability to keep their troops supplied, and to build necessary air fields, ports, and fortifications exceeded Japanese expectations. Indeed, one reason the Japanese had not feared an American invasion of Guadalcanal was because the airfield the Japanese were building there was still unfinished. Based on their own experience, the Japanese believed that it would take the Americans weeks to finish the airfield, giving Japan sufficient time to send more troops and warships to flush them out. But the Americans got the airfield finished and had warplanes operating on Guadalcanal by August 20, thirteen days after the Marines arrived. After that, it was one unpleasant surprise after another for the Japanese. By the end of 1942, the

Japanese officers who had participated in the Guadalcanal campaign had no doubts that Japan was going to lose the war.

For whatever reason, Guadalcanal has not retained the mythic status it was granted during World War II. In 1942 and 1943, Guadalcanal was the only battle that mattered to most Americans. It was like the Alamo, except that the Americans won, and for the rest of the Pacific war, there was never another campaign like it. After Guadalcanal, it was certain that America could not lose. But as World War II faded from living memory, the touch-and-go battle for Guadalcanal faded into the background of World War II history. Maybe it was the complexity of the battle, or the fact that America suffered some embarrassing defeats in the course of the campaign. Nevertheless, if you are serious about World War II history, you must pay attention to what went on at Guadalcanal. It mattered. It mattered a lot.

JAPAN AT WAR: AN ORAL HISTORY

by Haruko Taya Cook and Theodore F. Cook

NEW PRESS, 1993

Theodore F. Cook and Taya Cook, an American-born historian and his Japanese-born wife, spent several years in the late 1980s interviewing Japanese who had lived through World War II as soldiers or civilians. Some of the interviews are extraordinary. The now elderly Japanese speak frankly and with pride about their contribution to the war effort, or their disgust at the stupidity and waste of it all. Some speak casually of atrocities witnessed, or, in some cases, committed.

The veterans calmly describe the starvation and disease that was more of a killer than American firepower. The Japanese did not take care of their troops nearly as well as America did, regarding it as just another battlefield hazard. There were no starvation deaths among any American troops during World War II, but in the Japanese army such deaths numbered in the thousands. Guadalcanal, where Japanese and American troops fought for control in late 1942 and early 1943, came to be called "Starvation Island" by the Japanese because of the number of troops who starved to death there. Although the Japanese realized early on that they were going to have a hard time supplying troops on Guadalcanal (the Americans controlled the airfield, from which bombers were dispatched to attack any Japanese supply ships that ventured near the island), they nevertheless sent nearly 50,000 troops there, of whom some 37,000 died, 9,000 of disease and starvation. Many of the combat deaths were men lightly wounded who were unable to recover due to the lack of food and medicine. The interviewed ex-soldiers talk casually of dragging themselves out on patrol, even though they were weak from hunger and disease. As the war went on, American troops regularly took advantage of the poor logistical capabilities of the Japanese, and would try to literally starve them out.

But the suffering wasn't all inflicted on the Japanese; most of it was visited *by* Japanese troops upon local civilians. The majority of Japanese soldiers did not fight American soldiers, but the Chinese and other peoples in occupied countries. Most Japanese troops really believed they were "liberating" the people of East Asia from European and American domination. When the Japanese first showed up in Asian areas that had been European colonies for many generations, they were greeted as "brothers" and "liberators." East Asians took pride in the 1905 Japanese defeat of Russia in the Russo-Japanese war. Yes, it was racial, and not only because the European colonizers were arrogant and tended to treat the locals badly, but because the locals often felt (with some justification) that they were better people than these arrogant white men.

This accounts for the initially warm reception the Japanese received. However, ethnic pride was actually stronger in this part of the world than in Europe, and when the Japanese revealed the depth of their racism, there was an armed resistance in areas they occupied within a year. Retribution was savage. Since the people they were killing were not Japanese, any cruelty was considered justified. A number of such actions are described in *Japan at War*. Bad memories of brutal behavior during the war persist into the 21st century, which may explain why many of these elderly Japanese interviewed show little remorse.

The stories of the Japanese civilians are striking. Japan was a poor country at the outset of World War II, as much of its national wealth for the past two generations had gone into industrialization and building up its armed forces. Little of it reached the people. But the war brought a prosperity of sorts for a few years as the economy strained to produce weapons and equipment for the military. Then came the American B-29 bombers and the fire-bomb raids that proved more deadly than the later atomic bombs.

What's particularly striking about these interviews is the matter-of-fact attitude displayed by this generation of Japanese. They marched off to war, often to certain death, with an eerie detachment and resignation. Japanese civilians who were scraping by at home, getting pounded by the bombing of late 1944 and most of 1945, seem equally bland about it all. Some of the interviewees speak about how World War II history is taught in Japan and the impact the conflict had on their country, and report that the Japanese have tried to ignore their World War II experience. If they don't erase it exactly, they position it as "an unfortunate experience." (Germans, in contrast, felt a great deal of guilt and remorse about their wartime activities.) Many Japanese like to think of themselves as victims, forced to attack the United States, Britain, and Holland to save themselves from destruction. This may sound absurd to most Americans, but after reading *Japan at War*, you'll have a better idea of where the Japanese we-are-victims attitude came from. The Japanese had convinced themselves that East Asia would be better off if Japan ran the region. But none of Japan's neighbors agreed with that, and the Japanese refused to accept that, and many Japanese still see things that way. That's a valuable lesson, because most wars are fought between people who have some serious misunderstandings about what the other side is thinking.

SILENT VICTORY: THE U.S. SUBMARINE WAR AGAINST JAPAN

by Clay Blair Jr.

U.S. NAVAL INSTITUTE, 2001

Clay Blair Jr.'s book is considered the definitive account of American submarine operations in the Pacific during World War II. Through a combination of technical detail and narrative, he shows how sailors, most of whom were civilians when the war began, and submarines, most of which were built only after the war began, won the first—and so far only—successful submarine campaign against enemy ships. Blair not only describes what it was like to operate in a submarine for weeks on end, he provides a definitive list of statistics on the operations, and the losses and damage inflicted on the enemy. The American submarine campaign in the Pacific was a monumental achievement that rarely gets the credit it deserves. Blair tells the story as it should be told.

The submarine was an American invention. This is ironic, as most people think first of German U-Boats (*unterseeboot,* or "under sea boats") when the subject of submarines comes up. In both World Wars, Germany failed in its attempt to use submarines to isolate Great Britain, particularly from ships arriving from the United States. But in the Pacific, American submarines devastated Japanese shipping, and effectively cut the Japanese off from their overseas empire and the troops trying to defend it.

From the beginning, the Japanese had serious problems with getting supplies to the outposts of their empire: It took Japanese merchant ships 28 days to reach the Philippines, 52 days to get to the Dutch East Indies (the source of their oil and rubber), and 65 days to Burma. Their military bases in the Pacific were equally distant. Truk, their main naval base in the central Pacific, was 42 days from Japan. Their main base in the south Pacific, Rabaul, was 48 days. Hawaii was 60 days distant, which is one reason why the attack on Pearl Harbor was seen as so daring.

During the course of World War II, the Japanese lost 9.5 million tons of shipping (69 percent to submarines, 20 percent to aircraft attacks, 6 percent to mines, and the rest to miscellaneous causes). The average Japanese transport ship weighed in only at a few thousand tons. Japan began the war with 6.4 million tons of shipping, but by the end of the war only 1.5 million tons were left. Most of these were cowering in harbors because of the thousands of naval mines dropped by American submarines and B-29 bombers outside Japanese ports in 1945.

The American submarine campaign began slowly but impressively, with 875,000 tons of Japanese shipping sunk in 1942. In 1943, it was 2.2 million tons; it peaked in 1944 with 4.3 million tons. A relative lack of targets meant that only 2.1 tons were sunk during the first eight months of 1945. In addition to 1,294 merchant ships sunk, 188 Japanese warships (540,000 tons' worth) were also destroyed by American subs. Britain and Holland had subs in the Pacific, too, and their efforts accounted for about two percent of the Japanese ships sunk. But the most striking statistic is that only 50,000 sailors manning the Allies' submarines (including support staff), was less than 2 percent of Navy manpower, and it was these men who accounted for 55 percent of Japanese losses at sea.

All this was accomplished in spite of the fact that many American subs, early in the war, were inferior in performance to the German U-Boats, and the Japanese submarines had a far superior torpedo. There was also a problem with defective American torpedoes during the first year of the war. Quite a few of the American submarine captains during the early months of the war were also found to be inadequate, largely because peacetime training had concentrated on process and procedure, not independent thinking and initiative. The admirals were quick to pick up on this, and more energetic skippers were quickly found.

During the entire war, there were 1450 patrols by individual American subs (350 in 1941-42, 350 in 1943, 520 in 1944 and 330 in 1945). Each patrol lasted about three weeks. On three percent of those patrols, the U.S. subs failed to return (49 subs lost). The losses among submarine crews was larger, with 22 percent of U.S. submarine crewmen not surviving the war. There were accidents and illnesses that could kill you at sea. Moreover, the reward for one successful patrol was, after a month or so (for maintenance, repairs and training), another patrol. Eventually, the Japanese, or the hazards of the sea, would remind you that this was a dangerous job.

Instead of going after Allied merchant ships, the Japanese subs preferred to search for enemy warships, often ignoring transports or tankers that could have been taken down. The Japanese naval doctrine considered merchant ships unworthy targets for their submarines. Moreover, as a result of the superior Allied anti-submarine tactics and equipment, Japan lost 130 subs during the war, and Germany lost 11 U-Boats operating in the Pacific.

At the start of the war, Japan actually had more subs in the Pacific (67), than the United States (56). But the United States built another 200 for Pacific service while Japan was only able to build 120. The U.S. submarine fleet at the beginning of the war consisted of vessels from over a dozen different classes, built between 1914 and 1941. Later models, Gato-class boats (73 built 1941–43) and the nearly identical Balao-class boats (116 built 1942–45), were more than twice the size (at 1500 tons surface displacement) of the most common German U-Boat (the 626 ton Type VII). The Gatos were also more spacious than the Type VIIs, having a crew of 65, compared to 44 on the German boats. The Gato/Balao boats were superior in many ways. They could dive 600 feet deeper than most other subs, were easier to use, and were more resistant to damage and breakdowns. These subs accounted for most of the Japanese shipping sunk, as well as providing subs for the ace crews that racked up the highest numbers of enemy ships sunk. The top ten subs in the Pacific each averaged about 20 ships sunk, with the total tonnage varying from 100,000 tons (for the number one boat, the USS *Flasher*) to 72,500 tons of shipping (the USS *Snook*).

The Pacific covers a large area and many patrols resulted in no enemy ships sunk. Even though subs patrolled in high traffic areas, bad weather, enemy warships and aircraft, or just bad luck, prevented contacts. The record for ships sunk in a single patrol was set by the USS *Tang* which, during her third patrol, found and sank ten ships. *Silent Victory* is full of facts like these, which adds depth to one's understanding of the submarine campaign and puts it into better perspective. One issue the author did not know about was the extent to which Japanese coded messages had been decoded by American intelligence. The code used by Japanese merchant ships was actually decoded rather late, in 1943. But once we were reading Japanese messages, American submarine captains were fed this information, as if it were coming from spies in Japanese controlled ports, that Japanese shipping was in a specific location on certain dates. American sub crews came to look forward to these bits of "intelligence information," for they were usually quite accurate. So accurate, in fact, that U.S. subs began to operate in "wolfpacks" (groups of submarines) as the Japanese were forced, by losses of transports and escorts, to use larger convoys.

Unlike the American effort in the Pacific, which decisively destroyed Japanese merchant shipping, the German U-Boat force was defeated by mid-1943. The German subs were still a threat after that, but a minor one. For all their efforts (a thousand U-Boats put to sea), they only sank about one percent of Allied merchant ships crossing the Atlantic. It was not for want of trying, it was just that the Allies were more resourceful and energetic in meeting the challenge. The Germans sunk over 2,753 Allied merchant ships (14.5 million tons) during the "Battle of the Atlantic." About half those ships were sunk by 700 Type VII subs. These small subs were cramped, and sunk in large numbers (437 by enemy action, 165 by their crews at the end of the war).

The German effort was defeated by several factors. For most of the war, Allied code breakers were able to read the secret messages sent to and from the subs, making it easier to hunt down and sink the subs. Partly to protect this secret, the Allies made sure the Germans found out about other technical means that were used to track down subs. This included a highly efficient radio direction tracking system called Huff-Duff. This system had several receiving stations pick up transmissions from German subs and detect the direction the signal was coming from. Using triangulation, the reports from several listening stations would give a rough location for the sub that was transmitting. The Allies also had superior sonar (for finding subs underwater) and airborne radar (for finding subs when they were on the surface, which they were most of the time, especially at night, to run their diesel engines and recharge their batteries). The Allies also had excellent weapons, including depth charges that could be dropped from aircraft, and "depth charge throwers" that propelled depth charges up to 300 meters from the ship attacking a submerged sub. The Allies also had lots of long range aircraft (four engine heavy bombers) and, perhaps most important, half a dozen small "escort" aircraft carriers (merchant ships rebuilt to operate 20–30 warplanes) that each served as the key ship in a "hunter-killer" group. These groups then used their destroyers and carrier aircraft to search out German subs day and night. This approach proved the final nail in the coffin for German U-Boat operations in the Atlantic.

As the title *Silent Victory* implies, the submarine war in the Pacific was carried out by the "Silent Service," meaning that most of the submarine operations were kept quiet and, of course, were always carried out deep in enemy territory, where no media was able to observe and report.

Blair does an excellent job of describing the subs, crews, and how they operated, as well as, in effect, providing the missing wartime reportage. His accounts of some of the more exciting moments of wartime patrols gives more meaning to otherwise dry statistics of submarine operations. *Silent Victory* also gives the subs their due for all the other chores they were given—performing reconnaissance for the fleet, going after enemy warships, carrying raiders covertly to enemy beaches. Primarily, however, the American subs went after Japanese shipping, and sank most of it. Thousands of American soldiers, sailors, and marines owe their lives to the men in the "Silent Service."

SOLDIERS OF THE SUN

by Meirion and Susie Harries

RANDOM HOUSE, 1992

The performance of Japanese soldiers during World War II gave new meaning to the term "fanaticism." Before Pearl Harbor, Americans knew little about the Japanese military, except that it was responsible for committing atrocities in China, along with vague memories of Japan defeating Russian troops during the 1904–05 Russo-Japanese War. Suddenly, within six months after Pearl Harbor, Japanese soldiers began to look like supermen. They quickly defeated the British and Dutch in Southeast Asia. In the Philippines, Japanese troops invaded, brushed aside the American-led Philippine army, and spent months battling a determined American-Filipino force on the Bataan peninsula.

Reports came in from New Guinea, where American and Australian troops fought the Japanese in jungles and mountains. The Japanese soldiers were still mysterious, but now they began to seem fanatical, at least by American standards. By the end of 1942 most Americans were aware that Japanese soldiers didn't surrender—they fought to the death. When, in the summer of 1942, American Marines invaded Guadalcanal in the Solomon islands and captured a Japanese airfield, the Japanese tried to reclaim it by way of desperate attacks by infantry. The Japanese also liked to fight at night, and would march through swamps and jungles thought impassable.

Who were these guys?

As *Soldiers of the Sun* explains it, these soldiers were, well, typical of Japanese of their time. During the 1920s and 1930s, a wave of militarism gradually swept over Japan. This new attitude towards military service and the use of the army wasn't exactly fascism, though Americans during World War II often heard it discussed as such. No, the Japanese developed a new "religion" that was part traditional emperor worship, part "the way of the warrior," and part belief that the Japanese were selected by a higher power to control East Asia. The Japanese emperor was believed to be descended from the gods, and considered the "warrior in chief" of the armed forces. Such beliefs produced soldiers who believed, quite literally, that "death was lighter than a feather."

When the Japanese army defeated the Russians in 1904–05, giving Japan possession of Manchuria, it was the first time Japan had such a large overseas possession. They also obtained control of Korea around the same time. Such successes were intoxicating, and the Japanese began to believe their notions of being some kind of master race.

Soldiers of the Sun tells of how the years of fighting in China added to the Japanese sense of invincibility. Japanese soldiers were well trained and well led, while most of their Chinese opponents were not. The Chinese often resorted to guerrilla warfare, which the Japanese considered cowardly. The Japanese suffered thousands of casualties in more than a decade of fighting in China, but they enjoyed many easy victories. When Japan attacked British, Dutch, and American colonies in Asia, there were *more* easy victories, as Malaysia, Singapore, Hong Kong, and the Dutch East Indies all fell rapidly. Not so the Philippines. There American troops held out in Bataan until April 9, 1942, and nearby Corregidor didn't surrender until May 6.

The Japanese were able to use the superior maneuverability of their aircraft and control of the air to force American and Filipino troops into the Bataan peninsula, but the fanatical fighting power of the Japanese troops was not able to force their opponents to surrender. Initial Japanese attacks failed, and one Japanese division was practically wiped out, but reinforcements were brought in, and lack of food and ammunition supplies, more than Japanese attacks, eventually caused the Americans and Filipino troops to surrender. As a result of this tainted victory, senior officers were relieved of duty, as the Japanese believed that this was a case of bad leadership—well-led Japanese troops should have defeated the Americans quickly.

Later that year, Japanese troops again encountered American marines on Guadalcanal, which proved an even more traumatic experience. More Japanese divisions and brigades were wiped out. This time the American troops were not cut off from resupply by the Japanese navy, and the Japanese had a hard time of it. When one Japanese officer mentioned this to another, the other man quipped, "You're not fighting the Chinese any more."

The Japanese soldier of World War II was no superman, but he did have many special qualities. *Soldiers of the Sun* explains how a combination of Japanese custom, wartime propaganda, an attitude of racial superiority, and Bushido ("the way of the warrior") philosophy created a unique type of fighting man. The Japanese soldier was given hard training, in all weather, and much of it at night. Blind obedience was expected, and usually given. But the Japanese army was a conscript army. Given a choice, most Japanese would have remained civilians. But the generals who were running the country used propaganda, and preyed on the willingness of the Japanese to blindly obey authority figures. This worked as long as the Japanese were successful, but when the tide turned against Japan after Guadalcanal, the iron resolve of the Japanese soldier began to crack.

Soldiers of the Sun points out that the troops were often not too happy with their lot. Many of the atrocities Japanese troops committed were seen by Japanese officers as simply a way to improve morale by letting the troops take out their frustrations on the locals. After all, the women raped and men murdered were not Japanese, so what did it matter? This racist attitude influenced everything the Japanese soldier did. When fighting the formidable American soldiers and marines, the Japanese were particularly enraged. How could these barbarians dare defeat them? A combination of frustration and contempt made Japanese soldiers even more vicious. Prisoners often received particularly harsh treatment, not only because they were non-Japanese, but because the Japanese did not consider surrender an option. If foreigners surrendered, they were not real men, real soldiers. They had disgraced themselves and deserved whatever treatment the Japanese could devise, an attitude that led to things like using prisoners for bayonet practice, or live surgical subjects for Japanese army doctors.

It should be noted that much of the bad treatment given soldiers captured by the Japanese was not inflicted by Japanese soldiers. As the care of prisoners was considered dishonorable, most of the prison camp staff was Korean. So why were these Korean prison camp guards often so brutal? Unable to attack the Japanese who occupied their country (rebellions were put down with much brutality), they could take out their rage on other foreigners.

But Japanese soldiers were human, and morale problems arose when things got rough. In China, officers opened brothels and starved the local Chinese to provide more food for their soldiers, all in order to "improve morale." The Japanese also understood the importance of propaganda. Newspapers, radio reports, and newsreels all strove to cast the best light on the Japanese army. When a soldier was killed in action, strenuous efforts were made to return his remains to his family, whom the government helped by conducting appropriate ceremonies for such a national hero. The book makes it clear that the Japanese soldier didn't come out of nowhere, and wasn't a superman. He just seemed that way at times. But the Japanese did lose the war, and the Japanese army contributed to that by believing that fanatical and well trained troops could overcome Japan's lack of weapons and equipment. The basic problem was that Japan was basically a poor country in 1941. In the previous eighty years Japan had gone from a largely agricultural and feudal nation to one that was partially industrialized. But Japan could not build and maintain an air force, fleet and army to the same standards as the United States.

Soldiers of the Sun details the development of the Japanese army, and its experiences against the Chinese, and then Western armies. The Japanese soldier is demystified. Scary in combat, he was nevertheless found by American soldiers to be predictable and beatable, despite high casualties. The Japanese custom of rarely or never surrendering, along with their reckless bravery cost the Allies much. The legendary "banzai" charge, a desperate, fight-to-the-death charge of Japanese infantry, was used only when the Japanese troops were surrounded, or when being pounded to pieces by Allied bombs and artillery left them with few choices. Under such circumstances, their doctrine called for a desperate night attack on the enemy. In a perverse way, this made sense. If the Japanese stayed where they were, they would be smashed eventually, at no cost to the Allied troops. But if they launched their banzai charge, most likely they would inflict a few casualties on the enemy. This kind of logic was applied throughout the war by the Japanese. It led to Japanese soldiers quietly starving to death on Guadalcanal, or surviving for decades after the war ended on some other islands. Some Japanese soldiers just couldn't believe that Japan had surrendered.

It's hard to believe a lot of this. But after you've read this book, you'll understand, and believe. And hope it doesn't happen again. Even though it probably will with some other army of fanatics.

STILWELL AND THE AMERICAN EXPERIENCE IN CHINA, 1911–45

by Barbara W. Tuchman

GROVE, 2001

Tuchman tells the story of how China fell apart in the early 20th century, and became an unreliable and expensive ally of the United States during World War II. The Stilwell of the title was General Joseph Stilwell, who was the senior American officer in China during World War II until he was recalled late in the war at the request of the Chinese. And the problem, in that particular case, was not with Stilwell. Stilwell had not intended to become the U.S. Army's foremost authority on China, but wartime needs, his familiarity with China, and his ability to speak the language, thrust him into the job. Tuchman does an excellent job of interweaving Stilwell's affairs with the chaotic events in China during this period.

For over two thousand years, China was a mighty empire, but by 1911 the empire had been overthrown and a republic established. The republic was not strong enough to hold the country together, and it broke up into many parts, each run by a warlord who ruled by force, and waged civil war to determine who would control a reunited China. By 1930, the Nationalists, led by Chiang Kai-shek, appeared to have united the country, except for one rebel army led by Chinese Communists. In 1937, while trying to crush the communists, Chaing also faced the Japanese effort to conquer China. Communists and Nationalists agreed to unite against the Japanese, but neither was really willing to cooperate in fighting against the common enemy. Both Chinese factions fought the Japanese only when forced to and, after America entered the war, the Chinese adopted a watch-and-wait attitude, expecting the Americans to defeat the Japanese. Then, Nationalists and Communists believed, both could fight it out for control of China.

Stilwell found himself in the middle of China's chaotic politics several times before World War II began. In 1919 he was sent to China to perfect his Chinese, and stayed for three years. He returned to China in 1926 to command an American infantry battalion stationed there on peacekeeping duty. In 1935 he returned again as military attaché at the American embassy, and remained until 1939. Rapidly promoted afterward, by 1942 he was a lieutenant general, and was ordered to return to China as America's chief military representative and commander of all American forces in the area. But there were never many American troops in China and Burma. Stilwell's main job was motivating the Chinese to fight.

When America entered World War II at the end of 1941, China had, in theory, an army of 3.8 million troops, organized in more than 300 divisions. Only about forty of these divisions were well armed and trained, largely through the efforts of Russian and German instructors. Russia had also provided large quantities of weapons and equipment. However, some 80 percent of the Nationalist troops were actually controlled by the warlords. The Nationalists had not destroyed the warlords in the 1920s; rather, they had absorbed them. The warlords still had a lot of power in the areas they ruled, and their armed men, organized into haphazardly equipped "divisions," lived off the local population. The warlords were now de facto generals in the Nationalist army, but as Stilwell was to discover, these warlords were very independent and insubordinate generals.

The Communists had far fewer troops than the nationalists, but they were better trained. They were good to the local civilians and attracted new converts daily. The problem the Nationalists faced was that, as they were trying to unite China, they had to work with corrupt landlords and government officials who were unpopular with most of the Chinese people. The Communists, by contrast, promised to wipe the slate clean, to eliminate corruption and the wealthy families who were living off land obtained from the emperor centuries ago.

Stilwell understood what was going on in China. Back in the United States, however, the Nationalists were portrayed as the protectors of freedom and democracy while the Communists were seen as bloody-minded revolutionaries. Unfortunately for the Nationalists, as World War II progressed, more and more of the 400 million Chinese began siding with the Communists. Stilwell had the complete backing of the U.S. government in his attempts to turn the Nationalists around, but it proved an impossible task.

Stilwell faced additional problems. When Japan attacked Hawaii in late 1941, they also went after Dutch and British colonies in southeast Asia, including Burma, which in 1941 provided the only route to get supplies into China for the Nationalists. (The Japanese had taken control of the Chinese coastline in the 1930s, and occupied Vietnam as well by 1940. Russia had a peace deal with Japan, which meant no military supplies via the Soviets.) With Burma gone, the only way to deliver military supplies into China was by air, over the treacherous Himalayas. Stilwell tried to convince the Nationalists of the need to equip and train at least thirty Chinese divisions with modern weapons and tactics, even if this meant flying the soldiers to India for training, then flying them, and their new weapons, back.

Other American commanders suggested using air transport to move fuel, bombs, and spare parts to support American fighters and bombers based in China. In this way, the Japanese could be attacked from the air and the Nationalists would not have to worry about the possibility that Stilwell would take control of the divisions he was going to train. This appealed more to the Nationalists as, in principle, it meant that they got their own air force. But the strategy backfired when the Japanese decided that the American air attacks were becoming a problem. The Japanese launched an offensive in early 1944 against the Chinese airfields from which the American aircraft were operating. The Chinese, without those well-trained divisions Stilwell was still trying to form, were forced back. The airfields were lost and the American air campaign came to an end.

Stilwell was called home in October 1944, an indication that the United States was fed up with the corruption and unreliability of the Nationalists. Once Japan surrendered in the summer of 1945, the more popular, better trained and organized Communists made their move, and within four years, controlled China. Stilwell died of cancer in October 1946.

Stilwell and the American Experience is important because it illustrates the connection between the war in Burma and events in China. Although Stilwell's major concern was China, where over a million Japanese troops were confronting many more armed, but poorly trained and led Chinese, he was constantly distracted by problems in Burma, India, and back in Washington.

There was not a lot of movement in China, there was a lot of war. The Japanese suffered 1.1 million casualties (dead, wounded and missing) in China between 1937 and 1945. The Chinese came off a lot worse, with 3.2 million soldiers and nearly 20 million civilians dead. Many of the civilians died from disease and starvation that were a direct result of Japanese military operations. For example, the Japanese were in the habit of advancing right after the harvest was in, stealing all the food they could get their hands on, then withdrawing. This left millions of starving Chinese behind. Japanese treatment of Chinese civilians actually exceeded that inflicted on Russian civilians by the Germans.

While the Japanese never set up death camps, they managed to kill over ten million Chinese civilians with less organized mayhem. While the Japanese and Nationalists fought 22 major battles (involving at least 100,000 troops), there were over 142,000 lesser incidents. Most of these were guerilla raids and ambushes. And most of these were staged by the Communists, who concentrated on guerilla war and avoided major battles. In this way, Chinese Communist forces grew from 440,000 troops in 1941 to 910,000 in 1945.

For Stilwell, success in Burma was crucial, for if the Japanese could be pushed back far enough, the Burma Road could be reopened and more military supplies could reach China via truck. His efforts did result in an improved Chinese army of some 5 million troops by 1945, but the warlords still controlled many of them, or were apt to be insulted if Chaing tried to move troops out of a warlord's province without giving something in return (a large bribe would usually suffice). Stilwell was too much of a straight arrow to get into the bribery game, and he was appalled at how some Chinese (Nationalist and Communist) leaders considered deals with the Japanese simply business. The most troublesome custom was arranging local truces with the Japanese if it served their purposes (like allowing the Japanese to mass for an attack on the other Chinese faction). Stilwell could never get over the fact that, to many Nationalist Chinese, the war against the Japanese took a backseat to fighting the Communists, getting rich, or both.

Stilwell and the American Experience in China 1911–45 clearly (well, as clearly as possible) describes what went on in the second largest war zone of World War II. It was only in Russia that the forces involved, and casualties inflicted, were larger. The war in China was huge, but it was a very different kind of war from what was taking place in Russia, or anywhere else. Joseph Stilwell was in the middle of it all, and his story shows that one man can make a difference. Unfortunately, in this case, it was not enough of a difference. One of the great "what-ifs" of World War II asks: If the Nationalist government could have been convinced to deal with its own shortcomings and fought the Japanese harder, causing them to have insufficient troops for their attacks on American, British, and Dutch territories in Asia, would

a more powerful Nationalist Chinese government have pre-
vailed after World War II? We'll never know, but as *Stilwell and
the American Experience in China* makes clear, changing things
was a monumental task, and this time America did not succeed
at doing so.

THE JAPANESE NAVY IN
WORLD WAR II IN THE WORDS OF
FORMER JAPANESE NAVAL OFFICERS

edited by David C. Evans

U.S. NAVAL INSTITUTE, 1993

In the Imperial Japanese Navy, the United States faced a terrifying and unpredictable foe during World War II. It may have looked like a normal navy, but it didn't fight like any Western navy, and didn't think or do much of anything else in ways familiar to Western eyes. Still, the Japanese won a number of naval battles against Western navies, and were formidable even in defeat. The best way to understand the Japanese navy is via this book, a collection of articles most of which were written by Japanese naval officers who served during the war and lived to share their experiences. The first few chapters comment on Japan's early victories, and some of the authors still savor them as reminders of better days. But the tone turns decidedly darker.

Japan is an island nation yet, until the 19th century, never had much of a navy. The Japanese depended on their soldiers, not their sailors, to defend the nation from invasion. This arrangement worked, although a bit of luck was involved (storms coming along just as an invading Mongol fleet was about to land, for example). Once Japan decided to modernize their culture, one of the things they decided to build was a modern navy. Hiring British naval officers as advisors, and ordering warships from British shipyards, the Japanese sought to learn from the world's foremost naval power.

By 1905, the Japanese navy had decisively defeated the Chinese and Russian navies. After Germany's defeat in 1918, Japan was seen as the third most powerful fleet on the planet. But the cost of keeping up was killing Japan financially. Warships are expensive, and Japan's economy was still miniscule compared to Britain and the United States. But those two countries were feeling the fiscal crunch as well. So in the early 1920s, the three nations hammered out a naval disarmament treaty. Although offensive to Japan's pride, she accepted a 10:10:7 ratio (for the British, U.S. and Japanese fleets). The treaty did what it set out to do, but Japan announced it was terminating its participation as of 1936, and proceeded to expand its fleet. At that time, Japan was run by a military government, and saw war with the United States in the not-too-distant future. While still poor, Japan had discovered during the treaty period (1923–36) that its fleet was probably superior, on a ship for ship basis, to those of Britain and the United States. It discovered this in two ways.

First, Japan tried to overcome the unfavorable ratio the treaty imposed by training its crews to a higher standard. "Try harder," was an old Japanese custom. When applied to navy training it meant going out a lot at night and in bad weather. Japanese admirals believed that they could use the night and bad weather to their advantage, for all other navies avoided training in the dark and during storms. The reasoning was that it was too dangerous. But the Japanese saw the danger as an advantage. And they were right. In the opening months of World War II, Japanese sailors proved they had an edge over their adversaries at night fighting.

The Japanese qualitative edge was not unexpected. During the treaty period, hundreds of Japanese navy officers went off to visit the West and see firsthand how foreign navies operated. Western naval officers spent a lot of time talking shop with the Japanese and it was obvious that Japanese sailors trained harder, and were more skilled. But these officers also saw something else; that the industrial might of America and Britain towered above Japan (by a combined ratio of about five to one). In a long war, Japan would be crushed under a flood of new warships produced by Britain and, in particular, the United States. Japanese naval officers were aghast at the number and size of American shipyards. They were also impressed by the American work ethic, which seemed to match that of the Japanese. The Japanese navy steadily went from strength to strength.

Japanese officers who had observed members of other cultures in their own homelands, especially the United States, came away with the impression that in a naval war, the Japanese could win only in the short term. Over the course of several years, Japan would be crushed. Their response to such an insight revealed a virulent aspect of the Japanese navy: they were willing to fight to the death. And they did. Several of the chapters in this book describe how Japanese went about doing just that.

The chapter on the Kamikaze suicide pilots shows that there were limits to the dedication of Japanese sailors. Most of the Kamikaze pilots were from the navy, as it was the navy that handled most of the fighting in the Pacific. The first Kamikaze pilots (in the fall of 1944) were volunteers; by early 1945, navy pilots had to be energetically encouraged to "volunteer." Many such volunteers were bitter, but they obeyed. Some were more than bitter, as was the one who machine-gunned the living quarters of his commanding officer shortly after taking off on his suicide mission.

The Japanese navy was marked by much unsound decision-making. The intense warrior spirit among the officers, also caused problems in dealing with enemy submarines. Japanese submarine captains could not bring themselves to attack anything but warships. As a result, the thousands of American cargo ships and tankers moved troops, weapons, equipment, and supplies across the Pacific with hardly any losses from enemy action. At the same time, the warrior attitudes among Japanese navy commanders made them blind to the danger posed by the American submarines attacking Japanese merchant ships. *The Japanese Navy in World War II* features a frank discussion of such matters by a Japanese naval officer who was present, and later studied the subject in detail after the war. He sheds light on the question of how the Japanese could have ignored protecting their shipping for so long: by the time the Japanese began to use convoys, and deploy more anti-submarine ships and aircraft, they had lost most of their merchant shipping to American submarines.

Throughout the book, the Japanese authors make two fundamental points. The dedication of Japanese sailors, and their warrior spirit, contributed to their successes during the first six months of the war. However, their inability to adapt to changing conditions turned those successes into disasters for the rest of the war. Most of the reasons for this are cultural, and cannot be underestimated, but poor leadership and bad luck were also factors.

You can't really understand World War II in the Pacific unless you hear from the other side. This book helps you do that.

THE PACIFIC WAR

by Saburo Ienaga

RANDOM HOUSE, 1979

Events always look rather different when viewed from the "other" side. *The Pacific War*, written from the perspective of the Japanese, is not purely a military history, but speculates about what went wrong in Japan to produce the militarism that propelled Japan into a war with China, and then one of conquest in the western Pacific. Saburo Ienaga believes, as did many Japanese right after the war, that attacking the United States was a great folly and a hopeless undertaking. What was obvious in the summer of 1945 was not so clear in early 1942, when it was party time in Japan as everyone cheered the victorious soldiers and sailors. This book points out that the military men in charge of Japan did not have much confidence in their ability to defeat America, but felt compelled to wage war by their sense of honor (then, and now, of crucial importance to the Japanese) and the realization that by not going to war, Japan would have had to withdraw from China. Such a withdrawal would have made the military government appear stupid and ineffective—it might even have meant a return to democracy in Japan, something unthinkable to the generals who took control of the government in the 1920s. Most Japanese citizens took a dim view of war with the United States, but as the

Japanese tend to defer to authority (even if the authority was illegitimate), there was never a hint of rebellion throughout the war years.

But we forget that, a century ago, Japan was much admired in the United States. With a little nudge from some American warships in 1853, Japan swiftly moved from a medieval, low-tech society to a quite modern one. This achievement was considered a wonder by everyone, and Japan was thought to have excellent prospects going into the 20th century. This was the first East Asian country that embraced Western ideas, and the West saw success for this effort in Japan an encouraging sign that the rest of Asia would eventually follow.

But after World War I, when Japan allied itself with Britain and the other allies, it all went bad. That's a subject that this book addresses. Plus a bit on the aftermath of World War II and how Japanese try to forget what led them there and what they did during the war. Japan is still a strange place, and in ways we may yet come to regret once more. Today, Japan's neighbors worry about Japan building nuclear weapons, expanding its armed forces and going back to its aggressive ways.

In any Japanese version of the "Great Pacific War" the story will start in 1931, when Japan began military operations in China. It wasn't until 1937 that Japan made major moves to conquer most of that country. Throughout World War II, most of Japan's efforts were taken up with fighting Chinese on the Asian mainland, not in the Pacific. Only a small fraction of Japan's ground forces were sent to the Pacific, and most sat out the war on bypassed islands. From the Japanese point of view, it was a very strange war. The navy took the brunt of combat in the Pacific, and was destroyed in the process. The irony is that most admirals disapproved of the army's operations in China, and thought war with the United States was sure to fail. But, being Japanese admirals, they obeyed the emperor (who was under the sway of the generals) and followed orders.

Most Japanese soldiers did not face conditions nearly as harsh as those imposed on soldiers in Europe and Russia. The operations in China were relatively low-key most of the time, and the

Chinese resistance was often inept. China was more like a guerrilla war, and the Japanese were so vicious that they never lost the upper hand. When Southeast Asia was occupied by Japan in early 1942, it meant more occupation duty for Japanese soldiers, more "inferior" locals to abuse. (Residents of areas once occupied by Japanese soldiers still dislike the Japanese.) "Atrocities" were all in a day's work for Japanese soldiers fighting the Chinese or on occupation duty. The only real opposition the Japanese met was from Allied troops, against whom Japan put up a fierce fight and got clobbered anyway. As a result, the Japanese see themselves as the injured party, and can't understand why the Chinese and the peoples in Southeast Asia don't like them. To them, it is obvious that Japan had the right idea, that conquering East Asia would have brought superior Japanese rule to all who lived there. The "evil" Americans stopped Japan from carrying out this splendid plan, and in so doing killed many brave Japanese soldiers and civilians. To this day, the Japanese still regard themselves as the victims in their World War II defeat.

THE TWO-OCEAN WAR

by Samuel Eliot Morison

LITTLE, BROWN, 1989

Admiral Samuel Eliot Morison, a distinguished historian and a former Trumbull Professor of American History at Harvard University, wrote a fifteen-volume history of U.S. naval operations in World War II that is, in effect, the official history of the United States Navy during World War II. *The Two-Ocean War* is a classic, partly because it's a remarkable bit of writing, but mainly because it does justice to the enormous effort the American fleets put into fighting, and winning, World War II at sea.

Morison was dissatisfied at how military history was written. He was convinced that too many histories were written from the viewpoint of outsiders, often long after the events occurred. Historians, he believed, could do a much better job if they were present when the events they wrote about took place. More was to be gained by writing while in contact with the events, when the participants were alive, rather than after the ships were dispersed and the sailors had departed.

Following the attack on Pearl Harbor, Morison took his idea to President Roosevelt, who was enthusiastic. So was Secretary Knox. Before he knew it, Professor Morison was Lieutenant Commander

Morison of the U.S. Naval Reserves, and given the writing assignment that he had suggested.

For the remainder of the war, Morison spent more than half of his time at sea, on active duty on eleven different ships, attaining the rank of captain, with seven battle stars on his service ribbons. He was present at Operation Torch, the North Atlantic invasions; he served on Atlantic convoys; and his travels took him through most of the combat areas of the Pacific during the height of the conflict. He retired from the Navy with the rank of Rear Admiral, and died in 1976 at 89.

The fifteen volumes are very well written by a professional historian who also happens to be a very entertaining writer.

Volume One, *The Battle of the Atlantic*, covers U.S. Navy history between the World Wars and the plans for modernizing and expanding the navy in the years before World War II broke out. This volume also covers the ever closer contacts among American and British admirals, as well as between President Roosevelt and Prime Minister Churchill, from the start of the war in September 1939 and through America's entry into it in December 1941. This includes the "unofficial" participation by American ships in British convoy protection duty in the North Atlantic in 1940 and 41. Finally, there is the first fifteen months of official action for American sailors in the Atlantic. During this period German submarines had a field day on American shipping off the American coast and the U.S. Navy geared up to fight the Germans for control of the Atlantic. The convoy battles in the North Atlantic during 1940 and 1941 are particularly well described.

Volume Two, *Operations in North African Waters*, covers Operation Torch, a unique military operation, whereby an American fleet would transport across the Atlantic an army to be positioned in North Africa by November 1942. Such a feat had not been attempted since the British sent a fleet and an army to New York in 1776, to put down the rebellion in the American colonies. The German submarines were still a potent force in the Atlantic, and sending all those warships and transports across the Atlantic was risky. A British fleet, coming from Britain, merged with the American fleet at Gibraltar. The combined force of 340 ships then invaded French controlled North Africa. For the first time in history, American and French troops, sailors and pilots fought. But before the fighting got too intense, the French were persuaded to switch sides. Here, Morison describes the resulting land battles as well as the frantic diplomacy that followed, but it's mainly about one of the more daring, and underreported, naval operations of World War II.

Volume Three, *The Rising Sun in the Pacific*, describes the growth of Japanese military power in the Pacific, and the depressing first five months of the war in the Pacific, including the initial Japanese advance. Volume Four, *Coral Sea, Midway, and Submarine Operations* is rather more upbeat. The carrier battles of Coral Sea and Midway evened up the balance of naval power in the Pacific, and this volume ends with the planning for the invasion of Guadalcanal in the Solomon Islands. Also covered is the first year of U.S. submarine operations, including the Great Torpedo Scandal and the transformation of the submarine service from a cautious peacetime organization to an aggressive wartime force.

Volume Five, *The Struggle for Guadalcanal*, emphasizes naval activity during the six-month series of actions at six major naval battles (Savo Island, Eastern Solomons, Cape Esperance, Santa Cruz, Guadalcanal, and Tassafaronga) as well as more than thirty lesser encounters. This included the first (and one of only two), battleship versus battleship encounters of the Pacific War, as well as two of the five carrier versus carrier actions. On top of that, there were major actions on land as well as between land based air forces. The Americans won, the Japanese lost. Morison covers these engagements in excellent detail, and his accounts are still studied by professionals.

Volume Six, *Breaking the Bismarcks Barrier* covers one of General Douglas MacArthur's most successful, and least recognized campaigns—the effective coordination of air, land, and naval forces to flush the Japanese out of the Solomon and Bismarck islands during 1942 and 43. This was a more effective road to the Philippines and Japan. But the Navy's drive across the Central Pacific, starting in late 1943, ultimately grabbed more attention, even though it was more expensive in lives and resources. Moreover, MacArthur's campaign directly, and immediately, threatened Japan's greatest vulnerability, their oil supply in Indonesia. It's quite possible that this campaign got ignored because there were no big battles, just a lot of small ones. Morison does a good job of explaining the innovative techniques MacArthur developed to accomplish his goal.

Volume Seven, *Aleutians, Gilberts and Marshalls*, concentrates on very different campaigns: first, the rather large effort to expel the Japanese from the bases they had established on the Alaskan islands of Attu and Kiska. This was more of a political than a military effort, as the Japanese bases were not militarily significant, but they were on "American soil," and this upset many voters in the United States and Canada. So a highway was built through Canada to Alaska, large military bases were established in Alaska and a special American-Canadian commando brigade was formed to toss the Japanese out. The Japanese left without a fight before this overwhelming force arrived. There were casualties, mostly from friendly fire and aircraft accidents (Alaska, and the North Pacific have the worst flying weather in the world). Morison describes the start of the Navy/Marine drive across the central Pacific, beginning with Tarawa in the Gilberts, and later the Marshall islands. Also covered is the bold, and very successful carrier raid on the main Japanese fleet base at Truk, in the Carolines, a two-day series of air attacks that was instrumental in forcing the Japanese to withdraw their major ships from the central Pacific.

The first part of Volume Eight, *New Guinea and the Marianas*, focuses on MacArthur's campaign to run the Japanese out of New Guinea, one of the largest islands on Earth, and most varied in terms of climate and vegetation. The latter part offers an account of operations in the Marianas and the last carrier-versus-carrier battle ever—the Battle of the Philippine Sea.

In Volume Nine, *Sicily—Salerno—Anzio*, the focus shifts to Europe and looks in on three major amphibious operations in the Mediterranean from mid-1943 to early 1944. While these three operations were essential in the conquest of Sicily and the lower half of Italy, they also served as a tune-up for the Big One (Normandy). Morison shows how sailors, soldiers and aviators learned the skills needed for a successful amphibious operation.

Volume Ten, *The Atlantic Battle Won* covers the energetic, imaginative, and ultimately successful campaign against the German submarines. Among other details, Morison describes how the use of four-engine bombers and a succession of new radar designs and other electronic sensors, helped pilots to patrol nearly all of the waters Allied convoys had to cross. For that "gap" in the middle of the Atlantic, the novel "Escort Carriers" (merchant ships modified to carry a dozen fighters) were used to insure that German subs faced their most potent foe, air power, everywhere. Since the allies built over 50,000 four engine bombers throughout the war, there were plenty available for maritime patrol. While .50 caliber machine-guns, bombs and depth charges sank a lot of subs, aircraft were most dangerous because they confirmed where the slow moving subs were at a specific time and date. There was no place to hide, because World War II subs had to spend most of their time on the surface, charging their batteries. In early 1943, President Roosevelt overruled the admirals and ordered 250 four engine bombers into anti-submarine service. He knew the U-Boats were on the run. By the end of May, the Germans pulled their remaining subs from the North Atlantic, and concentrated on attacks closer to their European bases (which were also under steady bombing attacks). In that month, the Germans lost 43 U-Boats, and only sank 34 Allied ships. The Germans were only able to build about 24 new subs a month. Thus May 1943 is considered the point where Germany lost the Battle of the Atlantic. Anti-submarine operations in the Arctic (the "Murmansk Run" to Russia) and along the British coast are also covered.

Volume Eleven, *The Invasion of France and Germany,* is mostly about the amphibious operation in Normandy on June 6, 1944. Also covered are the August 1944 amphibious invasion of southern France, and the U.S. Navy's support for the campaign in Europe.

Volume Twelve, *Leyte,* covers the largest naval battle ever (the

Battle for Leyte Gulf in October, 1944). This was the last gasp of the Japanese navy. It was big and, for the Japanese, it was futile. The Japanese came close in several aspects, but they seemed to be cursed, as their luck failed them at every turn. This volume covers both sides' preparations for this battle, and this is most interesting for the descriptions of what the Japanese were thinking. The tragic amphibious operation on Peleliu is also covered.

Volume Thirteen, *The Liberation of the Philippines*, actually involved a lot of Navy activity during late 1944 and 1945. There were a lot of small amphibious operations (taking advantage of American control of the seas around all those islands in the Philippines), as well as combat support from carriers, surface ships and subs. This campaign also saw the first widespread use of Japanese kamikaze suicide aircraft.

Volume Fourteen, *Victory in the Pacific*, covers the last, and bloodiest, battles of the war. Iwo Jima and Okinawa were strenuously defended by the Japanese, and there was heavy, and effective, use of Kamikaze suicide aircraft. But by this time, the United States pretty much controlled the waters and the air above the Pacific. So carrier raids and extensive submarine operations are also covered, including the major use of naval mines to shut down what remained of Japanese shipping.

Volume Fifteen is a *Supplement and General Index* for the other fourteen volumes. A lot of statistical data here, especially for all the ships and aircraft types involved.

Morison later wrote a one-volume version of his naval history, not a condensed version of his full-length history, but a new book that used the earlier fifteen-volume history as its source. The shorter history is good, but obviously does not provide the detail of the larger set. Whichever version you select will provide an excellent education on American naval operations in World War II.

WAR PLAN ORANGE: THE U.S. STRATEGY TO DEFEAT JAPAN, 1897–1945

by Edward S. Miller

U.S. NAVAL INSTITUTE, 1991

In one sense, the Japanese attack on Pearl Harbor in December 1941 came as no big surprise. The United States had been expecting something like it for more than twenty years. Miller's book tells how the American military developed a plan to deal with a war with Japan, called "War Plan Orange," and why the plan was so successful.

For years, American military planners anticipated potential wars against foes likely (Japan) and unlikely (Canada). Plans for war with Japan were codenamed Orange. After World War I, the United States believed that war with Japan was the most probable conflict the U.S. would next find itself caught up in. Japan gained possession of Germany's Pacific island colonies after World War I, and promptly built naval bases, and eventually air bases, there. These bases were much larger than those needed merely for self-defense.

Through the 1920s, Japan grew more militaristic and aggressive, expanding into China and making noises about how it deserved to be the major power in the western Pacific. The problem with that was that the United States occupied the Philippines. The Netherlands held the Dutch East Indies (modern Indonesia) as a colony, as did Britain hold Malaysia and Singapore. And then there was Australia and New Zealand and America's smaller island possessions in the Pacific.

While Japan was identified early on as the potential foe, American planners had to deal with rapidly changing technology through the 1920s and 30s. This is where the book shines, as it clearly shows how all these new developments were confronted and, after many wrong turns and interesting debates, the American naval war planners largely got it right. The only thing that was not foreseen was the Japanese use of Kamikaze suicide bombers. But even the Japanese had no plans for that before 1944.

The major changes the planners had to deal with were the development of aircraft carriers, which took place during the 20s and 30s, and the rapid improvement in aircraft capabilities during the same period. Consider that aircraft went from largely fabric and wood construction in 1920, unable to carry much more than a pilot and some machine guns, to all metal, four engine bombers that could carry several tons of bombs to targets two thousand kilometers distant by 1937. Long range bombers changed the oceanic battlefield in several ways. Naval planners realized immediately that the longer range aircraft made it possible to spot fleets at sea earlier and more easily. Along with that, the long range aircraft could then attack any warships that had been located. This was all new at the time, and the American planners realized that naval warfare would be fundamentally changed because of such changes.

Although In 1918, naval power was still calculated by the number of battleships, over the following two decades naval planners had to consider the impact land-based and carrier aircraft would have on the primacy of battleships. Upon entering World War II, many in the navy (and the general public) believed that the battleships were still the ultimate naval weapon. War Plan Orange knew better. By the late 1930s, planners decided that sending American battleships to confront a Japanese threat to the Philippines would not work.

The search for alternatives led the U.S. Marine Corps to develop novel amphibious warfare techniques, as well as the Navy designing and building new carrier aircraft. The 1940 Naval Bill, which authorized the building of Essex-class aircraft carriers, made clear that the 1940 version of War Plan Orange was remarkably different that the 1920s versions.

The book also details the numerous arguments and disputes over which islands and routes would be the most useful for an advance across the Pacific, evaluating which offered the most military value (i.e., anchorages, land to easily build airfields). No one knew exactly what kind of fight the Japanese would, or could, put up. Given the general disdain for Japanese industry and technology among Americans, it's amazing that the U.S. planners were able to maintain a realistic view of who would do what to whom as the relative military strength of both countries changed during the 1920s and 1930s.

War Plan Orange is an easy-to-read account of how the war-planning process is carried out. It's not all a matter of simple decisions, but of wrestling with many unknowns and unforeseen events. In addition to the unanticipated threats of the Kamikazes, the planners found that they had underestimated the time and resources that would be needed to defeat Japan. Still, American preparations for war in the Pacific proved to be among the most accurate and effective of any done by the major nations embroiled in World War II.

Miller also points out that for several decades after the war, most people, in and out of uniform, were unaware how accurate and useful War Plan Orange was, a misperception that arose because key War Plan Orange documents had been kept secret until the 1960s and 1970s. The early assessment of some historians, that the War Plan Orange effort was wasted, became accepted as the conventional wisdom, and it was entirely wrong. There's a major lesson to be learned in that.

Five

LARGER ISSUES

---

*T*ECHNOLOGY—IN COMMUNICATIONS, media, security, and "special operations"—reaches across all theaters of war. The books covered in this section consider larger issues, such as the creation of the huge U.S. Army and Air Force from formerly miniscule organizations. The United States was the only major power in World War II that had to create large armed forces from practically nothing. Weapons and equipment were built from scratch. Special organizations were established that were unique, important, and generally unrecognized. This section also includes several important books that didn't fit into previous categories.

Commandos and Rangers of World War II

by James Ladd

St. Martin's Press, 1978

A number of books have been published on World War II's commandos, but they tend to concentrate on the action, and rarely explain where these units came from and what became of them. Ladd's book addresses this critical issue. The development, organization, and operations of the Allied commandos are covered, in concise and readable form. There were literally dozens of different commando organizations created by the Allies during World War II, and it's easy to get lost trying to sort them all out.

Commandos and Rangers of World War II provides excellent coverage of those units that took part in the majority of commando operations for the war, and how the units were organized, trained, and operated. And, because it was written for a general audience, it's an easy read.

The Germans actually invented most of the World War II commando concepts before World War II, and used them early and often. But they didn't call them commandos. More on that later. British Prime Minister Winston Churchill noted what the Germans were doing in 1940 and, remembering the World War I German *Stosstruppen* (Storm troopers), ordered the British armed forces to get with it. Thus were the commandos, and many other units of similar intent but different names, created.

Your basic World War II commando was a carefully selected infantryman who was given additional training and sent out to conduct raids in units of fifty to a hundred men. When the United States got into the game with its Rangers, they got inventive, and that proved disastrous. The Rangers operated in larger units, and didn't move as fast as the British commandos. Big mistake, and the Rangers took big losses. After World War II, the Americans got rid of the Rangers, despite the fact that these excellent troops could get the job done if they operated like the British.

The British are credited for developing what we today think of as commandos: a small group of under a dozen that takes on daring missions in enemy territory. The American Office of Strategic Services and the British Special Operations Executive invented what we today call Special Forces—not exactly commandos in the classic sense, but daring soldiers nonetheless, who worked with friendly locals in enemy territories.

The Allies used commandos and what we now call "special operations troops" in every theater of the war, and in great variety. Everything that came to be known as "special operations" after 1945 had its origins in World War II. Even the U.S. Army Special Forces were created in the 1950s out of World War II experiences. This was because the Allies wanted to support, work with, and if possible, control the large number of guerrilla movements that appeared during World War II. This proved difficult to do. Several different types of "agents" and "liaison officers" were parachuted into Axis-occupied territory, with varying degrees of success. Fortunately, many of the Americans who were involved in these efforts were attracted to the newly formed Special Forces in the early 1950s. Thus the current Special Forces can really trace their origins back to the daring and dangerous operations in enemy territory during the Big War.

Then there were the Germans and Russians. They are not covered in *Commandos and Rangers of World War II*, and here I'll tell you why, and what is important about them:

Few books have been written about the "Brandenburgers" (as the German commandos were called, after the area where they trained). There are several reasons for this. First of all, the Germans lost the war, so there was less interest in what their commandos were up to, with a few spectacular exceptions (like Otto Skorzeny's Jagdkommando). Another problem was that the Brandenburgers belonged to German military intelligence (Abwehr), not the army, Nazi Party or the Waffen-SS. Most interestingly, the Brandenburgers didn't get along with the Nazis, largely because the man who created the Brandenburgers, Admiral Canaris, was a secret (to stay alive) anti-Nazi. Canaris was caught and executed by the Nazis at the end of the war.

German officers began thinking of commandos, in the modern sense, right after World War I. The man who took the lead was Theodore von Hippel, a veteran of von Lettow-Vorbeck's guerilla operations in Africa. Paul von Lettow-Vorbeck's war in Africa was one of those unusual sideshows. He was in charge of the garrison of a German colony in East Africa when World War I broke out. The British forces in the area greatly outnumbered Von Lettow-Vorbeck's force, and thought that they would just go in and take the Germans' surrender. But von Lettow-Vorbeck fought back, even though most of his troops were not German soldiers, but German trained Africans. And von Lettow-Vorbeck won. He held off over half a million Allied troops throughout the war by waging a brilliant guerilla war, complete with commando raids to obtain arms and ammunition. Von Lettow-Vorbeck only surrendered when he learned that Germany had signed an armistice. A hero back in Germany, he was the only World War I German general to receive a victory parade.

Based on his experiences in Africa, Von Hippel came up with the idea of training specially selected troops to operate in small groups, deep in enemy territory, where they could destroy, or seize control of, critical installations (railroad bridges, radio towers). Von Hippel proposed using men who spoke the enemy language fluently and wore enemy uniforms. However, this was illegal according to the laws of war, and it was customary to execute such men if you caught them. But von Hippel was persuasive, and invoking the popular example of von Lettow-Vorbeck, he was allowed to recruit and train several hundred men during the 1930s. Von Hippel's commandos performed as advertised during the 1939 invasion of Poland.

However, many senior generals were offended by such deceptive tactics and the army disbanded von Hippel's commando after the Polish campaign. Too many German generals considered the commandos a bunch of thugs and criminals. Von Hippel and his commandos were saved by an admiral. Admiral Canaris was the head of Abwehr (German military intelligence), and saw what the commandos had done in Poland and liked what he saw. The Abwehr set up a training camp for the commandos outside Berlin, in the town of Brandenburg, and the commandos came to be known as Brandenburgers because of that.

Canaris didn't really try to change the minds of the army generals, he didn't have to. In the World War II German army, the Abwehr was more like the CIA than just a department of the military that took care of intelligence about the enemy. Canaris had a large budget and considerable authority. He expanded the commando force to several thousand troops. The Brandenburgers saw action throughout the war, but always in small groups, or even as individuals. Because the commandos were working for an intelligence organization, their operations remained even more secret than commando operations usually do. The German army and Waffen SS, however, were used to dealing with Abwehr and its agents. The German military were accustomed to getting good information from Abwehr, and thus tolerated Abwehr's offbeat methods. The Abwehr commandos were accepted as just another Abwehr operation, even though the commandos were doing a lot more than collecting information.

The commandos were less successful when the tide turned against Germany in 1943. Commandos are more successful with an advancing army, as they can go out into enemy territory with the expectation that advancing friendly troops would eventually catch up with them This does not work when you are retreating. So the Brandenburgers were sent to work on the

growing number of guerilla organizations opposing German occupation. This was more difficult than just wandering around in
enemy territory wearing enemy uniforms and speaking his language. Guerillas tended to know each other better, and didn't
wear uniforms. Although they had some success, it was not
enough for Canaris to justify the expense. So in May, 1944, about
1800 of the best men were transferred to the Waffen SS
Jagdkommando and the rest formed the core of the Brandenburger motorized infantry division.

The Brandenburgers were unique in that they worked for military intelligence, and were not considered a combat unit (although
they were capable fighters). While many of the Brandenburger
missions were to collect intelligence, most had a direct military
impact because that information enabled the Germans to outmaneuver the enemy. Most important, Brandenburger operations
were generally more strategic than those of most other World War
II commandos. In this respect, the Brandenburgers were operating more like today's Special Operations forces than World War II
commandos. After World War II it was recognized that commandos were more effective, not as super soldiers, but as skilled operators that could take care of important strategic missions. In this
respect, the Brandenburgers were ahead of their time, as well as
generally forgotten.

The Nazis noted the success of the Brandenburgers and established their own organization, called *Unternehmen Otto* or
Ottolagen, in July 1942, to perform sabotage and subversive actions in enemy territory. At first, the *Ottolagen* was not very successful, until colonel (SS-Obersturmbannführer) Otto Skorzeny
was brought in. Skorzeny was one of those natural born commandos. Skorzeny's troops, trained as commandos, became known as
the Waffen SS Jagdkommando (or Jagdverband der SS). Skorzeny's
men performed a daring rescue of imprisoned Italian dictator
Benito Mussolini from a mountain hotel in July, 1943. This so
impressed Hitler, that he ordered Skorzeny be given the authority
and resources to recruit and train several Jagdkommando battalions. In early 1944, Skorzeny took control of 1800 of the Brandenburger commandos and became a much feared special operations

threat for the rest of the war. Skorzeny escaped to Spain after the war, where he continued to dabble in espionage and other murky activities until his death in 1975. He didn't get as much attention after the war as he should have, and this was partially because he was a devoted Nazi and, after all, the Germans lost the war. But the Jagdkommando developed some useful techniques and engaged in many daring, and successful, operations. The Jagdkommando were also quite brutal, but their history should be examined as a model of how ruthless dictatorships will conduct special operations.

Russian World War II commandos are even more shrouded in secrecy than the Brandenburgers and Jagdkommando. Part of this has to do with the fact that Russia did not establish any commando units in the Western sense. What commandos the Russians did have either belonged to the NKVD (secret police) or were temporary organizations. The Soviet dictator Stalin was quite paranoid (often for good reason) and did not want any commando units around that might threaten his rule. The NKVD's commando units were largely concerned with counterintelligence (catching spies). These were of platoon and company size, and many of them were not commandos in the usual sense (they were not elite combat troops). The temporary commando units usually contained a high proportion of political officers and regular officers selected for their political reliability. These units were trained for a specific mission, and then disbanded (or returned to non-commando status) after the mission was completed. The Russians didn't get into the traditional commando game until the 1960s when they formed Spetsnaz units.

JANE'S FIGHTING SHIPS OF WORLD WAR II

CRESCENT BOOKS, 1994

Much of the fighting in World War II was done at sea. To understand the naval aspect of the war, you have to understand the ships, and the bible for warships during the 20th century is *Jane's Fighting Ships*. In 1947, Jane's published a compendium of information on what had been built, and destroyed, during World War II. Reprinted from time to time, and widely available secondhand, this book has become a standard reference, in spite of errors due to wartime censorship.

Jane's Fighting Ships reminds one that at the end of World War II the British Royal Navy remained a mighty, if threadbare, naval force, while, at the same time, the U.S. Navy was new, huge, and the obvious top dog on the high seas. There was no hint that the ramshackle fleet of the Soviet Union would make a run for naval supremacy over the next four decades, nor that the fleets of most other Europeans nations would shrink sharply.

For those familiar with naval matters, this book illustrates how much ship design has changed since World War II. Carriers, destroyers and submarines built before World War II are noticeably smaller than those built during and at the end of the war. Most aircraft carriers built before World War II were 20,000 ton displacement. In 1940, the United States began building the Essex-class carriers, which were 27,000 tons. Towards the end of the war, the Midway class was built, 45,000 tons each. Cruisers went from under 10,000 tons to 17,000 tons, destroyers from 1,600 to 2,100 tons. Submarines went from under 1,000 tons to over 2,000 tons. Battleships, few of which were built from the early 1920s to the late 1930s because of a disarmament treaty, were at about 32,000 tons in the early 1920s, and quickly went to over 60,000 tons once building began again. The major navies saw the trends early on and many battleship building projects were cancelled, the resources shifted to carriers, submarines and destroyers.

Battleships were more abundant than most World War II buffs realize. This was a time when no nation could consider itself a real naval power without them. *Jane's* provides the numbers and unbiased descriptions that show that many nations were paying for relatively ancient battleships of questionable value. *Jane's* also makes it obvious that the aircraft carrier was the new king of the sea in World War II. There were more carriers than battleships at the end of the war, and most of those carriers were new. While only five carrier-versus-carrier battles were fought during World War II, carriers made themselves useful in other ways. For example, 17 percent of the Japanese merchant shipping sunk during World War II was sent to the bottom by carrier aircraft.

Only about a fifth of *Jane's Fighting Ships* is devoted to the U.S. Navy, despite the fact that the American fleet was the largest and strongest in the world. The United States tended to build a large number of the same type of ship. There were 24 Essex-class aircraft carriers, and 37 Casablanca-class escort carriers. Among smaller warships, there were 105 Gearing-class destroyers, and 98 Fletcher-class destroyers (151 if you include the "improved Fletcher class" ships, both the same size but with slightly different equipment). And then there were those uniquely World War II ships, the destroyer escort. These were "destroyer lite," designed expressly for escorting merchant convoys. While World War II destroyers were about 2,000–2,500 tons, the destroyer escorts were one-third the size and with a third less speed, weapons, and crew. Many destroyer escorts were built, though most were scrapped soon after the war ended. There were 99 Rudderow-class destroyer escorts, 52 Buckleys, 81 Edsalls, 57 Bostwicks and so on. There were 120 of the Balao-class subs ordered, and 54 Gato-class subs built. There were 106 Admirable-class mine sweepers built. But where Jane's really sheds light on aspects of fleets that you rarely see is in the noncombat support vessels. Most nations had a relatively small collection of these transports, including a few amphibious ships, but the U.S. Navy had thousands.

However, what Jane's does not show is the largest fleet in World War II, the ships under the control of the U.S. Army. All these Army ships were support ships—not a fighting ship among them (although some had machine guns and light cannon for self-defense)—which is why they are omitted from *Jane's Fighting Ships*. During World War II, the Army had 111,000 ships under its control, the U.S. Navy, 75,000. The Navy also had over 1,400 combat ships. At its peak, the Army fleet controlled 17 million tons of merchant ships, while the Navy had only eight million tons. The Army total included 88,000 amphibious assault craft and 8,500 barges. Most of the crews were a mixture of soldiers and civilians. The Navy was reluctant to supply any manpower, pleading (with some justification) wartime shortages. But the civilian mariners did a good job. My own father, drafted into the Army in 1942, spent several months as the radio operator on an army PT boat that was being used to rescue crews of ships torpedoed in the waters off Louisiana. This was late 1942, when the German U-Boat danger was much diminished in the Caribbean. But he remembered having older civilian sailors, some with U.S. Navy experience, showing them how to run the boat. It worked.

It should not be surprising that the Army controlled so many ships, as most of the amphibious operations in World War II were run by the Army. In addition, the Army also begged, borrowed, bought and, in a few cases, stole shipping to support its overseas operations. Thus the Army had 1,665 large seagoing ships, 1,225 smaller (under 1,000 tons) seagoing ships, and 11,154 harbor craft (including tugs, mine planters, crash boats, fuel lighters, dredges, and so forth). The Navy was not happy about this, and keeping the Army fleet out of Janes did not mollify the sailors. As far back as the American Civil War, there were disputes between the Navy and the Army over who should control shipping that was used primarily for supporting army operations. The problem arose again during the Spanish-American War and World War I. The Navy believed, quite logically, that if it floated, it should belong to the Navy. The Army, being practical, knew that ships belonging to the navy would be used as the Navy saw fit (that is, Navy needs would come first).

So before World War II, it was agreed that the Navy would control everything that floated. The plan didn't survive Pearl Harbor, and the Japanese attack on the Philippines and their advance towards Australia. The Army was ordered to grab whatever it could, overseas, as well as in the states. A truce of sorts developed in this matter, and the Army was allowed to control most of the shipping it needed. Well, not always. The Navy generally got the newest and largest shipping, so the Marines shipped out in better stuff than did the Army. The Navy justified this approach by leaving all shipping problems for Army troops to the Army. While the Army ended up with a lot of smaller and older shipping, it didn't care as long as it had enough to get where it needed to go.

At the end of World War II, the Army fleet totaled 17 million tons, which was nothing in terms of combat power, when compared to the U.S. Navy's nearly six million tons of warships (1.1 million tons of battleships, 1.7 of carriers, .9 of cruisers, 1.7 of destroyers, and .6 of submarines) and about 7.2 tons of minor combatants, amphibious, auxiliary, and miscellaneous vessels. The Army had no warships. But the Navy insisted on a new agreement on who would control all shipping in the future, and got it. Once the Japanese surrendered and the returning soldiers were transported home, the Army had no seagoing ships at all. After World War II, the Navy finally took control of everything and the Great Army Fleet passed into history.

Many of the Army ships were identical to those used by the

Navy (and that show up in *Jane's*), and they were often built at the same shipyards. So the long lost Army fleet can be seen, sort of, in the coverage *Jane's* gives to U.S. Navy support ships.

This book is not a perfect reference, but it is a piece of history from the period, and a pretty unique one at that.

MARCHING ORDERS

by Bruce Lee

DA CAPO PRESS, 2001

One of the little-known aspects of World War II espionage was the existence of an American spy network in all the Axis capitals and in Moscow. These agents had direct access to Hitler and Mussolini as well as senior military and civilian officials. They sent back long, detailed, and frequent reports, which often were read by President Roosevelt. Most amazing was the fact that these spies were paid for by Japan, and served the Allied cause until the end of the war.

This is all true. But read on for the fine print.

The histories of World War II written in the first decades after the war ended were created without access to a huge number of vital documents. Historians knew they did not have access to Russian records, but they were unaware of the hundred thousand or so German and Japanese secret messages that American and British code breakers had deciphered. Then, in the 1970s, this code-breaking effort was revealed, and many of the secret messages were made available. Many more were not. Among those that remained unexamined for two decades were the Japanese diplomatic reports sent home from embassies in Germany and Russia. Bruce Lee obtained access to 14,000 of those messages, and learned what Allied leaders did with the information in them. This is the essence of *Marching Orders*.

Many historians had overlooked the fact that Japanese diplomats had personal access to Axis leaders Hitler and Mussolini, as well as senior members of the German and Italian armed forces and government. The messages that Japanese diplomats sent back to Tokyo were filled not just with the nuts-and-bolts information found in military dispatches (where U-Boats were being sent, how army units were to be deployed for battle, the supply situation, and so on), but with high-level strategic intelligence as well. The Japanese ambassador in Berlin, Baron Hiroshi Oshima, regularly reported on what Hitler had told him of German war plans. The ambassador also was able to travel freely, and he reported, in great detail, what he saw. This, for example, gave the British and Americans the best analysis of what effect their thousands of four-engine bombers were having on German civilians, industry, and military. The Japanese ambassador to Germany reported that, while the British night area bombing was consuming enormous resources (to deal with the wounded, evacuate and house the refugees and rebuild some of the damage), it was the American daylight precision bombing that was causing the most headaches. These attacks were actually taking out key factories and facilities. And Oshima's reports provided exact details.

American code-breakers had cracked the Japanese diplomatic code in the late 1930s, and were able to decipher these messages faster than most other secret Axis radio transmissions. Interestingly, it was American Army's Signals Intelligence Service that cracked the code, not the State Department, partly because the army did not want to depend on the State Department for the kind of military information that deciphered diplomatic dispatches could reveal.

The Signals Intelligence Service had only nineteen people on staff in 1939. By the time of Pearl Harbor there were 331 staff members, and at the end of the war, over 13,000. The decoding project was called "Magic" and was usually lumped together with "Purple," the U.S. Navy project that cracked the Japanese encryption machines (similar to the German Enigma machines).

They gave the Allies invaluable stuff. And we know it was considered as such, because copies of the messages placed in the archives still have notations on them by General Marshall (the head of the American army) and other senior civilian and political leaders. The most critical of these messages were sent directly to President Roosevelt. Naturally, because the code-breaking effort was the best kept secret of the war (even more so than the atomic bomb project), no mention of it could be made in Roosevelt's official White House documents or anywhere else. No biography about Roosevelt mentions the president's reliance on Magic, not because the existence of Magic wasn't revealed until 1948, but because the actual messages were classified. Nevertheless, the scribbled notes on the messages attest to the importance of these messages for news about how enemy leaders were reacting to Allied plans, and about the surprises the Axis had up its sleeve. Thanks to Magic, there weren't many surprises.

It didn't take American leaders long to realize how valuable such diplomatic reports were. Ambassador Oshima was particularly diligent and insightful (as was his staff of military and civilian analysts). In addition to reports on German strategic thinking, there was information on new German weapons and weapons production in general. In the months before D-Day, Oshima (conveniently) made a tour of the German defenses along French beaches and met with many of the German commanders. What he wrote about was key in assuring the Allies that their deception plan—to make the Germans think the Normandy landing was just a diversion—was working. After D-Day, Oshima's access to German generals produced more lengthy reports on how the Germans reacted, what their losses were, and what they would do next.

This feedback, direct from Berlin, was invaluable, especially so in 1942 and 1943, as the Allies were beginning their counterattack against a still very powerful German army and air force. You've got to put yourself into Churchill's and Roosevelt's frame of mind in 1942. At that time the Germans did indeed appear as supermen. France was conquered in six weeks, the British barely survived the Battle of Britain because of stupid German decisions, and the British knew it. A small German force in North Africa was giving a larger British army a hard time, and German submarines were sinking Allied shipping at a fearful rate.

Oshima's reports from Berlin told another story, one reassuring to the Allies. Germany was operating on a shoestring, and making some stupid decisions. This emboldened the Allied leaders; a British and American fleet dared to steam into the Mediterranean in late 1942 and invade North Africa while British troops routed Germany's Afrika Korps. By spring 1943, North Africa was free of Axis forces. Later, thanks in part to Oshima's revealing reports about shaky Italian morale, Sicily and Italy were invaded in quick succession. Japanese diplomatic messages revealed much about enemy plans in the Pacific and made it possible to turn the tables there as well. The American victory at Midway, in June 1942, would not have been possible without the decoding effort. And the American invasion of Guadalcanal two months later was another result of reading the enemy's mail. In less than a year, the Allies had gone on the offensive, all because of Magic.

Magic's reports helped enormously with defeating the German submarine campaign. Although other secret codes had to be cracked so that detailed information on German sub locations could be corroborated, the Magic reports provided high-level feedback on which Allied tactics were working and which were not. Same thing with the Allied strategic bombing campaign against Germany. Oshima's reports detailed which types of attacks did the most damage, and which were wasted effort. Bombing strategies were adjusted, and the aerial campaign delivered more devastating attacks as a result.

As Allied armies poured into Germany, other diplomatic reports helped American and British leaders figure out what the Russians were planning. Although allied with Britain and the United States against Germany, the Russians were not forthcoming about what the Red Army was up to. This was not a problem when the Russian Front was so remote from where the Allies were fighting, but in early 1945, American and British troops were about to meet up with their Russian counterparts. The diplomatic reports probably saved lives by preventing Western leaders from doing things that would trigger friendly fire.

Keep in mind that Japan and Russia were not at war through most of World War II. In the late 1930s, there were a few border battles between Russian and Japanese troops in Manchuria and Mongolia. The Japanese got beat, bad. Germany and Japan were already allies by then, and the Germans expected the Japanese to attack Russia when Germany invaded Russia. Didn't happen. In fact, in April of 1941, two months before the German attack on the Soviet Union, the Japanese signed a neutrality treaty with Russia. So when Japan attacked Pearl Harbor in December of 1941, the Germans promptly declared war on America. The Germans were hoping the Japanese would denounce their neutrality treaty and attack Russia. The Japanese didn't, they couldn't. The Germans failed to realize that Japan was actually a rather poor country and was fully occupied with the war in China and the attacks against American, British and Dutch forces in their neighborhood.

The Germans, however, realized that Japan was fighting the British and Americans, so they were, indeed, wartime allies. The neutrality with Russia was ignored, and Japan maintained diplomatic staffs in Russia and Germany throughout the war. The Japanese ambassador in Russia was kept on a short leash, not allowed to travel much or to meet with Russians from the foreign ministry. But even before Germany was defeated, intercepted reports indicated attempts to cut some kind of peace deal that would keep the current Japanese government in power. The Japanese ambassador's reports to Tokyo on these negotiations, and his fears that Russia might break its treaty of neutrality with Japan, were read with great interest by American officials. The ambassador was getting reports from his staff, particularly those who served as couriers accompanying mail and goods moving by railroad from Vladivostok to Moscow, that the Trans-Siberian Railroad was crammed with trains moving east carrying troops and weapons. The Japanese did not know that early in 1945 Stalin had promised Britain and America that Russia would attack Japanese forces in

China within ninety days of Germany's surrender. Germany surrendered to the Russians on May 9. Even before that, the Russians started to move men and weapons to their Far East territories. There was only one reason for sending that many troops all the way across Eurasia—to attack Japan. The messages from the Japanese ambassador in Moscow, as well as Japanese diplomats in Switzerland, made clear that more than a Russian attack on Japanese troops in China would be needed to persuade the Japanese to surrender. The Allies had agreed that they could not afford to let the current Japanese government stay in power under any circumstances, which is why they demanded unconditional surrender. It's interesting to read in their decoded exchanges the Japanese diplomats' questions about what exactly "unconditional surrender" meant.

Once the atomic bombs were dropped on Japan, the diplomatic messages quickly changed their tenor. Everyone knew it was over. But Lee's book does not end there, nor does the story. For some weeks after the Japanese surrender on August 15, 1945, the Japanese Foreign Ministry kept operating, and continued to issue orders to their embassies around the world. Within days of Japan's surrender American code-breakers read messages from Tokyo to Japanese diplomats overseas ordering them to start a campaign portraying Japan as a victim in the war. They were to downplay Japanese atrocities and emphasize Japanese civilian losses in the recent A-bomb attacks.

This secret war did not end with World War II. As it ended, Intelligence on French diplomatic maneuvers also began to turn up in decoded Japanese reports from Moscow. The French were trying to cut a deal with the Russians to form a new alliance to oppose America and Britain, and were also found to be meddling in Lebanon and Syria, attempting to reestablish their colonial control in those regions. British and American leaders did a slow burn as they observed their French "ally" saying one thing, and doing something quite different behind their backs.

And then there was the situation with cracking Russian secret codes. On October 29, 1948, a day known as "Black Friday" in the American intelligence community, the Soviet Union and its allies changed all of their codes, ciphers, and communications procedures. This was a disaster because the U.S. and Britain had cracked Soviet military codes at the end of World War II, and were reading the Soviets' secret messages. It was an American soldier, William Weisband, who tipped them off. Weisband, who worked in the army security organization that later became the National Security Agency, was not prosecuted, because it was felt that too many intelligence secrets would come out in court, but he was booted out of the army.

What happened was that, at the end of the war, American intelligence agents obtained one of the Soviet cipher machines and, working with the British experts who had cracked the German Enigma machine, were soon reading Russian encrypted messages. Other Russian codes were cracked as well. What is left unsaid, for the moment, is which Russian ciphers were cracked after 1948. The National Security Agency has had the tightest security of any American intelligence organization, and has been most successful at keeping its secrets.

As Bruce Lee makes clear in *Marching Orders*, reading other people's mail can help you win a war.

Reporting World War II

Library of America, 2001

Journalism, especially print journalism, played a major role in World War II. This was the first major war to be reported heavily by many journalists who were right up there with the troops. Volume One of this two volume set covers the war from 1938 to 1944, Volume Two from 1944 to 1946. Published on the fiftieth anniversary of the end of World War II, this collection of over 200 pieces, including magazine articles, radio transcripts, cartoons, and book excerpts is truly a time machine. Over sixty of the best writers and photographers of the 20th century are represented, among them James Agee, Margaret Bourke-White, Janet Flanner, Martha Gellhorn, John Hersey, Tom Lea, A. J. Liebling, Edward R. Murrow, Roi Ottley, Ernie Pyle, Robert Sherrod, William L. Shirer, Howard K. Smith, E. B. White, and many more. And what the authors cover is, well, everything.

Items written in 1938 document the buildup to war, and the terror and unease felt among Europeans at the prospect of another conflict. In later reports from France, as it was being overrun by the Germans in 1941, American journalists in Nazi Europe are seen to be able to move about somewhat freely because

America was as yet neutral. From this period, first-hand accounts describe the early years of the war from inside Nazi Germany.

Once America was in the war, reports were filed from all the battlefields where American troops were found. This includes Midway, Burma, and London under attack; the Philippines, Russia, the south Pacific and north Africa in 1942; and Italy and on bombers over Germany in 1943. There are stories from the home front, and at sea with the merchant marine. Stories from 1944 and after D-Day tell of more victories than defeats and, when American and Russian troops meet, in Germany in 1945, of the death camps they found. Many of Bill Mauldin's "Willie and Joe" cartoons are included, and to conclude the second volume is the John Hersey 1946 essay, "Hiroshima," the first of the revisionist looks at World War II.

Also featured in *Reporting World War II* are pieces that mark the start of the Civil Rights Movement. Black men and women served in great numbers and suffered considerable abuse from segregationist practices, a fact journalists could not ignore at a time when America's enemies were the openly racist Nazis and Japanese. More than a dozen pieces by Ernie Pyle appear, ample evidence to demonstrate why he was considered one of the premier front-line reporters ever. But nearly all the selections convey a sense of immediacy that can only be found in a journalist reporting an event on the spot. It's exhilarating stuff.

All these articles are from a different generation, and a far different time than our own. The style of writing is different, as journalists must adapt decade by decade to make their use of words and grammar more appealing to changing customs. But the thinking is different as well. Yes, there are many timeless elements. But it is the differences that will stand out the most. This is World War II, as the people who lived through it learned about current events. You are there, as the words bring the not-so-distant past to the present.

THE AMERICAN MAGIC

by Ronald Lewin

PENGUIN, 1983

The fact that the Allies had broken enemy codes did not become widely known until the 1970s, although early in World War II, the story of Americans code-breaking was talked about in the press. The FBI and senior government officials squelched such stories, however, so that the Japanese would not catch on. Although the cracking of the Japanese codes had an enormous impact on the war, both in the Pacific and Europe, American code breakers never got as much credit as their British counterparts, even though the American work was in some respects more important.

The reason for the Japanese smugness about their codes was their faith in the cipher machines, invented in the 1920s, and their unshakeable belief that these machines could not be beat. Since the Allies used similar machines, and Axis code breakers had been unable to make a dent in the encrypted messages they produced, the Japanese believed their messages were secure.

The Japanese continued to use code books for some uses, particularly communications between their overseas diplomats and Japan. This code was broken, and that was kept secret. U.S. Army and Navy code breakers also broke several other Japanese communications codes before Pearl Harbor. When, in the summer of

1940 Army code breakers unlocked the Japanese diplomatic code, this so impressed one admiral that he called it "Magic." The name stuck for the American code-breaking program.

The effort required to crack the Japanese code was considerable, and it's interesting to note that the early American work was done independently of the British, who were engaged in essentially the same work with German codes. Both Germany and Japan used cipher machines. The Germans were the first to develop a military version of Enigma (a 1920s commercial encryption machine intended to secure commercial communications), and they passed it on to the Japanese in 1937. The Japanese studied Enigma, but preferred their own machine, one that replaced the rotors that scrambled the text with stepper switches or a "sequentially shuffling cipher system." As the Americans had cracked an earlier, less formidable Japanese cipher machine, which they nicknamed "Red" (not be confused with the Japanese navy code called Red), once they had figured out the new version, they called it "Purple."

The American Army team that cracked Purple took advantage of some critical Japanese mistakes. For example, the Japanese would send out the same greetings or headings for many messages. Worse yet, for a while they sent duplicate messages via the older Red code. One of the U.S. team members was an engineer who knew of a switch, used by the telephone company for automatic calls, that could be used as a computer-like device to decipher the encryption methods the Japanese were using. With that insight, American engineers built machines that, while not identical to the Japanese Purple equipment, did essentially the same thing. Their work took eighteen months, and for a year before the Pearl Harbor attack, Japanese diplomatic messages were being decoded.

The Japanese Navy was another matter. The main navy code changed frequently, and in 1940 was designated JN-25 which rendered previous work worthless. That year, a new code, the "Flag Officers Code" (used for messages specifically going to admirals) was introduced. The U.S. Navy code breakers gave it priority, as it appeared to be a code that would contain valuable information.

This turned out to be false, and the Flag Officers Code was never cracked.

The U.S. Navy code breakers also went after JN-25 before Pearl Harbor, but they didn't have the staff to deal with it quickly, and did not get around to deciphering pre-Pearl Harbor messages until 1942. Although the diplomatic messages sent in Purple had not mentioned enough about military operations to give away details of the Pearl Harbor attack, the JN-25 messages did. Right after Pearl Harbor, the Navy got cracking on JN-25 and by the end of 1942 they had it pretty well cracked. The ability to read JN-25 was largely responsible for the victories at the battles of the Coral Sea and Midway.

The big problem with cracking Japanese codes was the tremendous growth in the number of coded Japanese messages sent over the years. From 1930 to 1935, the message volume of diplomatic and navy code increased twelve times. By the end of 1941, the Japanese Navy was transmitting 7,000 coded messages a month. There were many different codes in use and some were deciphered only to discover that the Japanese were not using that code for anything very important.

The diplomatic code remained readable throughout the war, resulting in several interesting developments. The U.S. Navy felt no urgency to speed up work on JN-25 when the Purple code could be read so easily. But Japanese scholars, decades after the war, compared the original Japanese messages to the Americans' Purple decrypts and now insist that inaccurate translations caused diplomatic problems and misunderstandings. This assertion points out the fact that the translations were imperfect. Many of the decrypts were accomplished with some guess work and "filling in the blanks," and the American intelligence people working on decrypts understood Japanese only as a second language. One can take these claims of inaccuracy as another attempt by the Japanese to portray themselves as victims in World War II.

American code-breaking was more successful with the Japanese than with the Germans for several reasons. Most of the key Japanese codes were broken early on, and the Japanese did not change their codes as frequently as the Germans did. Thus there was an unwitting but constant flow of information from Japanese sources. Of nearly equal importance was the inability of Japanese code breakers to crack many Allied codes (as the Germans did). The Japanese deciphered some low-level Allied codes, and Chinese codes were regularly broken since the 1930s, but their inability to break the principal Allied codes, particularly those produced by the British and American code machines (similar to Enigma and Purple), led the Japanese to believe that their own machine code was invulnerable—a costly error in a war where the Japanese were already out-matched in so many other areas.

THE AMERICAN SOLDIER

by S. A. Stouffer et al.

SUNFLOWER UNIVERSITY PRESS, 1949
(REPRODUCED ON REQUEST BY PUBLISHER)

One of the most important books about World War II is not a book-length work, but a series of opinion surveys conducted among U.S. Army personnel during the war, compiled by a group of academics (L. S. Cottrell, Jr., L. L. Janis, A. A. Lumsdaine, M. H. Lumsdaine, M. B. Smith, S. A. Star, S. A. Stouffer, R. M. Williams Jr.) who supervised this work for the U.S. Army. This collection of survey results makes for extremely valuable history. It gets inside the heads, so to speak, of the soldiers who fought the war. The surveys covered a huge range of subjects, and did so using statistical techniques that were then quite new, but which are now considered proven, classic tools for such work.

The surveys were conducted in Washington, DC, by the Research Branch of the Information and Education Division of the U.S. Army. The Research Branch was formed in late 1941, prior to the Pearl Harbor attack. Peak strength of the Research Branch in early 1945 was only ninety-three people (most of them clerical support), along with ten army officers and twenty-four opinion survey professionals. Several hundred additional Research Branch people in the field conducted the actual surveys.

The Research Branch was formed because senior Army officers

recognized the usefulness of opinion surveys. Such surveys had become a big business in the previous two decades, and World War II military commanders were quick to use new technology. The Chief of Staff of Army, George Marshall, gave the green light for the project and off the pollsters went.

The brass saw the benefit of getting feedback from the troops. It was understood that the raising of a multi-million man army was something never done by the United States before. Even the American Civil War and World War I did not create such a large force. In addition, the mid-20th century military force was going to be quite different in composition than any previous American force. Combat troops would only comprise about fifteen percent of the force. The rest would be support troops, and a huge air force.

But there was another major change that somewhat unhinged the generals in the Pentagon. There had been a revolution in American education during the first half of the 20th century. High school, previously seen mainly as "college lite" or a college preparatory experience for the few percent of students who went to college, was now seen as necessary for all students entering an increasingly technological workforce. In 1900, only 95,000 students graduated from high school, and only 29,000 from college. By 1920, there were 311,000 high school grads a year (but only 54,000 college grads). By 1940, there were 1.2 million high school grads a year. Since the draft weeded out those who were difficult to train, or just plain dumb, a very high proportion of those inducted were going to be high school graduates. This was when the army realized that going to high school (which was a lot more demanding sixty years ago) was producing recruits who were a lot more capable than those just a generation earlier.

The draft had been reinstated in 1940 and the generals were already getting reports from the basic training centers about these smart ass kids who were giving their less educated sergeants a hard time, and often getting away with it. The officers on the spot were quick to take advantage of the situation, and were rapidly promoting these capable young guys. One of my own uncles, who not only graduated from high school, but went back for some extra courses (which was allowed, and encouraged, during the

Great Depression of the 1930s), joined the Navy right after Pearl Harbor and by 1943 found himself a 26-year-old Chief Petty Officer on an aircraft carrier. The "Chiefs" basically run the Navy and in the past, you generally had some gray hair, and over a decade of service, before you became one. But that high school diploma was giving millions of eager young men a head start. The generals wanted to know what these kids were thinking, and how their NCOs and officers were reacting.

Opinion surveys were popular among the Army leadership from the beginning. In late 1943, a limited-circulation magazine was prepared, featuring troops' opinions selected from various surveys. Called "What the Soldier Thinks," it was distributed to commanders and staff officers down to the regimental level. This magazine was so popular that circulation was quickly extended down to the company level. In effect, every officer, and most senior NCOs, could read what the troops were thinking. For the more perceptive officers and NCOs, there were no surprises. But for the rest there was a collective "Huh?"

After the war, funds were provided by the Carnegie Corporation to transfer all the Research Branch records to Harvard University, so a final report could be prepared. The result was a four-volume work, two of whose volumes covered the Research Branch's methodology (which included much cutting-edge statistical work), while the other two volumes reported the actual survey results, and how Research Branch interpreted them.

What is in these two volumes is still very relevant, not just as a vital slice of military life during World War II, but also of how men adapt to military life and combat. I discovered this myself while I was in the Army in 1961–63. This is where I discovered these two books, in a post library in South Korea. Being in the army at the time, I found the two volumes fascinating. But I wondered, was my generation responding to the army experience in the same way that my father's generation had? To answer that question, I typed up a questionnaire based on some of the surveys in *The American Soldier: Adjustment During Army Life* and conducted the survey (with the help of a few friends) among the 200 lower ranking enlisted men in my artillery battalion. I compiled the responses (without benefit of a computer) and found that responses, and reactions to army life, had not changed in two decades. In many respects, it has not changed in the four decades since that survey in Korea. The all-volunteer military replaced the part conscript, part volunteer force that existed from 1940 to 1972, so the troops today can no longer complain about being in uniform involuntarily. But most of the other gripes remain the same. Troops today have many of the same attitudes first discovered among their grandfathers by the Research Branch.

The first half of *The American Soldier*, titled *Adjustment During Army Life*, is a compelling dissection of what the men who entered the army during World War II thought on a large number of issues. The surveys didn't merely ask things like, "Is your training too hard?" or "Do you feel promotions are given out on merit?" but framed such questions in terms of who the soldier was (education, army rank and experience, and so on) and where he was (army, support forces, or air force).

One trauma you are immediately made aware of was the explosive growth the army went through between 1940 (when the draft was reinstated) and the summer of 1945. In 1940, the army had 266,000 troops. By August 1945, there were 8.1 million men and women in the army. General Marshall and his peers saw this coming. And they could do the math. After a few years, the pre-war army men would be a tiny minority of the "New Army." While General Marshall and his pre-war officers and NCOs could mould this new army to a certain extent, all these new men would hold on to a lot of their own ideas, and impose them on the army. Marshall wanted to know what these guys were thinking. While his boss, President Roosevelt, paid close attention to opinion polls, and had to be concerned about the people being polled voting him out of office, Marshall knew he wasn't running a democracy. But he also knew that a more effective army was one in which the troops effectively absorbed their training. To do that, Marshall wanted to know more about who was being trained, so that they could become the most effective soldiers possible.

It's difficult to measure the impact these surveys had on the success of the American army during World War II. But the American armed forces, alone among those of the other major powers, started World War II with the weakest military tradition. America, despite all its wars, is a fairly pacifist nation. In peacetime, which is most of the time, there is no enthusiasm for maintaining a large army. The European nations and Japan not only had larger peace time forces, but much larger reserve (part time soldiers) forces. These nations made much of their military traditions and the "sacred duty" of all young men to be drafted into the army for two or three years. Equally important for the German or Japanese man was to then spend twenty years or more in a reserve unit. The American army was, by comparison, tiny. When war came, many men were mobilized from the state militias (now called the National Guard), organizations that, until this century, were more social than military. Many more civilians would volunteer, and the small number of regular soldiers would try to train them. The result was usually early defeats, followed by an enemy crushed by growing numbers of battle hardened (another word for learning to fight "on the job") American troops. When the Research Branch was formed, many senior army officers hoped that these surveys would shed some light on what was going well, or not well. For example, early surveys indicated that many NCO instructors (and some of the officers as well) were ill-equipped to teach the new troops. Recruits discovered that the instructors were under a lot of pressure to get them through training, and even if too many of them were failing, people would mysteriously pass regardless of whether they had learned all their lessons. The Research Branch alerted the brass to this, and instructors were given more supervision and their training methods were spot-checked by outside teams. It was also found that many well-educated new recruits understood more about how an army worked than their officers. There was, it appeared, a considerable "perception gap" between the troops and the officers. The NCOs, who were in the middle, were not always able to bridge this gap for the officers. Moreover, in the American system, the junior officers were usually just as green as the new enlisted men who had just finished a few months of training. At that time, the army was taking college grads and putting them through 90 days of training, and then making them second lieutenants. A year later, with millions of new men coming in and thousands of new units being formed, these same men were often captains, and still not very experienced. The Research Branch surveys pointed this out, and gave the brass a chance to attempt some remedial action.

The surveys also indicated that new troops and officers were more attuned to the radical changes in warfare than many of their seniors. While Marshall and the other generals grappled with the complexities of mechanized and aerial warfare, they were reassured to discover that many of their young troops were also aware that it was a new age on the battlefield and they were open to fresh ideas. This insightfulness, it turned out, was largely a benefit stemming from the recruits' prior education (30 percent were high-school grads, and 28 percent had attended, but not graduated).

These young guys had a healthy attitude, were quick to learn and adapted very quickly to army life. That additional education had included both technical and liberal arts courses. It was modeled on the classic college education, but without the specialization (choosing a major). While high schools specializing in learning a trade were popular, all students received an education that made them aware that there was a large, and quite different, world out there. For many of these high school grads, the army experience was an opportunity to do something with it. My own father was drafted in 1942 and, while not a techie (he was a jock), the army evaluation exams showed he had an aptitude for technical matters and he was sent off to be a radio technician. By the end of the war, he was working on the first American smart (guided from the bomber) bombs. As a high school graduate, his experience was not unusual. Many young recruits in that situation jumped right in to whatever the army offered and made the most of it. The surveys alerted the brass to the fact that they had an opportunity here. While the better educated recruits quickly acquired a reputation for mouthing off about the often irrational things that happened in the army, they also had the talent and attitude that made them better candidates for promotion. Thus came the policy of promoting men more on ability than on seniority (as had been the tradition for a long time). While many of these more educated young men would have gotten promoted anyway, because local commanders saw it in their own interest to do so, the encouragement from the very top made it all so much easier.

The surveys helped make decision-making for the senior commanders easier in other ways. For example, at the end of the war, they needed a method to prioritize which troops would be decommissioned first. Everyone was eager to go home once Germany and Japan were defeated, and it seemed an impossible task to work out a fair system that would not stir up trouble. The surveys also showed that the troops were pretty tired of the long war, and their families back home were as well. President Roosevelt saw this issue as one that could hurt him politically if not handled correctly. Surveys on this matter enabled army brass to come up with a point system (with points awarded for time in the service, overseas, and in combat) that satisfied most of the troops and their families. The generals and President were pleased as well, for the surveys also showed that there was some risk of mutinies if this matter was not handled to the troops' satisfaction. Other surveys also made post-war planning easier, not only illuminating otherwise unanticipated issues, but reassuring senior leaders that they were heading in the right direction and warning them when they were not.

One postwar area that was illuminated by the surveys was race relations. There is a chapter in *The American Soldier: Adjustment During Army Life* on "Negro Soldiers." The World War II army was segregated. Black soldiers served in all black units (although most of the officers were white). Many surveys were conducted in the black units and the results helped make it possible to begin integrating the army. For example, there was a shortage of infantry towards the end of the war. The surveys showed that black soldiers resented the fact that they were largely kept out of combat units and were eager to prove that they could fight. Knowing this, the generals ordered integration of combat units with black replacements toward the end of the war. This worked, as the surveys had indicated it would. The surveys of segregated units, compared to those of white units, showed that there was much resentment among black troops for the poor treatment they were getting (both in the army and before) and that white troops were generally clueless about the situation. These surveys made it easier for President Truman to order the armed forces desegregated in 1948, and for many senior officers to accept this as a practical policy. The surveys in this section make fascinating reading, then and now.

The second half of *The American Soldier,* titled *Combat and its Aftermath,* is valuable because it confirms what combat veterans have known for centuries. The lessons revealed in these surveys are pretty prosaic; train hard and select the most capable leaders. So simple, yet so often not done.

There was much more, however, that the Research Branch did to support the war effort. There were many army policies that were changed as a result of surveys. It was shown that many of the differences in casualties between units were related to leadership and training. This made it easier for senior generals to make the needed changes (relieving commanders and changing training) to eliminate the poor performance.

The surveys established the importance in combat of the formation of small groups of soldiers who knew and trusted each other well. It was also made clear that the combat troops did not want to let their buddies down. Mom, the flag, and apple pie had nothing to do with it—it was all about survival.

World War II was a unique war, but in different ways than twenty years earlier during World War I. The earlier war featured most troops spending months in muddy trenches, then getting slaughtered in set piece battles featuring headlong advances into machine-gun and artillery fire. World War II was more mobile, and added tanks and air attacks to the mix. There were more troops involved in World War II, and the casualty rate, at least for American troops, was lower than in World War I. But this brought out another problem: combat fatigue. Research Branch surveys showed the growing presence and impact of soldiers who had spent too much time in combat. This condition was first noted during World War I, and called "shell shock" (because it was thought to arise from men being pounded for too long by artillery). Before World

War I was over, many doctors realized that "combat fatigue" was a more appropriate term than shell shock; it was the result of the stress of modern combat. Subsequent research into the historical record showed that some forms of "combat fatigue" had long existed. But 20th century warfare placed a lot more troops under a lot more stress, thus producing a lot more combat fatigue casualties Those affected acted disoriented and uninterested in their surroundings, a condition similar to a nervous breakdown.

American commanders during World War II never figured out how to deal with combat fatigue, but the surveys left a vivid record of its impact. More and more troops, after a few months of combat, adopted a "don't give a damn" attitude, and desertions increased, even though the men were sure to get caught. But the combat-fatigued soldiers' attitude was, What can you do to me that could be worse than more combat? The Research Branch's work in this area provided a foundation for postwar treatment of combat fatigue.

The surveys of the combat troops eliminated, for the first time, much previous guesswork about what the soldiers were thinking while enduring considerable stress and danger. Aside from the value placed on belonging to a small group of trusted fellow soldiers, faith was reported to be important. Indeed, there were few atheists in foxholes. Prayer was also important when things really got grim. And the grimness often involved atrocities committed by American troops, which usually involved killing enemy soldiers trying to surrender, or who had already surrendered. The surveys don't reveal details, but indicate that some pretty bad things were happening in the trenches.

Back in Washington, many generals looked to these surveys for suggestions that would help them come up with new policies that would make combat troops more effective. The surveys clearly showed that soldiers at the front wished they had had more, and tougher, training. There was a big demand for more training with live ammunition. Commando units regularly practice using live ammunition, but that's because these units were generally composed of combat experienced troops who already knew how important this practice was. The commandos took it for granted and regularly trained with real ammo. This was more dangerous, but the commandos were better trained and more experienced, and felt a few training casualties were worth it. When the United States entered World War II, it immediately became clear that a lot of training accidents, as a result of using real ammo, would have negative political implications. In other words, parents (who were voters) would not put up with their kids getting shot and killed because of training accidents, so the army had backed away from this but the surveys made it clear that this was a mistake.

Another major mistake the surveys revealed was the American practice of sending new and generally inexperienced personnel in to replace casualties. The surveys made it clear that combat veterans were not going to trust their lives to some new guys. Division commanders noted this, and henceforth the replacements received additional training at a division battle preparation center, and were only sent to join their new infantry battalion when that unit had been pulled out of combat. Then the new guys trained with the experienced troops for a week or two until everyone got to know one another. The casualty rate among infantry replacements came way down when this was done. But it never became army policy, and the individual replacement system continued to be used, with the same disastrous results, in Korea and Vietnam. This in itself is an important lesson. Even if the generals have a problem staring them in the face, along with a clear explanation of why it is happening and how it can be fixed, they will sometimes keep making the mistake.

Another dark corner of combat on which the surveys shed some light was the often testy relationship between combat troops and the much larger number of "rear echelon" soldiers providing support. The surveys made it clear why this animosity existed. It went beyond the attitude of "I'm getting shot at and you're not." As the generals realized when they saw the surveys, stronger policies were needed to see that the combat troops got better treatment. Too often, the non-combat soldiers were more interested in their own comfort than in making life easier for the guys they were supposed to be supporting. This was mostly human nature. The support guys did do their job, and often went the extra mile. This was particularly true with the men and women running the military hospitals, or the truck drivers rushing more ammo, fuel and other supplies to the front. However, when the front line troops passed through where the support troops were set up, they noted the huge differences in the standard of living. A major problem was that the vast majority of the troops were in support units. The surveys showed that only fifteen percent of the troops were ever in combat (where they were being shot at and could shoot back) and only 25 percent were ever in combat or under fire (usually being shelled or bombed, something that happened occasionally to rear echelon units). For most men in the army, the only time they got to see weapons being used was in basic training.

The surveys also examined troops' reactions to getting shot at and the nerve-wracking (for many) experience of killing enemy troops. As was pointed out by the authors:

> Combat required a sharp break with many moral prescriptions of peacetime society. As easy as it seems to be for men to kill when their immediate group sanctions it, and as ambivalent as normal people often are about killing, it is still true that to kill another human being requires of most men from our culture an effort to overcome an initial moral repugnance. Under the requirements of the situation, men in combat were careful to hide this feeling, and it was not a subject of much discussion among soldiers. Killing is the business of the combat soldier, and if he is to function at all he must accept its necessity. Yet the acceptance of killing did not prevent the ambivalence revealed by such comments as that of a veteran rifleman who said, "I'll tell you a man sure feels funny inside the first time he squeezes down on a Kraut."

The surveys indicated that most troops had qualms about killing, and there was a wide variation in how men with weapons reacted to the opportunity to take a life. This led to postwar studies on how many infantrymen actually took part in the killing, or by shrinking back in revulsion and shock. The surveys opened a new area of scientific study on how men react in combat.

An issue that particularly rankled troops was the enormous difference in lifestyle between those soldiers who never left the United States and those who found themselves in some jungle or freezing forest getting shot in a muddy ditch. Guys back in the States lived in barracks, slept on beds with sheets, and ate cooked meals sitting down. Solutions to troops' resentments were few, but many were tried. For example, there was a constant stream of propaganda praising the combat troops for their sacrifice and courage in the face of danger endured. Efforts were made to come up with new equipment to make life at the front easier. But, as the surveys indicated, the quality of leadership was key. If the division commander paid more attention to the welfare of his combat troops, he could motivate the support troops to provide more supplies and services, on a timely basis, for the men in combat units. It takes an above-average officer to be sufficiently well organized to attend to his troops' welfare. As surveys pointed out, combat troops noticed this, and knew who was responsible. All the successful generals, including Patton, MacArthur, and Montgomery, were able men who took the time to look after the welfare of their combat troops. The surveys also made clear that there would have to be fundamental changes in how combat divisions were organized, to provide sufficient officers and resources to improve the troops' living conditions. Many new policies were implemented based on what the surveys revealed, resulting in fewer non-combat casualties (exposure, disease, accidents) and fewer combat casualties (because the troops were better fed and rested).

Surveys were also conducted among combat aircraft crews, because the largest air war in history was being fought over Germany during 1943–45. This was a unique situation, unlikely to be repeated. Today, air forces have fewer, but far more capable, aircraft. World War II bombers had a crew of eleven, while modern bombers have a crew of one, or two, and carry more bombs farther than their 1940s counterparts. But during World War II, there were 10,000 of these heavy bombers lost in combat or to accidents, plus many more aircrew who were killed or injured by anti-aircraft fire that did not bring their aircraft down. Ten percent of all combat casualties during World War II were people in aircraft.

Some 29,000 aircrew were killed and 44,000 wounded. There were serious morale problems, as aircrew in some areas realized that their chances of surviving the war were close to zero. The surveys' grim message to that effect led to limiting the number of missions an airman had to fly before being sent to a non-combat job, a policy that would give him about a 50 percent chance of survival. Medical personnel were warned to keep close tabs on aircrew who flew particularly harrowing missions. Spotting cases of combat fatigue before it disabled a man made it possible to head off a potentially disastrous situation. It was not unknown for combat fatigue to catch up with a man while he was in the air, which was really dangerous if the guy in question was the pilot. Usually, a week or two of rest would often make a man fit to fly again.

After the war was over, the Research Branch ran one last round of surveys, to determine how the army experience had affected men once they were civilians again. The surveys only covered men who were out less than a year, because Research Branch was shutting down, but the results were interesting. Most men felt they had been changed, largely for the worse. At the same time, however, the veterans became more involved in civic affairs and believed they had gained more maturity than they would have if the war had never happened and they had never served.

The social scientists who ran the Research Branch broke new ground in surveying and statistical techniques. One of the more powerful tools they used was factor analysis, a statistical method that searches for relationships between questions asked in a survey, to see if there are unexpected relationships. (There often are.) The technique was first developed early in the 20th century, and it was not widely used until cheap computer power became available three decades after the war ended. But with the primitive (by later standards) computing tools available to them, Research Branch did some investigation using this tool and found many unexpected relationships. These "multivariate relationships" usually explained earlier findings and pointed out areas that should also be investigated. Most of it, which is of use only to pollsters and statisticians, was included in the other technical volumes. But it's another important result of the Research Branch effort that doesn't get the credit it deserves.

While there are many books providing first-person accounts of the war experiences, *The American Soldier* lends substance to that experience. As such, it is among the most valuable books written about World War II.

THE GOOD WAR

by Studs Terkel

NEW PRESS, 1997

Studs Terkel has been writing oral histories for decades and has a real talent for it. In *The Good War*, he lets the troops and other participants speak for themselves. This book is a very easy read because of the way it's organized and paced, touching on everything from Americans who fought against the Nazis in the 1930s (whom the FBI called "premature anti-Fascists") to men and women in every part of the world caught up in the war. Most of the interviews were obtained in and around Chicago, where the author lives. Chicago has always been a vast melting pot of nationalities. Add in the tourists and other visitors, and it's easy to see how you can cover a worldwide event that happened four decades earlier by just going around Chicago with a tape recorder and a knack for asking the right questions.

Unlike some other books on the experiences of individuals during World War II, *The Good War* doesn't have a "cheerleader" quality about it. Terkel combines leftist politics and a large dose of journalistic cynicism to tell his stories with a sly bite. He talks to the right people and asks the right questions, which results in a more realistic take on momentous historical events. As combat veterans can be reluctant to talk about their experiences if they had a particularly hard time, many of those who served without getting shot at are happy to tell their stories with a wink and a nod (there were frequent opportunities in wartime to do a bit better than you were supposed to via the black market and other forms of crime).

Terkel lets his subjects talk about how the world-at-war really worked. Nothing really sensational, just the mundane details that often get overlooked in the official accounts. In real life, things tend to get a bit confused when there's a crisis. This book catches those moments. The author also casts a wide net. While combat troops are well represented, there's information on the home front, government officials, the people who built the weapons, and the supplies needed to keep the troops going. It was a big war that had impact on many more people than just the troops.

Additional interviewees were men who had been in Japanese and Russian POW camps (both of which had very high mortality rates). Included are details that you won't read anywhere else, (such as the bureaucratic drill POWs had to endure in a Japanese camp to have a dead buddy buried). There are also stories of Japanese civilians during the war, and Japanese-Americans in the United States, which make for strong contrasts.

And then there were the "V Girls" found in large American cities during the war—teenage girls swept up in a patriotic fervor, doing what they could for the troops: offering sex. Troops were delighted; cops and other politicians were appalled. Hell of a story, though.

Not surprisingly, there were opportunists out there. Although the U.S. government made a major effort to crack down on those who took advantage of wartime shortages and all those government contracts, there was still plenty of lucrative, legal and illegal, opportunities out there. And some of the operators were willing to talk after all those years.

The war made everything more vivid, no matter what you were doing. Movie stars and other entertainers found themselves in odd situations, even if they were not overseas entertaining the troops.

It was not only a World War, it was a somewhat Weird One as well. Life is not always heroic or horrible. Often it's just confused and, in an odd way, amusing. Here's the book that shows how that worked.

The Shadow Warriors: O.S.S. and the Origins of the C.I.A.

by Bradley Smith

Carlton Books, 1998

Massive intelligence agencies are a 20th-century development. And one activity of the modern intelligence agency is the operational mission. This is where James Bond comes in. "Special operations" are sexy and, understandably, quickly caught the attention of post–World War II authors of adventure fiction in search of story ideas among recent events.

During World War II, each of the major nations had one or more organizations that took care of undercover work and high risk missions. Among the Allies, the Russians had the NKVD, which was the largest, most ruthless, and secretive of the lot, and the British had several: MI-6 (foreign intelligence and operations), MI-5 (internal intelligence gathering and counterintelligence), and SOE (Special Operations Executive, a temporary organization set up to take care of additional missions created by World War II).

The United States, however, started from scratch in the intelligence business, but by the end of World War II, it had one of the world's largest. Until the CIA was established in 1947, there was the Office of Strategic Services. *The Shadow Warriors* describes how the OSS came to be and furnished the people and experience that laid the foundations for the CIA.

America was not unfamiliar with secret agents and messy missions in foreign nations, but until World War II such matters were done in an impromptu fashion. After 1941, a more organized approach was required. The OSS wasn't actually all that organized, but it did provide one-stop shopping when the U.S. government needed something unusual done in a dangerous place. More important, OSS could keep tabs on the intelligence activity that the Army, Navy, State Department, and FBI (along with a few other agencies) were involved in. The lack of coordination was noted by President Roosevelt in 1939. After asking nicely, several times, that he be provided with a unified picture of the war in Europe, and being ignored, Roosevelt appointed Wall Street heavyweight William ("Wild Bill") Donovan as Coordinator of Information (COI) in July 1941 and told him to get the job done.

Donovan had won a Medal of Honor during the first World War as an infantry battalion commander. He was well connected and well traveled, a lawyer with a reputation for making things happen. Underlying Donovan's reputation for action was his belief in thoroughly documented research. Even before Pearl Harbor, Donovan's COI researchers were providing Roosevelt with excellent reports on events in Europe. Once the United States entered the war, Roosevelt and Donovan saw a need for an agency that could concentrate on secret missions. Therefore, in June 1942, COI became OSS (the Office of Strategic Services). Donovan had, since COI was created, recruited heavily on Wall Street and the top universities and corporations. Everyone knew there was a war coming, and working for a war hero like Donovan on "special projects" was so appealing that few declined the offer. Despite hostility from the State Department and the military toward this new kid on the block, OSS quickly made itself useful by sending out skilled, eager, and daring operatives when the State Department or military needed them.

The OSS was never a large organization, peaking at some 13,000 men and women in 1944. About two thirds of OSS personnel were already in the Army or Army Air Forces, including many who joined as civilians and were given Army ranks and training to help them do their OSS jobs better. About a quarter of OSS people were civilians, including women, and many men who were too old for military service. About 10 percent came from other military services. Throughout the war, 7,500 OSS members served overseas, including 900 women. Actually, about 4,500 women served in the OSS, most in the United States. The OSS was a bargain, costing about $1.3 billion (in current dollars) for the entire war. Most work was done the old-fashioned way, with agents sneaking into enemy-held territory to collect information and work with local resistance organizations.

Nevertheless, OSS was eager to try just about anything, and its people were dispatched all over the world. However, everything had to be done in a hurry, and in the rush, mistakes were made and people got killed. The British, who had been at this sort of thing for centuries, cooperated with the OSS as much as possible, but were careful not to ally themselves too closely with the less experienced—and thus more dangerous to be around—OSS personnel.

One part of OSS, their analysis operation, was really unique in intelligence history. The work of the Research and Analysis Branch (R&A) was carried out by 900 academics, lawyers, and sundry other experts who carefully studied a variety of situations, sorted out all the details, and delivered clear, well-documented reports. This had never before been accomplished with the degree of thoroughness, speed, and accuracy shown by R&A. Whatever criticism OSS received for its World War II work, none fell on R&A. When the war ended, many in Washington wanted R&A retained. This proved to be difficult; R&A's roster read like a Who's Who of America's top academics, most of whom wanted to return to their universities. Enough stayed on to continue the OSS analysis tradition until the CIA was formed in 1947.

Among branches of U.S. intelligence, Special Operations (SO) received the most publicity. SO did then what U.S. Army Special Forces do today—work with resistance groups in enemy territory. OSS was active in Europe and in Asia; at one point, there were 2,000 OSS personnel in China alone. Their most spectacular success was Detachment 101 in Burma. There were never more than 120 people in this unit, yet they built up an army of 11,000 local tribesmen, armed with guns and other equipment flown in. Detachment 101's army created a major distraction for the Japanese, tying up thousands of Japanese troops. Detachment 101 not only collected enormous amounts of accurate data on Japanese operations in Burma, it got involved in driving the Japanese out in 1945.

The OSS also created a very useful psychological warfare unit called Morale Operations (MO), which was able to manipulate media (through rumors, and propaganda that didn't appear to be propaganda) to stir up resistance to the enemy or weaken the morale of enemy troops. (These activities were deemed so successful that, after the war, the U.S. Army created its own psychological warfare operation.)

Oddly enough, the OSS was not supposed to be an espionage agency. But Donovan felt he could improve how agent networks were set up overseas, and that the Army, Navy, and State Department had never really done a good job in this area. He set up the Secret Intelligence (SI) branch, and by the end of the war the worldwide network of SI case officers and local agents was producing so much excellent information that many people in Washington did not want to shut it down.

The OSS also was involved in the activities of the Ultra and Magic code-breakers. As it was extremely important that these projects be kept secret, the OSS set up a small, carefully selected group called X-2. This group was able to maintain secrecy while relaying essential information (from the sensitive Ultra and Magic decrypts of enemy messages) to OSS organizations. The mysterious and powerful X-2 agents soon became known throughout the OSS as guys who knew a lot, and could veto any planned operation without having to explain why.

Elsewhere in the OSS, however, counterintelligence (keeping enemy agents in the dark) was weak. In Europe and Asia, the OSS was penetrated many times by Communist and Nazi sympathizers. Some of these leaks were unavoidable, as the OSS often had to work with enemy soldiers and civilians to get the job done. For example, in the last months of the war in Europe, the OSS parachuted into Germany 200 Germans working for the Allies to act as secret agents. Some 18 percent of them disappeared or were killed by the end of the war, but others who survived proved excellent sources of information from within Germany. These men were recruited from German prisoners of war and trained by the OSS, a not uncommon practice, but not every one who was recruited stayed loyal.

The OSS also was the originator of the secret lab that developed odd, often useful, tools for agents and spies. While the British and other nations were already doing some of this stuff, the OSS took such research to a new level. Most of this was kept secret after the war because much of this technology continues to be useful.

"Wild Bill" Donovan stepped on a lot of high-ranking toes as he got the OSS organized and operating. Many offended worthies, including the newly installed president Harry Truman, were keen to put OSS out of business as soon as the war ended. This they did by October 1945. But Donovan had influence, and the State Department adopted the Research and Analysis division while the Army provided a home for the Secret Intelligence and X-2 branches. By 1947, many Washington big shots realized their error, and OSS was reconstituted as the CIA. In the 1950s, the U.S. Army Special Forces rebuilt a lot of the OSS Special Operations capabilities. In the 1980s, all the armed services contributed their special operations "operations" into the Special Operations Command. The OSS was now fully restored. New names, new agencies, but the same kinds of operators and jobs.

The Shadow Warriors clearly shows the OSS as the origin of the CIA and U.S. Army Special Forces.

THERE'S A WAR TO BE WON

by Geoffrey Perret

BALLANTINE, 1992

One of the wonders of 20th-century military history was the expansion of the U.S. Army during World War II. Averaging about 150,000 troops and three combat divisions during the 1930s, by 1945 there were over 8 million soldiers, 89 divisions, the world's largest air force, and the largest fleet of ships (transports and amphibious boats). *There's a War to Be Won* answers two important questions: How did it happen, and how did it turn out?

As if forty-fold growth in less than five years was not enough of an accomplishment, the Army was also faced with the torturous task of learning how to fight in several new arenas of war. Within a year of America's entry into the war, the Army units were fighting in terrains that ranged from Pacific jungles to North African deserts. In both theaters of war, the green American troops not only learned fast and improvised, they also defeated their more experienced opponents. In tropical New Guinea, American troops battled veteran Japanese troops across the Owen Stanley Mountains and used innovations like aerial re-supply and airmobile operations (landing transports in a combat zone to deliver troops and supplies) to defeat their more seasoned foe. In North Africa, Army troops used a trans-ocean amphibious operation and relentless fighting to defeat the fabled German Panzerarmee Africka at its own game. Again, it was a combination of innovation, persistence, and quick learning that won the battles. By the end of 1942, German and Japanese generals were no longer disparaging the U.S. Army.

There's a War to Be Won is not all good news. A lot of lumps were taken along the way, a lot of out-of-control egos were dealt with. The book makes the most of this and devotes many pages to the two biggest egos, and most successful battlefield commanders: Douglas MacArthur in the Pacific and George Patton in Europe. MacArthur began the war as the biggest talent, and biggest ego, in the Army. Chief of Staff of the Army in the 1930s, he went to work for the Philippines (an American colony preparing for independence in 1945), to organize the army of the future Republic of the Philippines. In mid-1941, as war appeared more likely, MacArthur rejoined the Army as commander of U.S. Army troops in the western Pacific. Defeated by the Japanese when they invaded the Philippines, he got another chance and went on to stop further Japanese advances, liberate the Philippines and ended the war as Japan's postwar ruler. *There's a War to Be Won* does a wonderful job of showing how MacArthur fit in with the rapidly expanding army, and how he feuded with the Navy over how the war in the Pacific should be fought. Patton, the American general most feared by the Germans, was another story. Outclassed by MacArthur in the ego department (but not by much), Patton practiced a vigorous and daring form of warfare that was out of step with the more plodding doctrine favored by most other American generals. At the time, Patton was seen as an exception, an eccentric who could do things in combat other generals could not. Decades later, Patton was proved prophetic, as his methods became standard in the American armed forces. His style of fighting was actually timeless, but required better training and combat leadership than the United States was able to provide during World War II.

Both MacArthur and Patton were innovators, but their new techniques had a hard time becoming part of the Army's standard tool set. *There's a War to be Won* shows that the new American Army learned to be cautious. Victory, not innovation, was the goal. American military leaders sought to make the most of what they had, and as quickly as possible. Taking too many risks was discouraged. Patton and MacArthur got away with being different and daring because they tended to win nearly all their battles, and (especially in MacArthur's case) with far fewer casualties than other U.S. generals. But other generals found they could not operate the same way MacArthur and Patton did. *There's a War to Be Won* shows why that was so, and why the U.S. was victorious anyway.

This book explains much more than why American military leaders were successful. It includes plenty of fascinating material on what it was like for millions of men (and some women) to step into a uniform and go overseas. There's even a fascinating section on what happened when soldiers were killed, wounded, or captured—another illustration of the Army's constant experimenting and striving to do things better. Handling the killed and wounded was no exception.

Early in World War II, nearly all of the Graves Registration troops, responsible for the bodies of troops killed in combat, were sent to Europe. Combat troops in the Pacific lacked Graves Registration, and bodies were easily lost in the jungle, not just because of all the vegetation, but because many early Pacific battles were desperate affairs. It was easy for dead soldiers to be overlooked as the living troops fought day and night against the Japanese; they were noted by the troops when the fighting was over. This became a morale problem. It was important that there be some kind of funeral service for the dead, a necessity that had been recognized in earlier wars and the reason specially trained Graves Registration troops were organized to recover, identify, and bury both friendly and enemy dead. Told that Graves Registration units would not be coming for a while, local commanders improvised. In some cases, the call went out for any troops who had been morticians in civilian life. These men were then briefed by old-timers (from World War I) on what Graves Registration units did, and then assigned more troops to help them.

Graves Registration units arrived in the Pacific in 1944. The improvised Graves Registration units had, by then, learned to cope with their own dead, but the Japanese were another matter, for the enemy favored mass attacks in the middle of the night which left hundreds of dead bodies piled up in front of American fox holes. Those bodies could be dumped in mass graves only once Japanese snipers had been cleared out, and the bodies were carefully checked to see if any Japanese were still alive (and, occasionally, waiting to pull the pin on a grenade as soon as a Graves Registration trooper got close enough). Because of this, it was sometimes days before enemy corpses could be buried. To complicate matters further, many more wounded Japanese would crawl or limp away and die in the bush because the Japanese did not provide as much medical care as did the American units.

One of the tragic consequences of the shortage of Graves Registration units in the Pacific was that bodies often were hastily buried without identification. As a result, thousands of soldiers still classified "missing in action" remain in unmarked graves hidden inside dense Pacific island jungles.

There's a War to Be Won fills in a lot of blanks in the history of World War II. Most people tend to take American participation for granted. But quickly forming, and sending overseas, millions of troops was no easy task. No other nation had to raise armies quickly **and** send them half war around the world while keeping them supplied on a scale never before seen in the history of warfare. Both German and Japanese generals complained that they were defeated mainly by America's abundance of material. This, of course, implied that American troops somehow lacked the traditional measurements of military success: skill and bravery on the battlefield. There's an element of sour grapes to that, because the Germans and Japanese both won victories where they had superior quantities of equipment and ammunition. What the Axis leaders didn't want to admit was that the Americans simply found new ways to win a war. The Axis warlords had high opinions of themselves, and hated to think that they had been out-thought and out-fought by amateurs. But that's exactly what happened, and this books shows how it was done.

THE UNITED STATES STRATEGIC BOMBING SURVEY

GREENWOOD, 1946

Even before World War II ended, Britain and America wanted to know how their investment in warplanes had contributed to ending the war. Together, Britain, America, and Germany devoted nearly 40 percent of their economic resources to building aircraft, and people wanted to know if it was worth it. Two survey teams, totalling 2,300 people, were assigned to conduct the U.S. Strategic Bombing Survey (USSBS). One team examined the impact of air power in the Pacific, the other the impact in Europe. The USSBS was unique in that the people working on it had first crack at surviving records and enemy personnel. The research material included movies the Germans had made during and after bombing attacks, and over 10,000 photos taken by the Germans and Japanese. There were also hundreds of interviews with people who had been bombed, which produced some startling conclusions about the effects of bombing. (It doesn't demoralize the victims as much as it makes them mad.)

Reports summarizing the survey's findings are available on the Web (www.maxwell.af.mil/au/aul/aupress/catalog/books/USSBS_B20.htm), and in print. The full reports run to more than a hundred volumes, with numerous charts, photographs, and maps. You'll only find these in some major libraries. But the summary reports, at a length of about 200 pages, tell a compelling tale.

The air war over Europe was of staggering proportions. In the bombing campaign against Germany, Britain and America dropped 2.7 million tons of bombs. To do this, 1.44 million bomber and 2.68 million fighter sorties were required. Losses were heavy; 40,000 aircraft and 159,000 aircrew. At the campaign's peak, the Allies had 28,000 warplanes and 1.3 million men in action. The impact on Germany was extraordinary. Some 20 percent of living quarters (houses or apartments) were destroyed or heavily damaged. Over a million civilians were killed or wounded.

But tallying up was the easy part. The really important, and harder, questions involved the relationship between the bombing campaign and Germany's ability to keep fighting. The bombing did affect German war production, but exactly to what extent continues to be a matter of debate. The major questions tended to be not whether bombing was effective, but what should be bombed, and when. These are questions that are still debated by political and military leaders. But during World War II, it loomed larger because of the amount of resources put into aircraft and bombing. Many still argue that some aspects of the bombing campaigns were not only ineffective but immoral. The USSBS clearly shows that there were no easy answers about this aspect of the war.

The bombing campaign in the Pacific was much smaller: 656,000 tons of bombs were dropped. Only 24 percent of that number was dropped on Japan itself, but the dropping of the first atomic bombs makes the use of the high-tech B-29 bomber of special interest. The B-29, whose development cost more than the Manhattan Project (that created nuclear weapons), dropped 22 percent of the bombs dropped in the Pacific, and all in less than a year. The B-29 was also the only American bomber that could carry the first atomic bombs. USSBS studies how well the B-29 performed. The first "modern" heavy bomber, its crew compartments were pressurized and other areas of the aircraft were state-of-the-art.

Reporting on the usefulness of the many dramatic new weapons used during World War II, tanks and aircraft being the most prominent, the USSBS was forward-looking. While many thought, at the end of the war, that nuclear weapons were the ultimate weapon, it didn't turn out that way. Nuclear weapons, especially when more than one nation had them, became too dangerous to use. Air power was another story. The U.S. Air Force, which became the premier air power for the rest of the century, learned much from the USSBS. While some lessons of the USSBS were generally ignored (like how often the people on the ground were able to deceive the bombers as to what they were hitting, or what they had hit), most of it was used as a road map for dominating the air in the future. What is amazing is how many air force leaders in other nations apparently ignored the USSBS. The report was not classified, and anyone was able to get a copy in the late 1940s.

The survey was an extraordinary piece of history. The amount of detail in the full report is overwhelming. This is historical research on steroids. The USSBS, which did not get started until September, 1944, was actually the continuation of three similar, but smaller research efforts;

Combined Bomber Offensive Survey (April–July 1944)

Strategic Bombing Effects Survey (July–September 1944)

U.S. Bombing Research Mission (September–November 1944)

While many cite the USSBS as proof that air power is overrated, the survey actually reaches the opposite conclusion. For example, the problem with bombing Germany out of the war was not that it was impossible, but that the campaign had to concentrate on the critical targets to succeed, and there were not enough bombers to destroy everything. One area where USSBS was most critical had to do with the inability of the Air Force leadership to pick the targets that would have best crippled German warmaking ability.

There were enough participating Air Force generals involved in the USSBS to ensure that it was not too harsh in criticizing where air power came up short. The air war partisans did not cook any of the USSBS data, but they were able to apply pressure to tone down censure of the air war effort. Air power was enormously popular during World War II, military and civilian leaders committing more than a third of the war budget to warplanes and air war. Moreover, the combination of hi-tech (and very expensive) B-29 bombers and the newly invented A-bomb gave air power an aura of invincibility.

The survey did demonstrate that targets were destroyed, although not with the accuracy the Allies thought. A good example is the attacks on three crucial chemical plants, at Leuna, Ludwigshafen-Oppau and Zeitz. Some 30,000 tons of bombs (over 7,000 bomber sorties) were dropped on these plants. The plants covered a fenced in area of 3.5 square miles. But only 12.5 percent of the bombs fell within that area. The Germans also noted that some 14 percent of the bombs did not explode (and those are still being dug up all over Europe to this day). The survey found that only three percent of the bombs actually hit plant buildings and equipment. But that 900 tons of bombs on target was sufficient to eventually cripple the production of these plants. The survey also revealed that the Germans learned from each attack. The Germans noted which parts of the plants, when hit, did the most damage to production. These tended to be water lines, gas mains, sewers, and electric cables. As a result, as the months of bombing went on, targets became harder to take out. This was because the Germans were encasing these key portions of the plants in concrete and stonework to better protect them. Allied photo reconnaissance aircraft could not pick this up.

So it was not enough to make several raids, examine aerial photos for enormous damage and conclude that you had shut down a plant. Even during the war, there were sometimes reports from spies that the Germans were constantly repairing damage, and using clever deceptions to make the Allies think they had knocked a plant out of the war. The Germans flew their own aircraft overhead to take photos, and then went to work to hide their repair work. This made the Allies think they had shut down a plant that was actually still producing. The Germans were quite successful at this, because many of these deceptions were not discovered until the USSBS teams came by on foot to check the damage.

But there was a larger problem, it turned out. The people tasked with selecting the most vulnerable targets chose the wrong ones.

The USSBS revealed that if the bombers had gone after the electric power plants, the German economy would have been crippled and the war shortened by a year or more. The panel of economic experts consulted miscalculated how vulnerable the German electrical generation and distribution system was. The error was pretty prosaic, the experts consulted to examine the vulnerability of the German electrical generation and transmission system were American and British. Seems that American and British electrical power systems are built with a lot more redundancy and flexibility than elsewhere. The German system was a lot more vulnerable, and knocking out two dozen major power plants would have dimmed the lights through most of German industry. The USSBS teams found the truth, and U.S. Air Force targeting staffs have, ever since, tried (not always successfully) to avoid the errors of their World War II predecessors.

The USSBS also studied naval operations, particularly in the Pacific. As the aircraft carrier was another weapon that made a dramatic entrance during World War II, U.S. Navy planners have studied carefully the USSBS Pacific survey and gone on to create a navy dominated by aircraft carriers. The survey also tracked the impact of air transport. China, cut off from the Allies by Japanese occupied territory in early 1942, was supplied for several years by American transports flying over the Himalayan mountains. Considering the transports available (primitive by today's standards), the amount of men (1.38 million) and material (1.18 million tons) moved was impressive.

By having access to American, British, and enemy records, the survey was able to confirm that pilot training was the most vital aspect of air superiority. The Japanese and German training and combat performance records, when compared to those of the U.S. and Britain (whose pilots received more flight training before going into combat), made it clear that attempts to turn out new pilots with too few flying hours easily gets them killed when they confront a better-trained foe.

The survey teams were disbanded in October, 1947, when their work was done. While some of the records were classified (primarily those relating to American air operations that were still current, and nuclear weapons–related information), most of the analysis was published for all to see. The USSBS is one of the more important government documents to come out of the war, and the summary volumes are accessible, and very readable.

UNITED STATES ARMY IN
WORLD WAR II

by various authors

U.S. GOVERNMENT PRINTING OFFICE, 1948–2003

This isn't one book. It's about 30,000 pages spread over the 78 volumes of the U.S. Army's official history of its operations during World War II, commonly called the "Green Books" because of their green covers. They were also known as "Greenbacks" and were further identified by color-coded bands indicating subject areas within the series. Red bands were combat histories; brown bands were technical services; green bands were special studies; and black bands were administrative histories. There were some exceptions, but those were the general rules. Many volumes were reissued in paperback editions for the 50th Anniversary of World War II.

The Green Books are generally considered to be the finest official histories of World War II. The authors were all professional historians, many of whom went on to write other popular historical works. They were given access to enormous quantities of documents, from enemy as well as American sources. The series has been slow to be finished; as of mid-2003, one last volume is still in progress. Many of the books are still in print, and many can be found free online. Go to www.army.mil/cmh-pg/collections/USAWW2/USAWW2.htm. Because they are U.S. Government publications, they can be reproduced freely, and some commercial publishers have done just that for the more popular titles.

These books are among the most underappreciated studies of World War II. Because they were published by the U.S. Government Printing Office, the books have received little publicity and no distribution to speak of to bookstores or book clubs. This is a shame, because many of these volumes are comparable to commercially published titles on the same subject.

In the last two centuries, it became common for nations to commission professional historians to write "official histories" of wars. These works varied tremendously in quality. Some were basically propaganda, trying to justify the government's decisions during the conflict. But some official histories are outstanding, and this is one of them. Many of the volumes that focus on specific campaigns could easily have been published as popular histories. Clearly written and well researched, the books in this series have been considered the definitive accounts of the actions they covered, and for parts of the war that never attracted much popular interest (such as the conflicts in southern France or Burma), these official accounts remain the gold standard for what went on there.

Even more important are the volumes covering how America prepared for war, and then kept the troops equipped and supplied. As the old saying goes, "amateurs study tactics, professionals study logistics." The Green Books know how to do logistics. Other volumes cover mobilization of industries and what it took to expand the Army from 200,000 troops to 8 million. A tremendous feat, and the Green Books explain how it happened.

Equally important are several volumes covering high-level planning and command. When the United States Army went from tiny to huge, there simply weren't enough West Point and staff school graduates to provide the professional manpower needed. The United States had to learn on the job and improvise. This remarkable story might have been lost to history without the Green Books.

The volumes on the Army's technical branches (especially engineering, transportation, quartermaster, signal, and medical) tell a generally unnoticed story—the degree to which the World

War II experience revolutionized how things are done in these fields. (Antibiotics, for example, first became widely available during World War II, and revolutionized medicine.) Engineer and signal troops developed new equipment and techniques that slid right into civilian use after the war. The Quartermaster Corps' development of new equipment and procurement techniques that set off a steady stream of innovation from World War II to the present.

Dipping into this series will be a rewarding experience. Most people interested in World War II never come across the Green Books. You know better. Don't miss the opportunity.

Following is a list of all 78 volumes in the series *United States Army in World War II*. Note that one volume (*The Medical Department: Medical Service in the War Against Japan*) is not yet finished, which, after 58 years, is pretty amazing. But that simply reminds us that getting the other 77 volumes written was itself a tremendous undertaking. That's a story in itself, with personality clashes, personal crises and unanticipated deaths and illnesses. But 77 out of 78 ain't all that bad.

The year after the author's name indicates first publication.

The War Department

Chief of Staff: Prewar Plans and Preparations by Mark Skinner Watson. 1950. A little-known story of how the pre–World War II Army struggled to modernize during two decades when the defense budget was miniscule.

Washington Command Post: The Operations Division by Ray S. Cline. 1951. The story of the small group of officers at Army headquarters who developed the plans for how to fight the Axis, a task no American army had yet faced.

Strategic Planning for Coalition Warfare: 1941–1942 by Maurice Matloff and Edwin M. Snell. 1953. Discusses the sometimes torturous negotiations with our British, Canadian, Russian, and Australian allies after America entered the war, as well as the scramble to gather resources and respond to the seemingly unbeatable Japanese and Germans.

Strategic Planning for Coalition Warfare: 1943–1944 by Maurice Matloff. 1959. Dealing with friendly nations once the Allies were winning proved to be almost as difficult as when they were losing. A lot of material on planning for the post-war world and the emergence of General George Marshall as *the* main force behind U.S. military planning during the war.

Global Logistics and Strategy: 1940–1943 by Richard M. Leighton and Robert W. Coakley. 1955. One of the more important and underrated books in the series. Logistics is the ability to mobilize men and supplies and get them to the combat zone. America organized a logistical operation that propelled the Allied war effort to ultimate victory. Details on the major decisions about where supplies came from, and where they went.

Global Logistics and Strategy: 1943–1945 by Robert W. Coakley and Richard M. Leighton. 1969. Covers the decisions and debates over the logistical support that made possible the major offensive operations that defeated Japan and Germany.

The Army and Economic Mobilization by R. Elburton Smith. 1959. The book to read if you want to know how a national economy is mobilized for war. Based on the experience the U.S. had doing this during World War I, things went a lot more smoothly in World War II. Also shows the planning for converting back to a peacetime economy, which was very successful as there was not a major economic recession after World War II, as there usually was after major wars.

The Army and Industrial Manpower by Byron Fairchild and Jonathan Grossman. 1959. Covers the tricky problems involved in keeping enough people out of uniform to fill all the jobs created by a booming war economy. Huge social implications here, as women were employed on a larger scale than ever before, and blacks were able to break into job categories previously closed to them.

The Army Ground Forces

The Organization of Ground Combat Troops by Kent Roberts Greenfield, Robert R. Palmer, and Bell I. Wiley. 1947. The decision-making that went into determining how the ground forces would be organized and equipped. Some of these ideas are still in use, and have been adopted by many foreign nations. Other ideas, however, are best forgotten, and this volume explains why.

The Procurement and Training of Ground Combat Troops by Robert R. Palmer, Bell I. Wiley, and William R. Keast. 1948. Many new problems emerged as America selected who among millions of new soldiers would be trained for which job, and how that training would be provided. A cautionary tale for those who like to come up with "new ideas" in this department.

The Army Service Forces

The Organization and Role of the Army Service Forces by John D. Millett. 1954. An interesting study of management in a new, temporary organization that needed to get supplies and services to troops all over the world.

The Western Hemisphere

The Framework of Hemisphere Defense by Stetson Conn and Byron Fairchild. 1960. Cultural and diplomatic history of our relations with Latin America during the war.

Guarding the United States and Its Outposts by Stetson Conn, Rose C. Engelman, and Byron Fairchild. 1964. Although the Navy provided most of the actual defense of North America during the war, this book covers the activities of Army troops in out-of-the-way places such as Greenland, the Caribbean, and the Panama Canal Zone.

The War in the Pacific

Strategy and Command: The First Two Years by Louis Morton. 1962. Fascinating study of how the Army and Navy got along, and sometimes didn't, in the United States and Japan, during a period of intense pressure and uncertainty.

The Fall of the Philippines by Louis Morton. 1953. The earliest authoritative account of the loss of the Philippines. The debates over what could or should have been done continue to rage; this book is an excellent description of what happened there.

Guadalcanal: The First Offensive by John Miller Jr. 1949. One of the earliest accounts of the campaign, and one of the best. Makes good use of captured Japanese documents.

Victory in Papua by Samuel Milner. 1957. Papua was a much more desperate campaign than Guadalcanal. A study of unprepared troops facing combat, and winning through innovative leadership and some very hard fighting.

CARTWHEEL: The Reduction of Rabaul by John Miller Jr. 1959. A classic campaign in military history. MacArthur used new technologies ("ship busting" aircraft, amphibious operations, and codebreaking) to isolate a larger Japanese force while defeating only part of it on the battlefield.

Seizure of the Gilberts and Marshalls by Philip A. Crowl and Edmund G. Love. 1955. Covers the early battles during the U.S. Navy's drive across the Central Pacific toward Japan. Tells the whole story of the joint Navy/Marine/Army operation, although from the Army's point of view, an angle that makes reading this book well worth the effort.

Campaign in the Marianas by Philip A. Crowl. 1960. Similar to the above volume, but focusing on later events in the drive across the Central Pacific. Some interesting material on the different ways Army and Marine divisions operate in combat.

The Approach to the Philippines by Robert Ross Smith. 1953. Covers one of the lesser known but interesting and successful campaigns of World War II. During 1944, Army troops conducted a complex series of amphibious operations, built airfields, and used novel tactics to clear out Japanese troops from the north coast of New Guinea, resulting in the capture of the southern Palau islands, which provided a base for the invasion of the Philippines.

Leyte: The Return to the Philippines by M. Hamlin Cannon. 1954. This was one of the most daring amphibious operations of the war, moving deeper into the Japanese rear area than the Japanese expected, who were so shocked they committed all that remained of their fleet to counter the Allies, resulting in the largest naval battle in history. Ultimately, the Japanese were more successful on Leyte island itself, as three feet of rain slowed down the American logistics build up and allowed the Japanese troops to hold out longer.

Triumph in the Philippines by Robert Ross Smith. 1963. Covers the invasion of the Philippine island of Luzon, in World War II's second largest amphibious operation after D-Day. Because American intelligence underestimated the number of Japanese troops on the island (it was 250,000, not the estimated 152,000), the Japanese were able to continue fighting in the hills until the end of the war (when 65,000 Japanese troops, hungry, diseased, and heavily armed, were still out there).

Okinawa: The Last Battle by Roy E. Appleman, James M. Burns, Russell A. Gugeler, and John Stevens. 1948. Although one often thinks mainly of marines fighting on Okinawa, the invasion was commanded by the 10th Army and most of the troops were Army. A detailed and intense description of how Okinawa was won.

The Mediterranean Theater of Operations

Northwest Africa: Seizing the Initiative in the West by George F. Howe. 1957. Covers the first major army operation of the war, the transatlantic amphibious assault on North Africa in late 1942, and describes how inexperienced American troops overcame that shortcoming.

Sicily and the Surrender of Italy by Albert N. Garland and Howard McGraw Smyth. 1965. Accounts of two more amphibious operations and the surrender of Italy during 1943—American Army's first major success of the war.

Salerno to Cassino by Martin Blumenson, 1969. From late 1943 to mid-1944, American troops battled Germans in very rough Italian terrain—some of the hardest fighting of World War II.

Cassino to the Alps by Ernest F. Fisher. 1977. From May 1944 to the end of the war, Allied troops pushed the Germans all the way up to the Alps.

The European Theater of Operations

The Supreme Command by Forrest C. Pogue. 1954. The story of one man, General Dwight Eisenhower, commander of Supreme Headquarters, Allied Expeditionary Force, from December 1943 to July 1945, and the decisions he made. Why an entire book for this? Because Eisenhower's command was unique in American military history. He was in charge of Army, Navy and Air Force units from several nations and conducted military operations from Norway to the Mediterranean, and his experience became the model for multinational military commands after World War II.

Cross-Channel Attack by Gordon A. Harrison. 1951. The story of the D-Day invasion on June 6, 1944, from the planning and preparations that began in 1942 (including what Germany did in anticipation of it) to July 1, 1944.

Breakout and Pursuit by Martin Blumenson. 1961. Covers the planning of the battles to break through the German lines at Normandy and the race across France (July 1 to September 11, 1944).

The Lorraine Campaign by Hugh M. Cole. 1950. The story of Patton's Third Army and the battles in Lorraine from September 11 to December 18, 1944, an interesting and rather neglected campaign. This book offers one of the best accounts available.

The Siegfried Line Campaign by Charles B. MacDonald. 1963. North of Patton's Third Army, the First and Ninth armies ran into even more resistance because they were closing in on Germany's industrial heartland. Army commanders cooperated with British units in the same area, and everyone suffered from worsening weather and greater German resistance.

The Ardennes: Battle of the Bulge by Hugh M. Cole. 1965. The first serious history of the largest battle the Army fought in World War II. Extensive detail on German preparations and operations.

Riviera to the Rhine by Jeffrey J. Clarke and Robert Ross Smith. 1993. One of the best accounts of the Allied invasion of southern France in August 1944, covering operations through the end of the year.

The Last Offensive by Charles B. MacDonald. 1973. Accounts of the final battles in Germany, from January 1945 until the German surrender in May.

Logistical Support of the Armies, Volume I: May 1941–September 1944 by Roland G. Ruppental. 1953. The story of the huge effort to bring in the troops and supplies necessary to support the D-Day invasion.

Logistical Support of the Armies, Volume II: September 1944–May 1945 by Roland G. Ruppental. 1959. The very different logistical problems encountered on the continent after D-Day, how they were handled, and how they influenced strategy. A fascinating story.

The Middle East Theater

The Persian Corridor and Aid to Russia by T. H. Vail Motter. 1952. When German naval and air power made movement of supplies to Russia via the North Sea nearly impossible in 1942, the Persian Gulf route became the main one. This book is about more than moving supplies, and chronicles the diplomatic efforts among the Iranians, British, and Russians that were needed to keep things moving.

The China-Burma-India Theater

Stilwell's Mission to China by Charles F. Romanus and Riley Sunderland. 1953. Relates American efforts to improve Chinese military capabilities between 1939 and late 1943. A tale of frustration and lost opportunities.

Stilwell's Command Problems by Charles F. Romanus and Riley Sunderland. 1956. Covers operations from October 1943 to October 1944—the diplomacy, logistical problems, strategic debates, and frustration with the Chinese leadership. The volume ends with General Stilwell's return to the United States.

Time Runs Out in CBI by Charles F. Romanus and Riley Sunderland. 1959. The Japanese are defeated in Burma, but reform comes too late to the Chinese army, as the war ends before the retraining and reforms can be completed.

The Technical Services

The Chemical Warfare Service: Organizing for War by Leo P. Brophy and George J.B. Fisher. 1959. A history of chemical warfare in the U.S. Army from World War I to 1946.

The Chemical Warfare Service: From Laboratory to Field by Leo P. Brophy, Wyndham D. Miles, and Rexmond C. Cochrane. 1959. The development and expansion of American capabilities for developing and manufacturing chemical weapons.

The Chemical Warfare Service: Chemicals in Combat by Brooks E. Kleber and Dale Birdsell. 1965. How the Chemical Warfare Service adapted to World War II, where chemical weapons were not used. Most of its efforts went into smoke generation, flamethrowers, and incendiary weapons, which all proved quite useful.

The Corps of Engineers: Troops and Equipment by Blanche D. Coll, Jean C. Keith, and Herbert H. Rosenthal. 1958. How the Army engineers prepared troops and gathered needed equipment for combat. American Army engineers probably were the most effective such force in World War II and this book does much to explain why.

The Corps of Engineers: Construction in the United States by Lenore Fine and Jesse A. Remington. 1972. Before the U.S. entered the war, responsibilities for military construction were shifted from the Quartermaster Corps to the Corps of Engineers, whose engineers were responsible for the largest military construction effort in American history.

The Corps of Engineers: The War Against Japan by Karl C. Dod. 1966. Covers the most heroic, seemingly impossible, and militarily critical engineering effort in history, much of the engineers' work done under very primitive conditions.

The Corps of Engineers: The War Against Germany by Alfred M. Beck, Abe Bortz, Charles W. Lynch, Lida Mayo, and Ralph F. Weld. 1985. Here the engineers did less building and more traditional engineering work, dealing with minefields, fortifications and obstacles in general.

The Medical Department: Hospitalization and Evacuation, Zone of Interior by Clarence McKittrick Smith. 1956. During the war, the

U.S. built and managed a huge complex of hospitals in the United States, and developed a system for bringing back wounded troops from overseas to these facilities.

The Medical Department: Medical Service in the Mediterranean and Minor Theaters by Charles M. Witse. 1966. Recounts the building and administration of hospitals near the battlefield.

The Medical Department: Medical Service in the European Theater of Operations by Graham A. Cosmas and Albert E. Cowdrey. 1992. Same as above, in Europe.

The Medical Department: Medical Service in the War Against Japan by Mary Ellen Condon-Rall and Albert E. Cowdrey (forthcoming). Same as above, in the Pacific.

The Ordnance Department: Planning Munitions for War by Constance McLaughlin Green, Harry C. Thomson, and Peter C. Roots. 1955. Covers the development and manufacture of wartime munitions, and looks back at the history of such efforts over the previous sixty years.

The Ordnance Department: Procurement and Supply by Harry C. Thomson and Lida Mayo. 1960. Manufacturing and moving all that ammo. A huge task.

The Ordnance Department: On Beachhead and Battlefront by Lida Mayo. 1968. Getting ammo to the troops is not easy, as ammo can blow up in your face if you make the least mistake.

The Quartermaster Corps: Organization, Supply, and Services, Volume I by Erna Risch. 1953. The story of efforts to provide housing, food, clothes, personal equipment, fuel, and hygienic services to nearly 12 million men and women who served in the Army during World War II.

The Quartermaster Corps: Organization, Supply, and Services, Volume II by Erna Risch and Charles L. Kieffer. 1955. More of the above.

The Quartermaster Corps: Operations in the War Against Japan by Alvin P. Stauffer. 1956. Discusses problems unique to the Pacific, such as feeding Hawaii and taking care of folks living in equatorial rain forests.

The Quartermaster Corps: Operations in the War Against Germany by William F. Ross and Charles F. Romanus. 1965. Similar to the above: problems unique to the European theater, such as the needs of millions of prisoners and refugees, and the distribution of cold-weather gear to the troops when winter arrived.

The Signal Corps: The Emergency (to December 1941) by Dulany Terrett. 1956. This and the following two Signal Corp volumes describe how an unprepared organization suddenly dealt with many new technologies (radio, radar, electronic warfare, signal security and intelligence, and photography) and supplied equipment to millions of new troops.

The Signal Corps: The Test (December 1941 to July 1943) by George Raynor Thompson, Dixie R. Harris, Pauline M. Oakes, and Dulany Terrett. 1957.

The Signal Corps: The Outcome (Mid-1943 Through 1945) by George Raynor Thompson and Dixie R. Harris. 1966.

The Transportation Corps: Responsibilities, Organization, and Operations by Chester Wardlow. 1951. The Transportation Corps was established shortly after the United States entered the war to coordinate the vast road, rail, air, and sea transportation industries that had developed over the previous decades. This volume describes how the Transportation Corps organized itself and moved millions of tons of material.

The Transportation Corps: Movements, Training, and Supply by Chester Wardlow. 1956. How the problems of training enough transportation officers was not solved by the end of the war, and how turf battles with other organizations affected control of various types of transports, particularly ships.

The Transportation Corps: Operations Overseas by Joseph Bykofsky and Harold Larson. 1957. Once material had been shipped overseas, ground transport proved to be an even bigger problem, as food, fuel, and ammo didn't make it over the last hundred miles to the combat troops in a timely manner.

Special Studies

Chronology: 1941–1945 by Mary H. Williams. 1960. Details of the war on a day-by-day basis. Main emphasis is on activities of the U.S. Army in Africa, Europe, the Middle East, Southeast Asia, the Far East, the Pacific, and the Western Hemisphere. Depending on how important an event was, activities at the battalion and lower level are noted. But most entries deal with regiment, division, corps, army, and army group level actions. Where appropriate, combat actions of the Army Air Force, Navy, and Marine Corps, as well as those of British, French, Soviet, and other Allied armed forces.

Buying Aircraft: Materiel Procurement for the Army Air Forces by Irving Brinton Holley Jr. 1964. An important topic, as the United States had no plan for mass production of combat aircraft (a very high-tech weapon at the time) in the 1930s, a situation that changed in 1938. The book describes the unending task of problem-solving and invention. A compelling tale for any student of industrial mobilization.

Civil Affairs: Soldiers Become Governors by Harry L. Coles and Albert K. Weinberg. 1964. Involvement in World War II was how the United States learned most of what it knows today about Civil Affairs. Covers mostly the experience in Europe. Very interesting stuff.

The Employment of Negro Troops by Ulysses Lee. 1966. A straight-forward history of the use of black troops during the war, one of the earliest key moments in the Civil Rights movement.

Military Relations Between the United States and Canada: 1939–1945 by Stanley W. Dziuban. 1959. The beginning of cooperative efforts in the defense of North America, encouraging Americans and Canadians to work together on other matters as well.

Rearming the French by Marcel Vigneras. 1957. The United States took responsibility for providing Free French forces with weapons, equipment, and military facilities. An interesting story, full of diplomatic and cultural angles that still resonate.

Three Battles: Arnaville, Altuzzo, and Schmidt by Charles B. MacDonald and Sidney T. Mathews. 1952. Detailed examination of small-unit combat in three battles fought in Europe. A remarkable effort, particularly because one of the authors (MacDonald) had extensive combat experience as a junior infantry officer. A classic.

The Women's Army Corps by Mattie E. Treadwell. 1954. The first full professional history of the role of military women in the Army during World War II. More than 100,000 women served in the Army, and this book provides valuable insights on health, fatigue, accident rates, psychological matters, training, housing, clothing, feeding, and military discipline as they relate to women in uniform.

Manhattan: The Army and the Atomic Bomb by Vincent C. Jones. 1985. The Army was the main military organization involved in the Manhattan Project, and this book describes the development of the atomic bomb from that point of view.

Pictorial Record

The following three volumes show a small fraction of the thousands of photos military photographers took during the war (along with some captured enemy photos).

The War Against Germany and Italy: Mediterranean and Adjacent Areas. 1951.

The War Against Germany: Europe and Adjacent Areas. 1951.

The War Against Japan. 1952.

The Medical Department

This 40-volume series was not part of the Green Books and was more of a technical record, intended for the medical community, of the enormous medical efforts made to support the Army during World War II. It's important to remember that many medical breakthroughs occurred just before, and during, World War II, and saw immediate widespread use, the most important of which were the development and large-scale manufacture of antibiotics (initially penicillin) and insecticides (such as DDT). Antibiotics made possible surgery that otherwise could not be attempted because of inevitable fatal infections. More than a third of the volumes in this series cover various types of surgery, much of it new at the time, and it was important to the medical profession to have recorded how many of these procedures developed. As troops were often laid low by disease, several volumes discuss preventive medicine. DDT controlled mosquitoes on a large scale, which reduced cases of malaria and other mosquito-borne diseases. New medicines also made it easier to treat troops who caught tropical diseases. As a result, it was not unusual for Japanese troops, who did not have access to all this new medical technology, to suffer 5–10 times as many non-combat losses to disease as the American troops they faced. Later in Korea, Vietnam and the Persian Gulf, the pioneering work of Army medical personnel in World War II continued to be one of the great, unheralded, "weapons" in the American arsenal. It's pretty tough going if you get into these books as they were written for medical professionals, and are highly technical, but the material is well written. Some volumes, such as those covering tropical diseases and cold weather injuries (frostbite and the like) are easy to understand. Be aware, however, that the illustrations are gruesome, particularly those in the volume *Wound Ballistics*, which has become a standard work on the effects of shell fragments and bullets on people. Nevertheless, the text is a goldmine of information for those interested in the medical details of World War II.

WINGED VICTORY: THE ARMY AIR FORCES IN WORLD WAR II

by Geoffrey Perret

RANDOM HOUSE, 1993

The U.S. Air Force as we now know it didn't exist during World War II. Until 1947, the air force belonged to the Army, and was called the Army Air Force. First dubbed the Army Air Corps, it was formed in 1909 after adventurous Army officers sought out the Wright brothers and were taught to fly from the very inventors of the airplane. The Army immediately saw the usefulness of aircraft, and by 1917 had built a large corps consisting of 227 aircraft and 5 balloons. At first, the Air Corps was seen as just another branch of the army, but during World War I, Army Air Corps officers noted how independent air forces were beginning to arise in some nations. Especially appealing was the British Royal Air Force, an independent service that also controlled aircraft used by the Royal Navy. The U.S. Army was not yet eager to establish a separate service for the Air Corps. Many Army generals were wary of exactly where all this air power was going. Eager, and sometimes slightly out-of-control, Air Corps officers had to make a good case before the Army would agree to cut them loose.

Between the two World Wars, the Army Air Corps had plenty of ideas, but not much money. When funds became available in the late 1930s, there was a lot of catching up to do, as the 1930s had seen an unprecedented growth in aviation technology. This was obvious from the constant stream of new aircraft models appearing on the civil aviation market, some of which, such as the DC-3, remain in commercial use more than sixty years later. But when it came to purely military aircraft, it was a different story.

Warplanes, as always, operated at the edge—the "bleeding edge"—of technology and this was nowhere more true than in Germany. The Me-109 first flew in 1935, when the Army Air Corps was still operating a lot of biplanes and open cockpit fighters. The Me-109 went on to distinguish itself in the Spanish Civil War (1936-9) where it spurred American legislators to give the Army Air Corps the resources it needed to design and build modern aircraft. There was a lot to be done, because as the Germans were building the Me-109, the Army Air Corps was introducing the P-35. The only thing the two aircraft had in common was their weight (three tons) and all metal construction. The Me-109 was faster, more maneuverable and better armed. In other words, it was a much better fighter aircraft. The P-35 had over twice the range (1200 miles) of the Me-109, a characteristic of American aircraft that was to persist throughout the war. America was a larger place than Germany, and long range was always considered a necessity. It wasn't until 1942 that the United States began to construct fighters that could cope with German and Japanese aircraft on equal terms. This was the year that the P-47 and P-51 appeared, along with the Navy Hellcat. The United States always had a good supply of light (one- and two-engine) bombers, but if you couldn't repel enemy fighters, your bombers would be just targets. However, before the war, the Army Air Force didn't believe that. It was thought that if you put enough machine guns on heavy bombers and flew them in large, tight formations, enemy fighters would not be a problem.

As a result, the Army Air Corps took the lead from the very beginning in one area—heavy bombers. Even before World War II, the highly competitive American aviation industry was the largest and most advanced in the world. Despite the Great Depression, there was a demand for air travel and transportation (particularly of mail). Several companies competed to come up with radical and effective new airliner designs every few years. The Boeing Company designed the first pressurized (high-altitude) airliner (the four-engine Boeing 307) in 1934. When the Army Air Corps solicited bids for a four-engine bomber, Boeing modified the design of the 307 (eliminating the pressurized cabin to save a lot of weight, since the crew could wear oxygen masks) and produced the B-17 bomber, which was an immediate success, with range, speed and carrying capacity unheard of at the time. The first B-17s entered service in early 1940, after the Army Air Corps convinced Congress that they were worth the cost.

The B-17 was, indeed, a marvelous aircraft, but it was not a wonder weapon. Despite the development of more precise bomb sights, it was still not possible for a single bomber to hit a target from an altitude greater than 25,000 feet. For that reason, the B-17 never proved very useful at sea, except when equipped with depth charges and bombs and trained to come in low. This proved useful against submarines, and sometimes against warships, but the return fire was more than most B-17s could handle. However, coming in at 200 feet or less did wonders for bombing accuracy, and the aircraft's .50 caliber machine guns also contributed to the damage.

The experience with the B-17 was repeated with every other type of aircraft. This was made easier for the Army Air Forces because they didn't get into the fighting until late 1941. Most of the other participants had been at it since 1939 (or, in the case of Japan, since 1937).

America had been building warplanes for foreign nations (especially Britain) for some years, and saw that the trend was toward heavier guns, leak-proof gas tanks, greater range, protective armor, and tail guns for bombers. The need for greater range led to the development of drop-tanks and more and more machine guns were added as the war went on. American engineers were among the best in the world, and by the end of World War II U.S. warplanes were seen as the best available in design and construction.

In building the world's largest air force from practically nothing, America had two very important advantages. The United

States had a large amount of aluminum manufacturing and vehicle-assembly capacity. Thus it was obvious that one way to get America into the war quickly was to build aircraft and train pilots to fly them. While major warships (battleships, large carriers) took several years to build, and several months to staff properly, aircraft units could be turned out quickly, with pilot and ground crew training only requiring nine months or so. Even before Pearl Harbor, plans were in place to produce huge quantities of aircraft when war came.

The Army Air Force realized that it would need a lot of pilots in a hurry. Civilian flying schools were mobilized to provide Primary Flight Training. New pilots were given sixty hours of flying instruction, and those who passed, moved on to Basic Flying School, where military flying techniques (night flying, and by instruments, in formation, and cross-country from one specific point to another) were taught. Pilots also learned to use two-way radio (still an innovation) while airborne, and to manage more complex aircraft. Those who passed this stage went on to Advanced Flying School. This took another nine weeks, but there were two different schools, one for fighter pilots (using single-engine trainers), another for multiple-engine pilots (bombers and transports). Overall, from 1941 to 1945, 325,000 trainees entered Primary Flight Training but only 60 percent of them made it out of Advanced Flying School and went on to another two months of transition flying for the aircraft they would use in combat. In all, trainee pilots spent over 200 hours in the air flying an aircraft.

As the war went on, it was realized that the more time trainee pilots spent in the air, the better they did in combat. So by late 1942, American pilots were getting at least 270 hours in the air before heading off for a combat unit. Eight months later, that was increased to 320 hours. By late 1944, it was increased to 360 hours. This increase in preparation was only possible because enough aircraft, and fuel, was being produced. The U.S. produced 283,000 aircraft for the war effort, and a third of them were used in various stages of training. At the time, the United States was the largest oil producer in the world, and had access to additional supplies in South America and the Persian Gulf. The United

States had the resources to increase the flying hours for its pilots in training.

Conversely, Japanese and German trainee pilots received fewer hours of training (about a hundred or less by 1945), which resulted in new Axis pilots more frequently being shot down during their first few combat encounters. For example, in 1940, during the invasion of France, German pilots lost about 6 aircraft per thousand sorties. By the summer of 1944, when new German pilots were getting less than half the flying hours trainees received in 1939–40, Germany was losing 111 aircraft per thousand sorties. Most of these losses were new pilots, straight from training. It had long been noted that if a new pilot could survive his first half dozen combat sorties, his chances of surviving the war went up considerably. By the summer of 1944, most new German pilots did not survive their first few sorties. The same thing was happening in the Pacific against the Japanese.

The Army Air Forces had a peak strength of 2.4 million troops, and 80,000 aircraft, but the American generals quickly learned that the number that really counted was the one that applied to sorties (how many aircraft took off, fulfilled an assignment, and returned). American officers noted that one of the reasons Germany quickly conquered France was that the Luftwaffe generated more sorties than the Allies, and that the British won the Battle of Britain in late 1940 by generating a high number of sorties, even though the Germans still outdid them. The U.S. Army Air Force got many chances to demonstrate how well it had learned its lesson, in the two months of air operations before D-Day and the battles that came after. The U.S. and British air forces put up 98,000 sorties, compared to 34,500 German. And then, for the three months after D-Day, the Allies generated 203,357 sorties, compared to 31,833 German. This was accomplished largely by the rapid build-up of the U.S. Army Air Force in Europe. By the end 1942, the U.S. had 1,300 combat aircraft operating in Europe. By mid 1943, the number had gone up to 5,000, then 7,500 at the end of 1943, and 11,800 by the time of D-Day. British air power had not gone up as much, being 9,500 aircraft in mid 1942 and 13,200 at

D-Day. At that time, Germany had only 4,600 aircraft in Western Europe and Italy. The Germans also had a million troops (including quite a few women) manning over 25,000 anti-aircraft runs and 6,000 searchlights. More than once, planes in the air, not guns on the ground shooting at them, determined who would control the skies.

Before the Army Air Forces reached its pinnacle of success in 1944, however, it had to spend some scary moments finding out what worked. As war loomed in early 1941, there were efforts to test U.S. aircraft and pilots in combat. One of the more daring of these efforts was the American Volunteer Group (AVG), better known as the Flying Tigers. Technically, the pilots of the AVG were volunteers, but they were in fact clandestinely recruited by the American government via discreet visits to Army, Navy, and Marine pilots. All of this, as well as the hundred American warplanes used, was paid for by the U.S. government. The aircraft for China were authorized by Congress, the hundred pilots were not. The pilots were told, unofficially, that they would later get their military jobs back, no questions asked, if they resigned their commissions to join the AVG and work for the Chinese government. Most of the pilots approached, selected for their flying skills and initiative, jumped at the chance to get into the war.

The Nationalist Chinese government already was using foreign pilots to man their air force in an effort to fight off the formidable Japanese air force. This was not working out well, as the mercenary pilots (mostly Europeans) flew obsolete aircraft that were no match for the well-trained Japanese. American public opinion was outraged at the Japanese aggression in China, but was also dead set against any American troops getting directly involved. Thus the AVG was assembled as if it were a private effort to aid China. Despite news stories that appeared about the AVG, this arrangement caused no problems.

By the fall of 1941, pilots and aircraft had arrived in British-controlled Burma. There, the pilots were going to train, get to know each other and their P-40 aircraft (which the Navy pilots had never seen, much less flown), before moving on to China.

The AVG was not a large organization, with only 340 men (pilots and ground crews). Then December 7th happened. All of a sudden, the Japanese were attacking everything in the Pacific, from Pearl Harbor to Burma. The AVG had not planned to officially start operations until December 18, but after Pearl Harbor was attacked on the 7th, they got down to business right away. The British appreciated the presence of the AVG, as these American pilots were quite good.

Unfortunately, the AVG never had more than 22 aircraft in flying shape at any one time, and were outnumbered by the Japanese, who had mustered over a thousand aircraft for the invasion of Burma. However, the AVG's leader, Claire Chennault, had been in China previously and had carefully observed how the Japanese air force operated. He developed tactics that enabled American pilots, in somewhat inferior aircraft, to defeat the Japanese, and they worked. His hand-picked pilots, using his tactics, tore the Japanese air force up. In ten weeks of combat over Rangoon, the capital of Burma, the AVG fought 31 air battles with the Japanese, destroying 260 enemy aircraft, and losing six pilots and 16 aircraft. The Royal Air Force destroyed 107 Japanese aircraft, and lost 22 during the same period, using a larger number of aircraft.

Other Allied air forces soon adopted the AVG's methods and saw their combat performance improve. When the AVG moved north into China as the Japanese army pushed south into Burma, these pilots were considered bona fide heroes—among the few bright spots for the Allies in those dark days. Walt Disney Studios designed a snappy logo for the Flying Tigers and the media had a field day with their aerial superstars. However, by July 4, 1942, the AVG was disbanded and absorbed into the U.S. Army Air Force, after flying 6,000 sorties during their short existence and doing it with style and success that cheered up millions of Americans.

The AVG also proved that the second rate warplanes the U.S. had in early 1942, particularly the P-40, could, with the right tactics and pilot training, deal with superior aircraft like the Japanese Zero (A6M) or German Me-109. It took over a year for better aircraft (P-47, P51) to show up in quantity. Until then, the P-40 (13,200 built), P-39 (7,500) and P-38 (8,600) were able to keep the Axis fighters at bay.

By 1944, about a quarter of the men and aircraft in the Army Air Forces were devoted to the bombing of Germany and the nations it occupied. It was the biggest operation the Army Air Force was involved in and the most expensive military operation of the war, costing $43 billion (nearly a half-trillion in current dollars). The Army Air Force lost 8,237 bombers and 3,924 fighters during the bombing campaign. This included some 29,000 airmen killed and 44,000 wounded. The number of casualties was about 10 percent of all American troops killed during World War II. The scope of the losses was not really noted at the time because the bombing campaign lasted about two years (from spring 1943 to early 1945).

To put it in perspective, the Army lost about 16,000 troops during several months of fighting in Normandy (after the D-Day landings), and some 19,000 dead in a month of combat during the Battle of the Bulge. Put another way, the Army Air Forces bombing Germany lost about as many men in combat as did the U.S. Navy for the entire war. Moreover, a young man joining the Marine Corps was more likely to survive the war than one headed for the 8th and 15th Air Forces (the units conducting the bombing of Germany) in Europe. The Marines lost 20,000 men during the war. Half of the bombing raids targeted Germany, about a fifth targeted France and the rest other occupied countries. About 20 percent of the bombs were dropped on military targets, the rest on economic targets such as factories or railroads.

While *Winged Victory* is a "popular history," the author does spotlight the key events that shaped the creation of the world's largest air force. Chief among these was the energy and drive demonstrated by the commander of the Army Air Forces ("Hap" Arnold) throughout the war. Arnold needed energy to deal with the many problems within the Air Force, with the army and, oh yeah, there was the enemy to deal with as well.

For much of the 1930s, most Air Force officers believed that bombers were the core of air power. The German use of bombers during the Spanish Civil War (1936–39) seemed to confirm this. But these were low flying, two engine bombers. American Air Force officers had upped the ante by getting behind four engine heavy bombers flying at over 25,000 feet. Hundreds of these heavily armed "Flying Fortresses" would—it was believed—rain destruction, with pinpoint accuracy, on targets below. It never quite worked out that way. In the end, the most effective warplanes were the low-flying two-engine bombers and single-engine fighters equipped with bombs. The Army Air Force generals greatly disliked this because those medium bombers and fighter bombers were mainly working at giving direct support to army troops. This would not do. The Air Force brass wanted an independent Air Force. The main reason they didn't get it before World War II (as had the British Royal Air Force and the German Luftwaffe) was because of opposition from Army and Navy leaders, and politicians. There were also practical considerations. With a major war approaching, a newly independent Air Force would not have time to build the support network it now got from the Army.

The supposed predominance of the heavy bomber became an obsession with senior Air Force commanders, who believed they represented the future. The Air Force gave out disproportionately more medals and promotions to bomber officers, in spite of the fact that fighter pilots received more press attention and were considered the most glamorous aspect of the Air Force. But the bomber fixation had nothing to do with reality, and everything to do with a quasi-religious faith in the ability of heavy bombers to do anything, including win a war, without much help from anyone else. In practice, this approach failed throughout the war, especially in Europe.

In the Pacific, generals claimed that the two atomic bombs dropped by bombers on Japan proved that the bomber was the ultimate air weapon. What the generals failed to notice was that the Russian invasion of Manchuria on August 9, the same day the second atomic bomb was dropped on Nagasaki, did far more damage to Japanese military power. Similarly, American submarines had accomplished a shut-down of Japanese shipping. This was crucial for a nation that had to import food, and then move it around by ship, because without a prompt surrender, by the end of the summer thousands of Japanese would start dying of starvation each week. And those deaths would skyrocket into fall and winter. In 1945, the U.S. had only three A-bombs, and their use was mostly a bluff. Hiroshima and Nagasaki could have been bashed just as thoroughly via conventional bombing raids conducted by 500 B-29s. Had the Japanese not folded after three bombs, the mass starvation would have been the ultimate weapon, plus the loss of the bulk of their army and food production in Manchuria. But the Air Force wanted none of this, and saw to it that items like this were played down in the post-war U.S. Strategic Bombing Survey (USSBS.)

In the rush to enthrone bomber pilots, the Army Air Force swept aside a splendid record of close-range air support. Air controllers rode with the lead tanks of advancing divisions, getting scouting reports radioed in from fighter-bombers overhead, and directed machine-gun, bomb, or rocket attacks by the fighter-bombers against enemy resistance. It was an excellent technique, but was phased out after World War II, when the Army Air Force became the U.S. Air Force. Nor did Army Air Force generals want to get involved in the business of air transport, and had to be tricked or bullied into doing it even during World War II. They even tried to avoid carrying paratroopers, or ordering air transports to do anything useful.

During World War II, the Army Air Force had to knuckle under to ground-force commanders who outranked them, an experience that made the Air Force commanders more eager to be a separate service. The Air Force crew was aware that they would soon have more money to play with than the Army or Navy in the post–World War II world. The reason was simple: the three most expensive World War II development projects (B-29 development, the atomic bomb, and radar research) were for the Air Force.

The Army Air Force went to great lengths to get the highest quality people, even when it meant depriving the other services of the smart and trainable people they needed even more. Much of what people did in the Air Force was high-tech and the Air Force leadership went out of its way to grab more than it needed.

A prime example was the way men were selected for pilot training. Air Force brass insisted that all pilot candidates have at least two years of college. (At the time, about the same number of people graduated from high school as graduate from college today.) The Air Force received bad press for this decision (which they eventually had to drop), when it was pointed out that few of America's World War II aces were college grads. The Air Force also refused to accept enlisted pilots, causing a law to be passed in 1942 to prohibit their participation.

The creation of the modern American air force was a mighty effort, and *Winged Victory* personalizes the process without forcing the reader to wade through masses of details found in the "official" history. Also, unlike the official history, this book spotlights the less admirable aspects (interservice rivalries, obsession with bombers and more).

APPENDIX

---

*M*Y INTEREST IN World War II has led me to write several books on the subject. Like many of the fifty I have described above, my books have strived to uncover really important aspects of the war that don't usually get much coverage. Below are descriptions of two of my World War II books that do that. Sort of a bonus. You get coverage on 52 books for the price of 50.

Some of them I wrote because there were no other books available on a particular aspect of World War II history. *Dirty Little Secrets of World War II,* coauthored with Albert A. Nofi (Morrow, 1994), is one of them. In my years of studying World War II, I have come across countless bits of useful and revealing (or simply interesting) information that appears nowhere else, or doesn't appear very often. It's not as if there haven't been thousands of historians searching for new revelations about World War II for the past half century. But many important, or at least interesting, items have been ignored, missed or buried. Okay, some of this stuff is basically interesting trivia, but the book was written for a mass audience of World War II buffs, not just a much smaller group of hard core World War II historians. There are over a hundred items covered in the book, in the form of brief, easy to read essays.

There were some important things we brought out in this book. For example, how many people actually died? Since the late 1940s, the most common number quoted has been about 50 million. Apparently no one has bothered to double-check the numbers. Actually, what got us going on this subject was the publication, in the early 1990s, of the actual Russian losses during the war (from the long secret Soviet archives). It was initially published in Russian. But I remembered enough Russian from my college days to read this book, and what a revelation it was. Thirty million Russians died during World War II. No wonder the Soviets kept it secret for so long. Actually, the Soviets kept it a secret because they didn't want the West to know how badly the Germans had hammered them. The data on losses became, literally, a military secret.

Then we started looking at what historians from other nations had been doing to revise their stats on World War II losses. In particular, we found that only rough estimates were being used long after better numbers had been researched and published. When we were finished compiling all this data we came up with the astounding total of a hundred million dead.

Among the other items in the book was a list called "Great Conspiracies, Betrayals, and Cover-ups that Weren't." A less charitable observer might call this section an examination of the worst historical research to come out of the war.

A lot of the items in the book are simply straightforward analysis of information that has always been right out there, but never looked at in quite the way we did. An example of that is the examination of naval battles in the war. In doing this we point out that there were nine battles in which battleships fought each other, but only five in which aircraft carriers fought other carriers. And there haven't been any since.

We also present little bits of information that, well, say a lot. Like a chart of spending on armaments by the major nations during the war. Very revealing, and doesn't require more than a minute to get the point. Most books on the economics of World War II require a lot more time to get the same information.

A lot of the stuff fills in the gaps of one's World War II knowledge, even if you have read extensively about it. Like the bits on the extent to which accidents destroyed nearly as many combat aircraft as enemy action. And the role of disease, especially in the tropics. There's also a lot of analysis in the book, bringing together a lot of information from many different sources and putting it all in one, easy to comprehend chart. Like the one for who had how many combat divisions at the end of every year in the war. I'd been meaning to do that one for years.

And so it goes, on to things like how the blitzkrieg actually worked, what happened if you got wounded, the glorious history of World War II cavalry, women in the war (and in places you never expected to see ladies with guns) and finishing with the lingering costs of the war (which were substantial).

It's a book that will fill in gaps in your World War II information that you didn't even know you had.

Another book of mine, *The War in the Pacific Encyclopedia,* also coauthored with Nofi (Facts on File, 1997), contains even more details.

The war in the Pacific was the largest naval war in history. There is unlikely to ever be another like it. But because of the vast size of this war it's hard to keep track of it all. And there's a lot to keep track of. So, when asked (by Facts on File, naturally), I jumped at the opportunity to do an encyclopedia of the war. In this volume (originally published as a two volume hard cover set, later available as one very thick paperback), we crammed 440,000 words on well-known subjects (the major battles, ship and aircraft types) as well as the many obscure details (all the islands that played a role in the war, critical security breaches, and Pacific islanders who fought for the Japanese). Any time you are plowing through a compact history of the war in the Pacific, or an account of an individual battle or campaign, mine is the book you should have at hand when you wish to have something explained.

We covered stuff not just completely, in the kind of detail that was meaningful. For the major leaders, we included key information like when they entered military service and what they then spent most of their time involved in during their careers. We only covered the senior leaders, so these are guys who entered service before World War I and had already established some kind of reputation by the time World War II rolled around. We briefly (a sentence or two) sum up their World War II performance. Very compact, very handy. For the battles, we do it all in 200–300 words. We place the battle in time and place, briefly describe the numbers involved, who won and why. Not as exciting as a book on the subject, but a lot quicker.

Islands are something I've always had an issue with in books on the Pacific War. That war was all about islands, except for some stuff in Burma and along the China coast. But nowhere could I find any one source that described all those islands and their military significance. If an island was mentioned, only fragmentary information was readily available. Very frustrating. Why not provide adequate and consistent information about the islands? We did it for this book, and what a chore it was. In the descriptions, we locate the island in reference to some larger, well known, territory (Australia, India, Hawaii, etc.). We then describe the island's resources in terms of anchorages, building airfields and infrastructure (local population and resources). Briefly described who used it and why, or why not. You'll never get lost in the Pacific again with this, at least in reading history of the Pacific war.

And then there are ports. Anyone who lives near a large body of water (and most people, world wide, do) know that some ports vary considerably in their capacity for ships, and their ability to handle them. We included all the significant ports for the Pacific during World War II. Some of these never showed up much in any battles or campaigns, but could have. So we include them as well, because the existence of any port influenced military operations, whether it was used or not.

Ship and aircraft types are something that military history books do cover, but often not in a consistent fashion, and minor (but sometimes important at one point in the war) models are often left out. We give the most important features of ships (number in class, number built, how useful it was and what happened to it) and aircraft (years of manufacture, number produced, top speed, comments on usefulness and bomb load). There are charts giving more details (weight, weapons, speed, etc.) for major classes of ships as well. The ship and aircraft charts make it easier to compare the aircraft and ships of the different nations, years, and so on. Non-combat ships and aircraft are also covered, as these played a critical role in the Pacific fighting. The vast distances in the Pacific meant that supplies, and just moving stuff around, became a crucial military advantage if you could do it.

Ground forces get described in terms of how they are organized, which ones were in the Pacific, what they did and how well they did it. Makes a lot more sense that way.

And then there are all those items you never think of until you come across them in a book and find yourself still wondering. Aircraft carriers get several items, covering things like how they operated, shortages, and differences between American and Japanese.

To give you an idea of the extent of the coverage, consider just the items beginning with the letter "G":

G3M Nell Japanese Bomber
G4M Betty Japanese Bomber
Gay, George H., Jr. (1917–1994)
Gearing Class, US Destroyers
Geiger, Roy (1885–1947)
Genda, Minoru (1904–)
Generals, Proportions in the Service, Allied, 1944
Geneva Convention
George VI, King of Great Britain (1895–1952)
German-American Commanders in the Pacific War
Germany in the Pacific War
Ghormley, Robert L. (1883–1958)
Gibbs, William Francis (1886–1967)
Gilbert Islands
Gona, New Guinea
Goto, Aritomo (1890–1942)
Graves Registration
Great Marianas Turkey Shoot
Gridley Class, US Destroyers
Gripsholm, Swedish Ocean Liner
Guadalcanal, Campaign for
Guadalcanal, Naval Battles of

There are a lot of entries on logistics, and things like how aircraft carriers actually operated. If you have any question about the Who? or How of World War II, you'll find the answer in here. After the *Encyclopedia* was published, I was pleased to receive reports from people who sat down and read it straight through. Something of a random-access way to approach the War in the Pacific, in my opinion, but apparently it works for some.

INDEX